M000105788

RACE AND THE CHILEAN MIRACLE

Pitt Latin American Series
John Charles Chasteen and Catherine M. Conaghan, Editors

RACE and the CHILEAN MIRACLE

Neoliberalism, Democracy, and Indigenous Rights

PATRICIA RICHARDS

University of Pittsburgh Press

Published by the University of Pittsburgh Press, Pittsburgh, Pa., 15260

Copyright © 2013, University of Pittsburgh Press

Manufactured in the United States of America

Printed on acid-free paper

10 9 8 7 6 5 4 3 2 1

Library of Congress Cataloging-in-Publication Data

Richards, Patricia, 1971–
  Race and the Chilean miracle : neoliberalism, democracy, and indigenous rights / Patricia
Richards.
      pages cm. — (Pitt Latin American series)
  Includes bibliographical references and index.
  ISBN 978-0-8229-6237-3 (pbk. : alk. paper)
  1. Mapuche Indians—Chile—Araucanía—Government relations. 2. Mapuche Indians—Civil
rights—Chile—Araucanía. 3. Araucanía (Chile) —Race relations. I. Title.
  F3126.R53 2013
  323.1198083—dc23   2013007085

A mi familia: Oscar y Menina
To my parents: Jim and Peg Richards

Y a Chiñura Morales Chihuaihuen

CONTENTS

ACKNOWLEDGMENTS

I express my heartfelt appreciation to all Mapuche and Chileans who participated in this study. It is my sincere hope that this book might contribute, in however small a way, to new forms of understanding in southern Chile. Special thanks go to Jose Alywin, Álvaro Bello, Gabriela Calfucoy, Jaqueline Caniguan, Sergio Caniuqueo, Serena Cosgrove, Ximena Cuadra, Chris Cuomo, Kirsten Dellinger, Melissa Forbis, Susan Franceschet, Charlie Hale, Diane Haughney, Lynn Horton, Jeff Jackson, José Mariman, Eduardo Mella, Rosamel Millaman, Anita Millaquen, Millaray Painemal, Wladimir Painemal, Yun-Joo Park, Amy Ross, Alfredo Seguel, Carolijn Terwindt, Gwynn Thomas, Marcos Valdés, Heinrich Von Baer, Sarah Warren, and Christine Williams—all of whom contributed to this work by reading drafts, commenting on talks, clarifying events, taking the time for conversation, and bestowing friendship.

Audiences at talks at the University of Georgia, the University of Mississippi, the University of Texas at Austin, and the Universidad Católica de Temuco contributed to the book's development with incisive comments and observations. I received essential institutional and collegial support from the Observatorio Ciudadano, the Department of Anthropology at the Universidad Católica de Temuco, and the Universidad de la Frontera. Magaly Ortiz transcribed the interviews. My research assistant, Jeff Gardner, provided support in bringing this manuscript into publishable shape. Grants from the Exposition Foundation, the Willson Center for Humanities and Arts at the University of Georgia, and the University of Georgia Research Foundation funded this project. Anonymous reviewers for the University of Pittsburgh Press gave incredibly attuned and helpful comments that vastly improved the manuscript. Acquisitions editor Joshua Shanholtzer and managing editor Alex Wolfe provided crucial guidance. Bill Nelson drew the map.

Copyeditor Amy Smith Bell was a pleasure to work with, and her expertise has made this book infinitely more readable. Portions of chapters 1, 2, 3, 4, 5, and 7 were published as "Of Indians and Terrorists: How the State and Local Elites Construct the Mapuche in Neoliberal Multicultural Chile," *Journal of Latin American Studies* 42 (2010): 59–90, and are included here with permission of the journal and its publisher, Cambridge University Press. Material from all chapters previously appeared in different form in Patricia Richards and Jeffrey A. Gardner, "Still Seeking Recognition: Mapuche Demands, State Violence, and Discrimination in Democratic Chile," *Latin American and Caribbean Ethnic Studies* 8 (2013, doi:10.1080/17442222.2013.779063), and is included here with grateful acknowledgment. Very special thanks goes to Eduardo Rapiman for permission to use his painting *Purrún* for the cover of this book.

Last but not least, I thank Oscar Chamosa for his perceptive comments and criticisms, his flair for style, his nearly limitless patience, and his loving encouragement. I also thank Menina, for bringing us joy.

ABBREVIATIONS

CAM	Coordinadora de Comunidades Mapuche en Conflicto Arauko-Malleko (Arauko-Malleko Coordinating Organization for Mapuche Communities in Conflict)
CASEN	Encuesta de Caracterización Socioeconómica Nacional (National Socioeconomic Characterization Survey)
CITEM	Coordinación de Identidades Territoriales Mapuche (Mapuche Territorial Identities Coordinating Organization)
CMPC	Compañía Manufacturera de Papeles y Cartones (Paper and Cardboard Manufacturing Company; parent company of Mininco Timber Company)
COM	Coordinación de Organizaciones Mapuches (Coordination of Mapuche Organizations)
CONADI	Corporación Nacional de Desarollo Indígena (National Indigenous Development Agency)
CONAF	Corporación Nacional Forestal (National Forestry Agency)
CORA	Corporación de Reforma Agraria (Agrarian Reform Agency)
COREMA	Comisión Regional de Medio Ambiente (Regional Environment Commission)
CORFO	Corporación de Fomento de la Producción (Economic Development Agency)
CORMA	Corporación Chilena de la Madera (Chilean Wood Association)
IACHR	Inter-American Commission on Human Rights
IDB	Inter-American Development Bank

INDAP   Instituto Nacional de Desarrollo Agropecuario (National
                Agricultural Development Agency)

LYD   Libertad y Desarrollo (Liberty and Development; a conserva-
                tive think tank)

MCR   Movimiento Campesino Revolucionario (Revolutionary
                Peasant Movement)

MIDEPLAN   Ministerio de Planificación (Ministry of Planning Social
                Development)

MIR   Movimiento de Izquierdista Revolucionaria (Revolutionary
                Left Movement)

PRODESAL   Programa de Desarollo Local (Local Development Program)

SERNATUR   Servicio Nacional de Turismo (National Tourism Service)

RACE AND THE CHILEAN MIRACLE

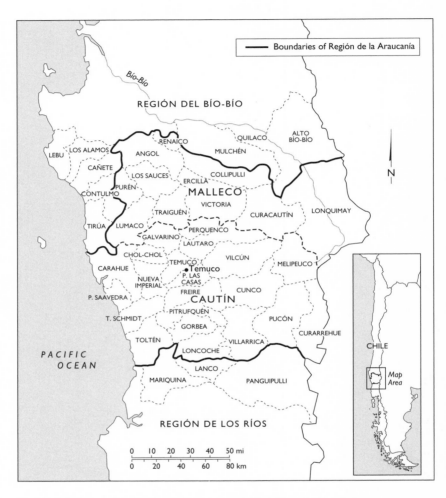

Región de la Araucanía and Adjacent Comunas with High Mapuche Populations.
Map by Bill Nelson, drawing in part from a map accompanying Nagnil (2005).

CHAPTER 1

RACE AND THE CHILEAN MIRACLE

Chile is often portrayed as a successful example of a peaceful transition to democracy sustained by high rates of economic growth. Enthusiasts refer to a "Chilean Miracle," the notion that free-market reforms imposed during Augusto Pinochet's dictatorship (1973–90) put the country on the road to development and stability. They cite Chile as a success story, a model for other countries to follow. This picture, although true in some respects, conceals a more complex reality of social inequality and conflict brought about in part by the very political and economic models implemented by Pinochet and later perpetuated by the center-left Concertación de Partidos por la Democracia (Coalition of Parties for Democracy), which held the presidency from the return to democracy in 1990 until 2010.

This situation is aggravated by the persistence of entrenched racism. The southern region of the Araucanía, part of the ancestral territory of the Mapuche indigenous people, is a forceful case in point.[1] The Mapuche were one of the last large indigenous nations in the Americas to remain free and sovereign. Their vast domain, the Wallmapu, spanned the Andes, encompassing significant portions of what is today Chile and Argentina. In the 1880s new military technology allowed the resource-hungry Chilean government to conquer Mapuche territory on their side of the border, just as the Argentines had done a few years before on theirs. In Chile, Mapuche survivors were relegated to humiliating conditions. They retained a small fraction of their ancestral lands, divided into isolated communities aptly called *reducciones* (reductions). Meanwhile, Chilean and European settlers, or *colonos*, obtained prime farming and forested lands where they established profitable *fundos* (medium to large farms). The conquest of the Araucanía thus created a two-tier rural economy exacerbated by distinctions of race and culture. Adoption of transnational racist discourses naturalized the power of fundo-owning colonos and the local representatives of the Chilean state, imprinting on the post-conquest Araucanía the unmistakable character of a colonial society.

This colonial character remained an indelible feature even as, during the twentieth century, the descendants of European colonos became Chilean and the Mapuche partially assimilated into the mainstream. In the early 1970s, many Mapuche participated in the social and political movements associated with the Unidad Popular government led by Salvador Allende.[2] Subsequently, they became targets of the systematic repression of Pinochet's regime. Pinochet's neoliberal reforms benefited colonos and other local elites as well as the large timber corporations that entered the Araucanía, surrounding Mapuche communities with soil-damaging, water-depleting pine and eucalyptus plantations. Politically persecuted, economically exploited, racially oppressed, the Mapuche were now paying the environmental consequences of national development.

Beginning in the 1990s, several years after the return to democracy, conflicts erupted between Mapuche communities and private and state interests over territorial claims and development projects, including the construction of hydroelectric dams and the massive expansion of the timber industry. In some cases, these conflicts reached a level of violence reminiscent of the dark days of the dictatorship, involving arson, equipment sabotage, raids on Mapuche communities, and charges of terrorism. Faced with rising Mapuche mobilization, the Concertación governments instituted multicultural policies to recognize some indigenous rights and promote diversity. These reforms, however, failed to address the ongoing colonial dispossession at the root of the conflicts. Moreover, local elites of European descent resisted both Mapuche demands and the government's palliatives, resorting to racist discourses and practices that challenged the notion of a multicultural Chile and further fed the conflicts. This dynamic and conflict-laden context presented an opportune moment to observe the disjunctures between new state and transnational discourses about democracy, multiculturalism, and indigenous rights and enduring local beliefs about race and belonging.

It was in this context that I visited Gonzalo Arellano, a young employee at INDAP (Instituto Nacional de Desarrollo Agropecuario, the National Agricultural Development Agency, a government agency within the Ministry of Agriculture). I sought Gonzalo out because of his work in helping to found a rural community called Bellaruka made up of Mapuche and poor farmers of European descent. The community has *personería jurídica,* meaning that it is legally recognized as a community and can derive state benefits as such. I thought Gonzalo might be a good resource for ideas about how to rework intercultural relationships in the region.[3] Nevertheless, it did not take long to realize Gonzalo was fraught with the racial anxiety that prevailed throughout the Chilean South. My visit began in his office in a small city in Malleco, where his responsibilities involved keeping tabs on Orígenes interventions in nearby Mapuche communities.[4] Orígenes is an intercultural development program financed by the state and the Inter-American Development Bank (IDB). It funds projects related to health, education, community and institutional strengthening, and productive development.

I asked Gonzalo how discrimination was manifest in the area. He answered by first asserting his expertise on the issue: "I have a lot of experience with the Mapuche."[5] Foreigners like me come to the region and are quick to see racism on the part of Chileans, he observed, when in reality there are "intractable cultural differences." He illustrated his point by running through a list of Mapuche faults:

> The government has bought land for them but the Mapuche don't respect fences and they don't work the land . . .
>
> INDAP gave one community fruit trees and equipment, and the Mapuche just pulled the fruit trees out of the ground . . .
>
> The Mapuche aren't farmers . . .
>
> They keep living like they have a half-hectare when they have 80 now . . .
>
> They have very aggressive leaders, which makes it difficult to work with them . . .
>
> They aren't willing to live together with others . . .
>
> They want to impose their culture on Chileans . . .
>
> And their property is covered with garbage.

Gonzalo's complaints are commonplace in the Araucanía, and many of these complaints have taken on an almost mythic quality. These are the stories non-Mapuche people tell, the examples they give, when they wish to assert that things are not as they seem in southern Chile. Gonzalo went on to clarify his point about culture, noting that it is not just about *convivencia*, or coexistence, but about things that are inherited, "like the animals." "The Mapuche's character is more sullen [*huraño*]—not to be pejorative—he's, like, silent and closed—that's the difference!" Gonzalo said with excitement, as if he had at that moment discovered the essence of the problem. It is difficult to talk about this without being subjective, he said, as if perhaps to say: forgive me, I know it sounds racist.

I asked how relations between Mapuche and non-Mapuche had changed over time. Gonzalo believes they have gotten worse, and I asked how. He said he would have to talk about politics to answer that question and he did not want to do that. He did, nonetheless, observe that the Concertación had given the Mapuche many rights but few responsibilities. As a side note, he reflected that we in the United States have the same problem with liberties and responsibilities. 'It is good to give the Mapuche land,' he thinks, 'but without responsibilities, they leave it *botada* [messy and abandoned].' Fleshing out this point, Gonzalo relapsed into another jeremiad: 'They don't take care of trees, they let their pigs run all over, they don't take responsibility, their non-Mapuche neighbors keep everything prettier. A Mapuche drunk in the street when you go out with your daughter on a Sunday throws rocks at you; it's an attempt against your liberty, your liberty is invaded.' For all that, he concluded: "The Mapuche are generating resentment instead of intercultural spaces," making already bad relations worse. "Chileans want less and less to do with the Mapuche." Gonzalo looked a little panicked and implored me not to tell anyone he said these things, because it could cost him his job.[6]

Gonzalo's co-worker, Ximena Ortíz, joined the conversation and tried to soften the tone. Things look different from the outside, she insisted. "Just like among Chileans, there are good and bad, there are also good and bad Mapuche. They aren't all victims. . . . They think because they are Mapuche, we have to give them everything without them contributing anything." Although Ximena began by recognizing a certain equality between Chileans and Mapuche, she too ultimately portrayed the Mapuche in negative terms. Having to deal with the complexity of intercultural relations in the context of high levels of conflict over land and other resources may partially explain why Gonzalo and Ximena voiced their frustration in this way. Yet, as agents of the state, they eschewed neutrality to adopt the point of view of colono farmers and local elites who felt vulnerable in the context of growing Mapuche activism.

After demonstrating the disdain he felt toward the Mapuche, Gonzalo surprised me by saying that interculturality fascinated him. I was curious what he meant, and he explained he was involved with a student exchange program and had spent some time in a European country. He also pointed out that in his *comuna* (municipality) there are colonos whose families came from Switzerland, France, Italy, and England, as well as the Mapuche, so there is potential for tourism.[7] But he regretted that the diversity among those groups had merged into the Chilean mainstream ("we put everything in the blender here"), where differences are perceptible only to those willing to "excavate." I found this confusing; these statements contradicted Gonzalo's earlier ones, when he insisted that differences between Mapuche and Chileans were racial in nature and deplored how the Mapuche tried to "impose" their culture on Chileans.

Even more perplexing, when Gonzalo spoke of the creation of Bellaruka, he began by saying, "here the Mapuche" but he stopped himself, saying, "well, *all* of us are descendants of the indigenous here." Those Mapuche who live in the communities have a different structure than the rest of Chileans, he went on to say, and there are strong cultural differences: "They don't like to live among Chileans." But again, Gonzalo returned to the assertion that "here [in Chile], we deemphasize differences. It's when someone comes from the outside that you notice them more." He seemed to want to assert that everyone was the same but was reluctant to do so when it came to Mapuche, who continued to live in rural communities, maintaining ways that by Gonzalo's standards could not be considered "Chilean."

Later I observed Gonzalo in action. Along with Ximena, we drove to a Mapuche community where Gonzalo had some Orígenes work to do. On our way, he reiterated how much he loved Europe and wanted everything to be equal in Chile, as it was there. I was confused because it was clear by now that he was not talking about relations between Mapuche and non-Mapuche. I asked what was at the root of inequality in Chile and he said it is cultural, citing differences between Catholic Chile and Protestant Europe and the work ethic, among other factors. Gonzalo also spoke of how European-descended colonos (those from countries other than Spain) were very racist and discriminated against the Spanish-descended people who settled the country. He found this very unfair, exclaiming: "Imagine that!"

Gonzalo's narrative was strikingly contradictory. Mapuche, especially those who live in rural communities, are racially and culturally different, and apparently odious to him. But he also felt that such differences are not incredibly relevant in Chilean society; it is only when outside observers visit that these differences are noticed (perhaps implying that outside observers *create* the differences—an assertion I would come to hear in various forms over the course of my fieldwork). And finally, Gonzalo opposed discrimination against people like himself but implied that discrimination against the Mapuche was their own fault.

As we approached the meeting place, we passed land the Mapuche community recently had purchased with help from CONADI (the Corporación Nacional de Desarollo Indígena, the National Indigenous Development Agency). It bordered their original community and was pretty rough looking, covered in tree stumps. Gonzalo and Ximena made fun of the community for buying this land. Gonzalo laughed as he asked me, "Would *you* buy this land?" He continued, "I wish the government would buy *me* land. Just 20 hectares is all I'd need." When we arrived, we sat down with Don Amado Kayupi and two other men from the Mapuche community. Amado's wife listened in, doing housework as the meeting proceeded. Gonzalo set about his Orígenes work.

Orígenes is a decentralized program, and communities select consultants who coordinate the labor associated with projects the communities choose to carry out. Gonzalo asked what the consultant had done, and the men told him the consultant had not come out as often as he was supposed to. Gonzalo scolded them: "If the consultant doesn't fulfill his role, it is *your* responsibility." This seemed rather audacious to me, given that part of Gonzalo's job was to assess the work of the consultants. Amado suggested there was a lack of communication about the rules of Orígenes. Gonzalo again passed the buck, saying the consultant should have given them a copy of the plans. Later, he asked how many sheds the community had constructed with money received from Orígenes for that purpose. Amado seemed irritated, asking: "How am I going to build the shed when I don't have a house yet?" Gonzalo questioned whether they were following the recommended design. Amado said, "I think we know by now how to design what we need." Amado and the other men complained about the number of meetings they had to attend in order to receive Orígenes benefits. During the conversation, Gonzalo not only held the community leaders responsible for his own duties, but he seemed to assume they had no knowledge, skills, or insight into their own reality.

As he prepared to leave, Gonzalo asked if there was anything else they wanted to talk about. Don Amado hesitated and then said yes. At a recent meeting, he said, people had complained about Gonzalo's manners. They feel he always tries to find things wrong with what they are doing. Gonzalo became very defensive, responding that it wasn't true. "Am I doing that now?" he sputtered. "I do the exact same thing in all the communities." His defensive response led Amado to go further, saying that people think Gonzalo is arrogant and lords it over them. The tension escalated. On several occasions while Amado was talking, Gonzalo turned to Ximena and said, "I don't understand what he is saying to me." Ximena found herself obliged to repeat exactly what Amado had just said. The interchange became almost surreal. *I* understood what Amado was saying. It may be that Gonzalo simply did not want to hear the complaints and criticisms. Or maybe he was so afraid of the Mapuche that he got worked up to such an extent that he really didn't understand. (Indeed later, when the three of us debriefed over lunch back in town, he said he sometimes worried that "they could do something to me.")

Don Amado complained that Gonzalo was inflexible because he would not let them buy a different type of cow than they had requested in their Orígenes proposal. Gonzalo angrily replied: "I'm not the one who makes the rules and if I don't obey them, I'll lose my job." But Amado was referring to a real problem that needed to be addressed: animal sellers were price-gouging Orígenes beneficiaries. He was frustrated and observed that Chileans complain about all the money the government is giving the Mapuche through Orígenes, but the ones who actually get that money are the same as always: Chilean shop owners, landowners, animal sellers, and consultants. He seemed to be indicating that the rich remain rich and the poor remain poor, just with more government intervention into their lives.

Every point Amado made, Gonzalo either argued or claimed he "couldn't understand." Amado grew visibly frustrated and told Gonzalo there was a saying in Mapudungun: "You're going to wind up without anybody to love you." He insisted Gonzalo needed to change his tune and stop being so arrogant and defensive. Gonzalo continued arguing, and Amado said, "You know, if I do something, I ask forgiveness." But Gonzalo refused to stoop to that level. Before we left, he filled out a required form recording what had been accomplished in this meeting. Even then, he made the community look like the source of the problem. He recorded their complaints in a general sense but ended his report by observing: "I tell the leader I am just following the rules established by the program." Gonzalo actually read this aloud as he wrote it, and when he got to the end, all the men shook their heads and rolled their eyes. Amado said, "Sure, you make yourself look good." Gonzalo pleaded innocence. He may have let the subaltern speak (Spivak 1994), but he still refused to listen.

I found myself nodding in support of Amado and the others. On the way out I told Gonzalo such situations are often best resolved by apologizing. Gonzalo said I was probably right, but the meeting left him with a bitter taste in his mouth. Ximena commented that Amado is a good leader because he will talk these things through and say them to your face. But she also said: "The thing is, you start this work and you think you can change things, but you realize things are really complicated and tiring." Gonzalo said he wanted a different job.

So much could be said about the interview and field excursion with Gonzalo. It gets to the heart of many of the attitudes Chileans in the south hold about the Mapuche and the myths they invent to keep them in their place. It speaks to the continued invisibility of the Mapuche as a legitimate people, as Gonzalo is clearly more interested in intercultural interchange among people of European descent. But it also indicates a certain amount of "racial ambivalence" (Hale 2006), as Gonzalo did facilitate the creation of Bellaruka and seemed less opposed to "urban" Mapuche. Yet he also hinted that "good" Mapuche are those who integrate, particularly for market-oriented ends. Finally, this vignette simultaneously demonstrates the persistence of attitudes of racial superiority, the exhaustion that results from doing work that, for a host of reasons, seldom sees positive results, and the absolute difficulty of intercultural exchange when one partner is considered a racial and cultural inferior. It offers a glimpse of the contradictions that can emerge between new state discourses and policies regarding indigenous rights on the one hand and enduring sociocultural beliefs about race and ethnicity on the other.

"RACE-ING" THE CHILEAN MIRACLE

Although notions of racial and cultural mixing have occasionally sprouted up over the course of Chilean history, Chile does not adhere to the myth of mestizaje dominant in Mexico and parts of Central America.[8] Nor does it have a "white country" myth along the lines of Argentina, although some Chileans claim to be "the English of the Americas." The nation does not identify as a "racial democracy" like Brazil either. Chileans are more likely to elide race altogether, preferring to emphasize class as a social marker. But that people do not talk about race as a part of national identity does not mean it has not shaped the substance of the nation as well as socioeconomic policies. Indeed, race and cultural difference have played a pivotal role in shaping social relations throughout the country, especially in the Araucanía.

Just as race and cultural difference tend to be elided in Chile, they are also neglected in most academic studies of postdictatorship Chile. Although there is a growing historiography regarding the Mapuche and their relationship to the Chilean nation, rarely is race addressed in accounts of Chilean nation building. Nor has the "Chilean Miracle" been examined in terms of its racial consequences. Today the Mapuche make up nearly 6 percent of the Chilean population and about a quarter of the population in the Araucanía.[9] While most indigenous people (well over 60 percent) in Chile now reside in urban areas, the Mapuche population in the Araucanía remains predominantly rural (around 70 percent). Urban and rural Mapuche alike are disproportionately poor. In the context of the Chilean Miracle, some aspects of Mapuche culture are promoted but substantive claims for recognition and distributive justice are denied, and Mapuche territory and the natural resources it holds—timber and water among them—continue to be appropriated for the enrichment of others. Such a situation, I argue, requires that we examine the racialized aspects of Chilean society—particularly in the south and as the south relates to power brokers at the national level—and understand Mapuche interests as distinct from those of Chileans, even as they may overlap in some circumstances.

In this book I show that racial and cultural hierarchies not only played a pivotal role in shaping social relations in the Araucanía in the past, but also pose serious stumbling blocks for the future of Chilean democracy. I focus on two levels of analysis: state policy and local subjectivities. I examine the production and consequences of "neoliberal multiculturalism" as a political project. In much of Latin America, multicultural policies have been used to generate consent for neoliberal reforms emphasizing free markets, decentralization, and small government. As the first country in the region to adopt neoliberalism (but one of the last to embrace multiculturalism), Chile is a particularly compelling case to examine this trend. I also examine how Mapuche activists, colono farmers, elites, and state workers mobilize competing views about race, ethnicity, and nation in the context of the conflicts. Examining these competing worldviews shows that local histories and social imaginaries are not always easily scripted into the neoliberal multicultural agenda. Historically woven local realities can reinforce, reshape, contradict, or challenge processes driven by state and transnational forces.

NEOLIBERAL MULTICULTURAL CITIZENSHIP

Transitions to democracy at the end of the twentieth century in Latin America were commonly accompanied by neoliberal reforms impelled by international financial institutions such as the International Monetary Fund (IMF) and the World Bank. These reforms entailed establishing an export-based economic strategy, opening the economy to international investment, eliminating trade barriers, privatizing state industries, devaluing currency, and replacing universal social services with programs targeting particularly needy sectors (Portes 1997). In Chile neoliberal reforms occurred much earlier, during the Pinochet dictatorship, and were arguably more severe.[10]

The imposition of neoliberal reform represented a transformation of the content of citizenship. Citizenship is the relationship between citizens and the state. It involves the substantive experience of belonging to a nation and the rights and responsibilities associated with that membership (Richards 2004). Building on the work of T. H. Marshall (1950), much theorizing of citizenship focuses on civil, political, and social rights as granted to and exercised by individuals. Although neoliberal reforms have generally upheld political rights (to vote, to be represented or elected) and civil rights (to private property, to individual liberties), social rights to public goods like healthcare, education, nutrition, and housing have been vastly curtailed. An important aspect of neoliberalism has thus involved inducing nongovernmental and community organizations to perform what were once state responsibilities (Roberts and Portes 2006; Vilas 1996). The role of citizens in the democratic process, indigenous and nonindigenous alike, is reduced to voting, consuming, and participating in community projects to make up for the loss of state services rather than making demands on the state, leading some to refer to postdictatorship democracies in Latin America as partial or "low intensity" (Gills, Rocamora, and Wilson 1993).

The rights of indigenous peoples generally have not rested easily with the concept of citizenship, not least because the existence of indigenous peoples preceded the creation of nation-states in their territories. The state represents that which usurped their land, committed genocide on their people, and binds them in an ongoing relationship of colonial dispossession. While the indigenous too are holders of individual rights, indigenous movements often focus on the importance of cultural rights (to language, traditions, ways of life) and collective rights (to territory, autonomous self-government) to their ongoing survival as peoples. Because they often are practiced by collectivities, these rights come into conflict with citizenship regimes based on the notion that rights inhere in the individual.

In an apparent contradiction, however, from the late 1980s to the mid-2000s, many Latin American neoliberal governments enacted multicultural reforms. Multiculturalism refers to "the efforts of liberal democratic governments to accept and embrace . . . ethnic differences" among their citizenry (Postero 2007, 13). These reforms entailed the recognition of cultural rights and, to a lesser extent, collective ones. For example, most Latin American states have ratified International Labor Organization (ILO) Convention 169, which recognizes indigenous rights to identity, language, consultation, territory, and self-governance. Social programs, such as intercultural education and healthcare, which are intended to be culturally inclusive, often accompany states' discursive commitment to multiculturalism. Several Latin American states even have incorporated indigenous participation and consultation, along with limited versions of autonomy, into their policies.[11] Multiculturalism thus has accompanied neoliberal reform in many parts of the region, representing, at least on the surface, a transformation in the relationship between indigenous citizens and the state.

Scholars have come up with various hypotheses to explain the apparent contradiction between the relatively restrictive form of democracy that prevails in much of the region and the aperture toward indigenous rights. Some maintain that democratization necessarily led to the expansion of rights for the indigenous as well as other citizens (Brysk 2000). Others suggest that together with neoliberal cutbacks, incomplete processes of political liberalization unintentionally led to expanding indigenous demands for political access, local autonomy, and participation (Yashar 1999). In fact, the increased role for community organizations and decentralization associated with neoliberalism may be necessary—if not sufficient—conditions for exercising some form of autonomy. Others argue that Latin American states incorporate indigenous peoples into politics and implement multicultural reforms to prove their legitimacy as democratic actors while also reducing potential instability (Van Cott 1994, 2000).

Still, rights and recognition are granted to the indigenous only insofar as they do not threaten state goals in the global economy. Thus Charles Hale (2002) has argued that many of these analyses exaggerate the power of indigenous movements and play down the extent to which multicultural and indigenous policies are part and parcel of neoliberal strategy. He suggests that rather than completely denying indigenous rights, states have granted some reforms to undermine pressures for more radical change. Bret Gustafson (2002) likewise sees indigenous policy reform as a strategy to insulate elite interests from the growing power of popular movements. The result is what Hale (2002, 2006), Nancy Grey Postero (2004, 2007), Lynn Horton (2006), Nina Laurie, Robert Andolina, and Sarah Radcliffe (2003), and others have referred to as neoliberal multiculturalism: a new form of governance in which cultural recognition is promoted without the economic and political redistribution that would lead to greater equality. Latin American states highlight diversity and grant a limited measure of autonomy, but construe demands for radical redistribution, autonomous territory, and self-determination as counterproductive for multicultural society (Hale 2002; Richards 2004).

Scholars and indigenous activists alike have voiced skepticism about multiculturalism as it has been incorporated into state policies in the neoliberal context. Much of this skepticism has focused on the tendency of states to promote formal recognition of indigenous rights without accompanying it with the redistribution of socioeconomic resources that could make that recognition meaningful (Assies, Ramírez, and Ventura Patiño 2006; Becker

2011; Hale 2006; Lucero 2009; Postero 2007; and Stahler-Sholk 2007). State-driven multiculturalism is thus criticized for recognizing diversity without addressing the power inequalities entailed by systemic racism and ethnocentrism. Bolivia and Guatemala each provide a case in point. According to Postero (2007), the neoliberal multicultural era in Bolivia (from the late 1980s to the early 2000s) was marked by demands for recognition and indigenous rights as well as state-driven multicultural reforms that, through decentralization and incorporating participation into budgetary decisions, responded to some of those demands but did not result in redistribution of power or resources because structures of inequality remained in place at the local level. Postero (2007, 4) has argued that despite the presence of multicultural policies, neoliberal reforms "reinforced the racialized inequalities long existing in Bolivia, laying bare the continued monopoly of power held by dominant classes and transnational corporations." Postero contends that with mass protests in the early 2000s and the election of Evo Morales, Bolivia entered a "postmulticultural" period. In contrast to neoliberal multiculturalism, this has involved a shift away from recognition as a central demand of indigenous protest and toward making demands for a new citizenship relationship on behalf of the Bolivian people as a whole.[12] This includes putting an end to structured inequalities (on the basis of race as well as class) and assuring that development benefits the people, resources are fairly distributed, and Bolivian patrimony remains in the hands of the people.

Hale (2006) has classified Guatemala as in the midst of a neoliberal multicultural moment, and yet he observes that, as in Bolivia, recognition-related demands have lost their prominence: "If the quintessential indigenous demand in the formative phase of Maya identity politics was to achieve state recognition, the greatest challenge now is to prevail in negotiations over what that recognition actually means in practice. Even the demand for autonomy, the culmination of indigenous empowerment in the previous era, faces this dilemma. The neoliberal state no longer opposes indigenous autonomy in all its forms; its preferred response, rather, is to concede limited autonomy, in the form of decentralization, participatory budgeting, and various other types of limited local control, and to draw the line there" (ibid., 37). A 2010 issue of *NACLA Report on the Americas* goes further, suggesting that indigenous movements in Latin America are now "after" recognition. Because recognition as achieved has been of little substance, NACLA suggests, indigenous peoples throughout the region are transferring their energies to demanding socioeconomic redistribution and combating the ravages of capitalism.

Despite what seems to be accepted as a general pattern in the region, the case of Chile shows that recognition continues to be an important part of the struggles of at least some indigenous peoples and a point of contention in their relationship with national governments. In Chile recognition and autonomy remain very contemporary—and contested—demands. Like those of many indigenous peoples, Mapuche demands have long centered on both redistribution of resources and recognition of Mapuche status as a people with the rights that entails (Richards 2004).[13] The state has responded with some recognition but to a much more limited extent than other Latin American states. In the 1990s, while other Latin American states were engaging in however-limited recognition, the Concertación framed Mapuche demands largely as a problem of poverty. This was the case despite the creation of CONADI in 1993 and Orígenes in 2001, even as the creation of a Comisión de Verdad Histórica y Nuevo Trato (Historical Truth and New Deal Commission) in 2001 and passage of ILO 169 in 2008 represented steps toward formal recognition of indigenous rights. All of these measures are discussed in greater detail in chapter 4.

In part, the limited scope of recognition in Chile is related to the fact that the country remains exceptionally centralized. As a result, even the limited local or regional autonomy granted in other countries is not seen in Chile. Consultation or participation of indigenous communities in decisions and policies is highly constrained, when it exists at all. In addition, conflicts over development projects and territorial claims created a situation in which the Concertación had to respond to Mapuche rights claims at the same time it answered to demands from the political right for harsher penalties against Mapuche activists. All told, although Chile under the Concertación did share some overlap with other countries, these factors make it unique in being, if not an exceptional case of neoliberal multiculturalism, then at least a particularly reticent one.

Most understandings of neoliberal multiculturalism view the state as nonmonolithic in its actions and intent, and rely on the work of Antonio Gramsci and Michel Foucault for theoretical guidance (e.g., Hale 2002; Park and Richards 2007). For Gramsci (1971), ruling class hegemony is built not simply through force or coercion, but rather by incorporating some of the interests of a broad range of social groups into the state agenda. Social movement activism may expand the scope of citizenship, but expansion of rights by the state simultaneously integrates citizens into the hegemonic project and generates consent for state objectives. The movement goals taken on by the state usually cohere with, or at least do not openly challenge, hegemonic material and cultural objectives. This helps explain why only some aspects of indigenous claims are incorporated as part of state-driven multiculturalism.

Nevertheless, the Gramscian approach does not capture the extent to which the advancement of these objectives involves the construction of new types of citizen-subjects. The work of Foucault is vital in this regard. For Foucault, individuals become subjects of a given regime through a dialectical process of "self-making and being-made" involving techniques that include "surveillance, discipline, control, and administration" (Ong 1996, 737). He referred to this process as "governmentality." A wide range of actors—in the state as well as in civil society—may participate in subject-making on the part of the state (Gordon 1991). Conversely, others may construct subject positions that contradict state objectives. Gonzalo illustrates the indigenous subjectivity promoted by the state in the context of neoliberal multiculturalism: willing to engage in personal improvement according to the rules of the market, respectful of private property, and eager to promote diversity. Don Amado's self-asserting manner is unacceptable in this context; rather than questioning what the state provides, the indigenous subject should be humble and grateful. The consequences faced by Mapuche who resist this paradigm are revealed in later chapters.

SYSTEMIC RACISM

Assumptions about race and racism are built into the neoliberal multicultural project. As Hale (2006, 20) has observed, neoliberal multiculturalism simultaneously "affirms cultural rights and endorses the principle of equality, while remaking societies with ever more embedded and resilient forms of racial hierarchy." Racial discourses (like class and gender ones) are integrated into social and economic policy and permeate struggles over national identity and indigenous rights. They are transmitted through citizenship regulations, education, religion, and the mass media, and they inform daily experiences and relationships.

The story of Gonzalo shows how notions of race and culture are interwoven in the Araucanía. In fact, Gonzalo seemed to use two different conceptions of culture. On the one hand, he used "culture" as a synonym for knowledge, skills, and work ethic. He implied that the Mapuche do not have culture and resorted to a racially infused nineteenth-century dichotomy of civilization versus barbarism. On the other hand, Gonzalo also referred to culture as ancestral beliefs and customs. This is the "culture" that he complains mainstream Chilean society has erased. Had European immigrants more fully retained their ancestral idiosyncrasies, the area would be a tourist beacon with festivals, colorful dress, and varied culinary traditions. If that context were a reality, it might be possible for the Mapuche to be another attraction in the local tourist package, particularly if they were willing to perform their culture in accordance with Western norms. Yet Mapuche insistence that they are not just a tourist attraction, in combination with the obstinacy of racist notions of indigenous barbarity, makes this seem like a distant possibility.

It may seem strange to use words like "race" and "racism" in describing indigenous peoples, who perhaps more often are conceptualized in terms of ethnicity. "Ethnicity" refers to the social meanings associated with cultural difference. Ethnic identities are often tied to the concept of place—being "from" somewhere in particular (Wade 1997). However, as Peter Wade has pointed out, understandings of indigeneity also contain elements of race. Race can be defined as the social meanings, conflicts, and interests attached to particular differences in phenotype—the range of human bodies' observable characteristics (Omi and Winant 1994). In fact, there is a great deal of overlap between social understandings of race and ethnicity. For example, the cultural and the phenotypic are often mutually implicated in popular understandings of where purportedly racial and ethnic attributes come from; both are treated as inheritable traits built into our genetic makeup, such that we can speak of cultural racism as well as racism based on skin color and other physical attributes. In fact, most racism is likely a combination of the two types (Hooker 2009). I favor the terms "race" and "racism" over "ethnicity" throughout this book, in part because of the social reality of this overlap, and in part because indigenous peoples generally distinguish themselves from ethnic groups by noting that they are not immigrants to a given place, but a nation or people possessing rights to a territory that was invaded and appropriated.

I turn to the work of Michael Omi and Howard Winant (1994), Joe Feagin (2006), and Eduardo Bonilla-Silva (2001) for theoretical guidance on race and racism. I am also especially indebted to Hale (2006), who has theorized the intersections of neoliberal multiculturalism and race based on the case of Guatemala. Although they use different terminology (Hale follows Omi and Winant in referring to racial formations; Feagin refers to systemic racism, and Bonilla-Silva to structural racism and racialized social systems), all of these authors view race as a sociohistorical construction. They see racism as embedded in social institutions, ideologies, and discourses—pervasive in all aspects of social life. I also draw from Anibal Quijano (2000, 2007) and his colleagues, who argue that racism is rooted in the experience of coloniality, with both economic and epistemic consequences.

These authors draw attention to the fact that race is not a natural or objective fact; rather, it comes to exist through a sociohistorical process, which many of them call racialization. That is, groups come to be categorized as races through a process in which social meanings are attached to phenotypic, cultural, or other differences. Those categories then become a central part of how society is organized; race influences the shape of social structure, politics, the economy, and other institutions (Bonilla-Silva 2001; Omi and Winant 1994). The related concept of racial formation refers to "the socio-historical process by which [particular] racial categories are created, inhabited, transformed, and destroyed" (Omi and Winant 1994, 55). In the case of Latin America, R. Douglas Cope (1994) has shown how Spanish colonization was accompanied by the creation of a *sistema de castas* (caste system) that ranked categories of people based on their racial purity (judged in terms of blood). The Spanish were at the top of the hierarchy, Indians and Africans at the bottom, and different "mixed" groups at various spots in between. As Postero (2007) has observed, social markers (dress, language, place of residence, and so on) eventually supplanted biology in determining racial identity, especially as intermixing made policing biological boundaries impossible. Nevertheless, these initial categorizations continue to shape racial formation throughout Latin America.

Race is a social construction, but it has very real material consequences. Racism is more than attitudes and discriminatory actions; it is built into social systems. The "effort to reorganize and redistribute resources along particular racial lines," accompanied by the representations and interpretations that explain race and race relations, make up what Omi and Winant (1994, 56) have called a "racial project." We can understand colonialism in Latin America as a racial project, as it was designed to facilitate the oppression of some (people of African as well as indigenous descent) and the appropriation of their labor and resources for the benefit of others. To a significant extent, this colonial dispossession continues to this day. In fact, Quijano (2000), Arturo Escobar (2007), and others have argued that global capitalism is the contemporary manifestation of modernity, which they see as rooted in the conquest and colonization of the Americas. The domination of non-European peoples on the basis of race, involving the "subalternization of [their] knowledge and cultures," is a necessary dimension of global capitalism (Escobar 2007, 184). Indeed, it is racial classification, first applied in Latin America to indigenous peoples, that has provided the justification for Eurocentric dominance in the global capitalist system (Quijano 2000, 2007). "In America," Quijano (2000, 534) has written, "the idea of race was a way of granting legitimacy to the relations of domination imposed by the conquest." Today, coloniality is the condition that remains, sustaining this inequality, even after formal colonialism has ended (Quijano 2007). (Many indigenous people would argue that formal colonialism is still in place, as their territories remain occupied.) This perspective drives home the importance of studying race and racialization in Latin America. It also adds to the analysis of neoliberal multiculturalism, suggesting its connections to a long history of colonial exploitation.

I am sensitive to the limitations of the wholesale application of U.S.-based concepts to social reality in other parts of the world. Nevertheless, given the process of racialization that has occurred in the Americas, and its links to coloniality, the concept of systemic racism is useful for understanding the Chilean context. Acknowledging that many societies are racially structured is not the same as saying race functions in the same way everywhere and at all times. This is what we mean when we say race is socially and historically constructed. As a product of global discursive flows associated with colonialism and slavery, race has impacted a broad range of societies, but it has done so in different ways in different places. As Hale (2006, 12) has observed, that the indigenous "have been systematically and structurally subordinated as indigenous people" is itself a compelling reason to analyze race in Latin America. Hooker (2009, 74, 81) adds that while many indigenous peoples self-identify in cultural rather than racial ways, indigenous peoples and Afro-descendants alike suffer negation of collective and cultural rights (to language, practices, territory, and so on) as well as straightforward racial discrimination, such as "denial of access to public establishments [and] labor discrimination." Facts like these make it worthwhile to specify how race and racism function in Latin American societies.

Hale and Hooker both note, however, that the impulse to look at racial formation in Latin America stands in tension with academic trends focusing on deconstructing race. It also conflicts with the position that "any generalized notion of racial formation would do violence to the rich and extensive heterogeneity in the ways that race is signified across space and time" (Hale 2006, 204). I stand with Bonilla-Silva, Hale, and others in maintaining that we can argue that race structures social systems while also specifying how that happens in particular ways in particular places; indeed, this is precisely what is necessary.

I address this central question: How has race shaped the Chilean social system, particularly in the Chilean South, and how does it continue to do so? To what extent did neoliberal and multicultural agendas under the Concertación represent a break with or a perpetuation of systemic racism and coloniality? As Patricia Hill Collins (1998) would have it, I am interested in examining the power relations that have shaped racial difference in Chile, recognizing race as a social construction at the same time as I analyze its powerful material and symbolic effects on Mapuche/Chilean society.

The state is a central focus in many studies of systemic racism. As Bonilla-Silva (2001) and Feagin (2006) have pointed out, state policy is only one means through which structural racism is perpetuated. Omi and Winant (1994, 82) insist that as "the focus of collective demands both for egalitarian and democratic reforms and for the enforcement of existing privileges," the state, while not unitary in action or intent, is a central actor in the process of racial formation. Throughout Chilean history the state has been a central focus of Mapuche demands as well as those of elites seeking to encroach upon Mapuche territory and resources. Through indigenous and broader economic policy, the state has shaped (and disciplined) indigenous subjects and built racial inequality into the system. Those inequalities—beginning with the original colonial assault and continuing in the present-day imposition of development projects and timber plantations in ancestral Mapuche territory—represent a systematic dispossession of the Mapuche to the benefit of elite Chileans. This book traces that history and shows how, to the extent that they represent an effort to consolidate the hegemony of the neoliberal model, indigenous and multicultural policies under the Concertación are a central part of an ongoing racial project.

Although I recognize that structural racism transcends the state, much of my attention is given to how shifting state policy and discourse have changed the racialized social system. I describe the conflicts that have emerged from a combination of Chile's racial legacies and contemporary policies that promote export industries and large-scale development projects. The Chilean version of multiculturalism developed in response to these conflicts. As elsewhere in the region, this has entailed promoting some indigenous behaviors as legitimate and criminalizing others that are perceived to threaten national development. Chile nevertheless differs from other countries, both in its reticence to recognize the legitimate existence of indigenous peoples and in its particularly enthusiastic application of state violence and charges of terrorism against Mapuche activists. Chile thus reflects not only wider regional trends but also continuity with its own racial history. Altogether, the Chilean case shows how, paradoxically, racism can be reinscribed by policies that on their face are about diversity and acceptance of difference. Chile is an extreme case, but one that sheds light on the persistent racism entrenched in democracies around the world.

At the same time, I argue that these state-driven changes are contradictory and incomplete. This makes it necessary to examine not just state processes but also the discourse and actions of local-level actors, which may draw from resources that contradict the state's aims. Scholars focusing elsewhere in the Americas have referred to new forms of racism that have emerged in the contemporary era. Bonilla-Silva (2001) has written of covert racist practices accompanied by an ideology of "color blind racism" in the United States, whereas in Guatemala, Hale (2006, 11) has recorded the emergence of "racial ambivalence," in which nonindigenous *ladinos* embrace egalitarianism and simultaneously "believe, and continue to benefit from the structured belief, that ladinos are 'más que un indio' [more than an Indian]." As part of this process, Guatemalan ladinos tend to leave biological explanations of race behind, embracing cultural ones instead. In both cases, although the shape of structural racism has shifted, racial supremacy is maintained.

While patterns of racial domination in the Chilean South are shifting, the concept of "new racism" does not settle easily with the Chilean case. Because of recent conflicts over resources and indigenous rights in the south, the state has slowly begun to promote multicultural policies that are similar to those in other countries in the region. But there has not yet been the convincing shift in racial discourse that Hale and Bonilla-Silva have observed. This may be related to the conflicts, which lead Chileans at the local level to resist multicultural discourses, or it may be related to a reluctance to acknowledge the Mapuche at all. The commitment to cultural equality that Hale has observed in Guatemala did not exist among my Chilean respondents. Although the government promoted cultural equality and the principle of equality did come up in conversation with local elites, most often culture was invoked to contend that the Mapuche were inferior and needed to change.

Finally, cultural racism is not new in Chile; rather, race and culture have always been mixed in Chileans' narratives about the Mapuche. Purportedly "old" ideas about racial inferiority persist in the Chilean South, contradicting the government's message of cultural equality. In turn, the new state policies do not totally challenge these views and in some respects rely on them, thus allowing racial dominance to be maintained. So although it is worthwhile to think about the Chilean case through a lens of systemic racism—recognizing that it is not the only organizing principle of the Chilean social system but one of the most important in the south—I am reluctant to say a new racism is operating there. I am more interested in *how* local manifestations of racism contrast or align with versions promoted by the state.

TALKING TO PEOPLE: SUBJECTIVITY AND RESISTANCE

One of the limitations of structural approaches, such as the approach to describing racism just outlined, is that they tend to fall short in explaining the role of human actors in reproducing and resisting the system. Sometimes the focus on systems and structures blinds us from remembering that humans create them, and they are sustained through social interaction. This is true not only of structural approaches to racism but of structural approaches to explaining social phenomena more generally. Light Carruyo (2007, 7), in reflecting on development scholarship, has observed that the field "has not yet found a vocabulary to connect large structural processes to the ways in which people live, love, and labor" or to understand "the ways [people] challenge and negotiate broader structural processes." She draws attention to the role of humans in creating social structure, living out their lives in contexts constricted by it, and resisting domination.

Many advocates of structural approaches to understanding racism recognize people play a role in reproducing and resisting it. For example, Bonilla-Silva (2001, 63) has emphasized that although ideology is built into and reinforces social structure, it is not an explicit roadmap for action and belief, but rather, it "furnish(es) the basic principles individuals use to sift through contested and often contradictory information in order to make sense of social reality." He sees a role for interviewing people to ascertain commonalities in how they talk about race that would indicate the existence of a changing racial ideology. Feagin (2006, 25) has advocated interviewing the racially dominant in order to reveal the elements of what he calls the racial frame—"an organized set of racialized ideas, stereotypes, emotions, and inclinations to discriminate," associated with discriminatory behaviors and embedded in social institutions.[14] Conversely, Feagin suggests that interviewing the racially oppressed provides insight into how racist social structure impacts individual lives.

Omi and Winant (1994, 59) take a Gramscian approach, suggesting that looking to the micro-social level allows us to see how people engage in and reproduce "common sense." Gramsci, they explain, defined common sense as the set of popular ideas and practices that ruling groups establish, through education, religion, the media, and other means, to consolidate hegemony. "It is through its production and its adherence to this 'common sense,'" Omi and Winant (1994, 67) tell us, "that a society gives its consent to the way in which it is ruled." Thus for all of these authors, even though racism is built into social structure, it involves individuals. Micro-level analysis is worthwhile not simply to establish individual-level attitudes and prejudices but to ascertain how structural racism and power pervade everyday life.

These approaches are useful in explaining contemporary racism in Chile, because they focus on how the entire social system is founded on racism as opposed to racism being the mean-heartedness of some individuals. In addition, they draw attention to how systemic racism persists even as particular racial formations change, and they highlight the roles of actors in producing and reproducing racism to derive systematic advantage at the expense of the racially oppressed. And yet the Chilean case presents additional quandaries that required talking to people and observing the "everyday" for other reasons as well. The shift toward multiculturalism in Chile under the Concertación suggests that the country was following the rest of the region in establishing a new racial project, at least in terms of policy and official state discourse. These changes seemed to do little to challenge racial hierarchies and, to a great extent, reinforced them. Local elites did not simply reproduce state-driven ideologies and frames but instead seemed to struggle with them, accommodating them in some ways and resisting them in others. It may be that in this particular historical moment, it was possible to observe competing racial discourses especially clearly; there were important disjunctures and points of conflict between new state and transnational discourses and local-level "common-sense" understandings. But the state at times also made use of elite resistance to justify its own reticence in addressing some Mapuche claims. Even within the state, there were two competing discourses: one of cultural acceptance, which was used to generate consent among the indigenous, and one of terrorism, which allowed the state to use coercion when consent was not conferred.

Racial discourses in the Chilean South did not always match up easily with those promoted by the state. These disjunctures—suggestive at the very least of competing elements within racial ideology or the racial frame—are an important part of how race is organized and organizes society in the south. I do not contest the basic premise that racism is systemic and structures all of society, and that this is reflected in "common-sense" understandings and practices at the micro-level. However, I seek to understand the differences between the dominant racial project and local articulations of race, difference, and belonging, and how people negotiate and make sense of those differences as the dominant racial project changes.

In doing so, I turn for guidance to approaches on how people negotiate social structure, draw from multiple discourses, and accommodate or resist contradictory discourses in their everyday lives. For example, while Ruth Frankenburg (1993) has agreed that race structures social reality, she suggests that actors learn, enact, and draw upon various "discursive repertoires" in thinking through race. She argues that it is necessary to situate actors' race talk in relation to this range of repertoires as well as material reality in particular historical moments and places. In her analysis of competing views on human rights in Chiapas, Shannon Speed (2008, 69) has pointed out that national and transnational discourses are filtered through "local understandings and political subjectivities"; people's history and lived experience impact how they interpret these discourses and put them into play.

Horton (2006) has made a similar point. She argues that multiculturalism is both a top-down process that advances neoliberalism and a bottom-up one that challenges it, and that these processes "interact in complex ways as mediated by national and local experiences" (ibid., 847). Moreover, as Postero (2007) has noted (speaking of the indigenous but making a point that can be extended to the racially dominant as well), subjects do not only or always consent—they evaluate, measure options, and may reject, refashion, or resist. This suggests that even if these new discourses are reflective of an overarching racial frame or ideology, they are used in complex ways on the ground, and investigating them can give us a better sense of how racism operates in a given society at a given historical juncture. This point is particularly important in the Chilean case, where multicultural discourses filtering down from the transnational and national levels are confronted with competing worldviews at the local level.[15] Focusing on what people say and do on the ground allows us to look at the interplay between how "difference" is "done" and the fact that, as Hill Collins (1998) has pointed out, difference is not inherent to groups but rather produced by power relations. That is, talking to people about racism allows us to examine the interplay between race as a structure and race as actively produced through interaction (and thus possible to resist in interaction).

Postero has also pointed out that sometimes competing discourses draw people in opposing directions. Neoliberalism as a discourse is not all powerful; race and class discourses often construct individuals and groups in different ways: "While one discourse may create Bolivian neoliberal subjects responsible for their own governing, the other reminds those subjects that they are lazy Indians" (Postero 2007, 187). While Hale might suggest (and I agree) that this contradiction is part of how racism operates in the neoliberal multicultural context, Postero's observations are important; even if both tendencies are reflective of a new racial reality, they pull in opposing directions, and it is only by talking to people at the local level that we can begin to make sense of that.

I appreciate Hale's (2006, 17) take on this tension. On the one hand, he is committed to "situating ladinos within a power-laden racial formation." On the other, he insists: "My emphasis on ethnography, and more specifically, the ethnography of social interaction and political process . . . stands in tension with those who, in their salutary focus on racialized power, end up neglecting how people negotiate, contest, and maneuver within these spaces of structured inequality." He concludes: "Theoretically, racial formation analysis focuses primarily on how political subjectivities are constituted by powerful external forces (subject formation), and needs to devote greater attention to how collective and individual actors actively give meaning to the world around them (self-making)" (Hale 2006, 209). Hale's reference to subject formation and self-making reflects the Foucauldian approach described earlier, with which the desire to acknowledge the structural aspects of racism stands in tension in some respects. But while the Foucauldian perspective helps us understand how racial discourses are used to shape subjects, not unlike structural approaches, it is less helpful in understanding how subjects push back. Although Foucault draws attention to subjects "being made" as well as to "self-making"—and argues that wherever there is power, there is the possibility of resistance—the bulk of his work focuses on techniques of domination. Much of Foucault's theorization of "self-making" focuses on the internalization and expression of domination—the process of being subjugated or made subject to (Foucault 1983, 212).

In his later work, Foucault focused more on resistance, but he conceptualized it, as well as the subject, from a highly individualized perspective, making it difficult to theorize collective resistance (Best and Kellner 1991). This limitation is problematic when we seek to consider how groups reject or resist subject formation—from the perspective of those who wish to retain racial hierarchies and feel threatened by the state's shifting racial project, but especially from the perspective of the indigenous who reject the state's project as more of the same. Indeed, the struggles of subjugated groups—the indigenous, women, formerly enslaved peoples of African descent, the colonized—have focused not just on material equality but on recognition that they have a right to be subjects of the social world (Auyero 2003; DuBois [1903] 1969; Hartsock 1990; D. Smith 1979; Tuhiwai Smith 1999). This liberatory aspect of subjectivity—the sense of a desire and a right to be self-defining subjects—should not be ignored when theorizing these struggles.

Understanding resistance to systemic racism demands that we pay attention to material inequality as well as (mis)recognition, and thus the roles subjectification and self-construction play in everyday experience. Likewise, understanding how nonindigenous elites think of themselves as legitimately dominant in society, the subjects of the social world, requires a theory of systemic racism and processes of power, but it also requires a theory of subjectivity. As Quijano (2000, 541) has pointed out, part of racism is claiming universality for Eurocentric forms of knowledge and repressing the knowledge of the colonized (for instance, see Bacigalupo [2007] on how colonization shaped practices, meanings, and resistance among Mapuche Shamans). In the end, although the shifting structures of systemic racism involve forming a certain type of subject—subjectification, in Foucault's terminology—understanding the day-to-day functioning of racism and resistance requires looking at how subjects assert themselves, interpret and reproduce the discourses around them, and demand to be self-constructing subjects in their own right.[16]

The story of Gonzalo that opened this chapter shows just how much is at stake when changing state policies and discourses butt up against individuals' and groups' understandings of themselves and the other. Throughout the book I draw attention to this issue: the intersections and disjunctures between state-driven changes in systemic racism and local understandings and actions. These intersections and disjunctures are key to understanding the persistence of racism in contemporary democracies. States' disinterest in substantively addressing issues related to redistribution and the recognition of the rights of indigenous peoples and other subordinated populations, *as well as* the resistance of people at all levels of the state and society to incorporate those principles into their everyday practices, together allow racism to thrive. In this sense the Araucanía is not an exception to the rule but paradigmatic of how racism operates in contemporary democracies.

METHOD, SITE, AND SAMPLE

I have been conducting research in southern Chile since 1999. Most of the fieldwork for this study was carried out over ten months between 2004 and 2007. I completed seventy-five qualitative in-depth interviews, most of which were audio-recorded. Most of these interviews were conducted with colono farmers and other local elites, state workers, and Mapuche activists from four comunas located in the Araucanía. Each of these comunas consists of a small to medium-sized town surrounded by Mapuche communities, farmland, timber plantations, and sometimes a smaller village. I chose to do in-depth interviews because I was interested in how these actors described and explained their beliefs, actions, and interactions with others, the motivations behind them, and their interpretations of the actions of others. By understanding and contrasting individuals' motivations and explanations for their behavior and attitudes, I could begin to understand conflicts over indigenous rights in the Chilean South and the extent to which these were mediated by multicultural discourses disseminating from the state and transnational levels. I also conducted ethnographic fieldwork, which included informal conversations with the actors involved, observations of state workers on the job, visits to Mapuche communities and the farms of *atentado* victims, and attendance at terrorism trials, meetings, seminars, and other activities and events.[17] These activities provided the valuable opportunity to corroborate or clarify what interview respondents had told me but also to deepen conversations and observe intercultural interactions in person. Finally, I collected a variety of secondary and media sources as well as organizational and agency documents.

Two of the selected comunas were located in the province of Malleco (the northern part of the Araucanía) and two in the province of Cautín (the southern part). I have chosen not to call the comunas by name to preserve the anonymity of respondents. As the comunas in each province displayed many commonalities with each other, I generally refer to them as "a Cautín comuna" or "a Malleco comuna." I selected the four comunas for several reasons. The Malleco comunas were sites of some of the most extreme conflicts between timber companies and/or colono elites and the Mapuche. One of the two comunas has a majority Mapuche population, and both have high colono populations. The Cautín comunas both have a Mapuche majority and had experienced little conflict along the lines of Malleco at the time of my fieldwork. Timber plantations have been rapidly taking over the territory, however. The Cautín comunas also have a long history of Mapuche political influence, whereas Malleco is one of the areas where the Coordinadora Arauko-Malleko, many of whose members have been accused of terrorism, has been most active.[18] Although about two-thirds of my interviews were conducted in these comunas, others were conducted with local elites, colono farmers, and Mapuche activists from other comunas as well as with regional-level state workers, representatives of NGOs, the Catholic Church, and universities, and a couple of individuals linked to the timber companies. Interviews took place wherever respondents' preferred: in their homes, places of business, local cafés, or at an NGO in Temuco, the centrally located regional capital, where I had use of office space. I conducted purposive as well as snow-ball sampling, meaning that in some cases I sought out key players in the region or conflicts, and in others, respondents recommended additional people to interview. I also relied on assistance from colleagues at local universities and NGOs. During my fieldwork I resided in Temuco and traveled regularly by car or bus to the other comunas.

Many respondents chose to appear by name when they signed their consent form. However, given the ongoing conflicts, I have decided to use pseudonyms for all respondents. In a context in which colonos were experiencing attacks on their property and Mapuche were being tried as terrorists, I simply did not want to risk the possibility of contributing to their further endangerment. Nevertheless, comments extracted from the media are attributed to their actual source. This means that some interviewees whose comments to the media are quoted in this book appear under their real name in those comments, and under a pseudonym in excerpts from their interviews with me. Similarly, there are Mapuche activists and scholars I interviewed whose work I cite; they appear by name when I cite their written material but by pseudonym in excerpts from our interviews. I also have chosen to conceal the identities of rural Mapuche communities; because they are small, revealing their names could jeopardize respondents' anonymity. Larger organizations to which respondents belonged are identified by name, unless doing so would reveal the identity of the respondent. There are a few exceptions to the rules described here. In chapters 3 and 4, I describe several well-known and reported conflicts in detail and by name; several individuals involved in those conflicts appear by pseudonym elsewhere in the book.[19]

The respondents I refer to as "local elites" include medium-scale colono farmers who have been targets of land recoveries or arson as well as lawyers, politicians, businesspeople, and local historians. Most were men, middle-aged or older; their wives and children often participated in the interviews as well. Some were not only relevant political actors at the local level, but through their involvement in regional and national politics, agricultural associations, and development initiatives, they also had broader influence. Others, including many of the colono farmers, came from families that once had a great deal of local and regional (and in some cases national) power and stature. Today they had less influence than they once did, but by virtue of their names, family histories, and direct involvement in the conflicts, they still exercised significant influence in shaping public opinion. "Local elite" is obviously a catchall term, and as much as possible, I try to describe particular respondents over the course of the book. "Colono" carries a number of meanings in Chile; for the purposes of this book, it refers to the descendents of Europeans who immigrated to the Araucanía after Chile defeated the Mapuche in the late 1800s.

Most of the state workers interviewed worked at the local level, either for municipalities or for national or regional programs with local operations. A few worked at the regional level. They worked for INDAP, Orígenes, intercultural health programs, departments of education, schools, forestry programs, social development offices, and other agencies and programs. Most held either technical or college degrees. They were women and men, Mapuche and nonindigenous, and ranged from their early twenties to advanced middle-aged. I focused on local state workers because I wanted to learn about and observe indigenous policies in action and to talk to the people who represented the state in Mapuche individuals' and communities' daily lives. In the case of non-Mapuche workers, I wished to ascertain the extent to which their exposure to Mapuche communities might contribute to less stereotypical or, conversely, hardened racial attitudes. In the case of Mapuche workers, I was interested in how they grappled with what many characterized as a hybrid existence, simultaneously of the state and of the movement.

Mapuche respondents included leaders and members of a wide range of organizations and communities. Many of the organizations focused their efforts broadly (beyond a single comuna), but even then I tried to interview members who lived in the four focus comunas. Some Mapuche respondents were directly involved in the conflicts; others were not. They included young people as well as "historical" leaders, active since the Allende years and before. Although my previous work (Richards 2004, 2005, 2006) focused on Mapuche women, the majority of Mapuche respondents for this study were men. In part, this is related to the fact that most visible leaders of the movement were men. I tried to combat their overrepresentation by interviewing women whenever possible and by addressing the issue of gender within the movement in chapter 6.

Despite the fact that at least 80 percent of Chilean citizens are mestizo, very few identify as such (Bacigalupo 2007). The informal system of social classification in the Araucanía refers to two oppositional categories of identification: Mapuche and Chilean or *winka*.[20] These are the terms people in the Chilean South use to refer to self and other, and there are places in this book that I make use of this dichotomy. However, I want to emphasize that although the categories are used oppositionally in the region, distinctions between the two groups are not absolute, and it is important to avoid reifying them. Although dichotomous understandings of self and other often attend social conflict, and the Mapuche and local elites I interviewed do not share much in terms of social experiences, economic location, and political cache, Mapuche and Chileans—particularly when we extend the analysis to members of the poor and working classes—may share political perspectives, experiences of economic uncertainty and vulnerability, as well as social understandings and practices.

Moreover, neither group is internally homogeneous. Mapuche individuals are represented across the political and religious spectrums. Not all are involved in the movement, and those who are hold a range of views. The Mapuche in the Araucanía are also Chilean citizens, and some are proud of that fact. Conversely, some Chileans in the region, albeit a minority, actively support the Mapuche cause. Despite the fact that this book tells a story of conflict, competing worldviews, lack of mutual respect and understanding, and the systematic oppression of one group on the basis of race and culture, I wish to leave open the possibility for social change; doing so requires that we recognize the ways that these identifications are in fact fluid and sometimes transcended. To the extent that I am able to do so while also maintaining anonymity, I therefore have tried to contextualize my respondents and make note of the variations that exist within these categories of identification, even as the differences among them are often difficult to transcend.

THE POLITICS AND ETHICS OF CONDUCTING RESEARCH ON RACE AND CONFLICT

After having worked in Chile for several years, I was puzzled by attitudes about race and indigenous rights there. I wondered why so few nonindigenous citizens in the Araucanía were willing to stand up for the Mapuche, why seemingly archaic attitudes about race and culture thrived in local discourse, and what all of this had to do with the state and global capitalism. Perhaps predictably, conducting fieldwork in the context of low-intensity conflict presented several methodological and ethical quandaries. Many of these quandaries involved interviewing local elites. The views they express throughout this book may seem so virulent as to be unbelievable at times. Nevertheless, I am confident that the views expressed by my respondents are representative of those of local elites in the region, regardless of age or sex. (There was some variation on the basis of proximity to the conflicts.) The wives and adult children who participated in interviews concurred with the men's views. Likewise, interviews conducted with only women yielded similar results, as did those with younger respondents. Although no social attitudes are totally universal, the quantitative findings of María Eugenia Merino and her colleagues (2003, 2004) suggest that the views presented in this book are dominant throughout the Araucanía.

I grappled with how to present myself to non-Mapuche respondents and how to respond to statements that were deeply offensive to me. I presented my research topic to all potential respondents in relatively neutral terms: I was interested in looking at the conflicts and intercultural relations in the region from a variety of perspectives. I did not, however, always state my own position on the conflicts explicitly: I think indigenous rights should be recognized and substantively supported, and I am against violence and dehumanization in any form. Still, I felt strongly that I had a responsibility to protect the rights of all my respondents—including the ones whose positions and actions I deplore. But the fact that I often found myself bearing witness to views that were repugnant to me made it difficult to balance that obligation with my responsibility to be true to antiracist principles. Customary interviewer behavior intended to make respondents comfortable and willing to keep talking, such as nodding or saying "mmm hmmm," seemed to implicitly condone their views.

But, on the other hand, just as with Mapuche respondents, I was deeply grateful for the time and trust colonos and other local elites invested in me as an interviewer. Even though I felt Mapuche claims on the territory were just, I was often touched by colonos' pride in their families' accomplishments in the region and saddened by their sadness about what they saw as their way of life being threatened. Over time, I became more skillful at refusing to be tacitly included in the "we" of local elites, but I also had to come to terms with the fact that the conflicts I describe were not always black and white, and my opposition to all forms of violence and dehumanization had to include those instances of violence and dehumanization committed by Mapuche. However, even though I think colonos and other local elites told me the story they believed to be true from their point of view, I cannot understand their observations in anything other than the context in which they and the Mapuche lived: one in which the Mapuche were systematically discriminated against and dispossessed of their resources for the gain of the Chilean state, corporations, and elites.

I was also confronted with the realization that it was my own race and nationality that gave me access to these interviews in the first place. More than once I was told that maybe Chile should have done what the United States did and just kill all the Indians. Many local elites seemed to feel comfortable with me because I am a white citizen of the United States—a country with its own repugnant racial history in which I, by virtue of my race and citizenry, am also implicated, regardless of any progressive commitments I might hold. To what extent does conducting research on the racially privileged in Chile allow me to ignore that fact?

Researchers from the Global North conducting fieldwork in the Global South must acknowledge and address the troubling ways our work might reinscribe the colonialist relationship (Speed 2006). I have been very conscious of this in my ongoing relationship with Mapuche activists and communities. My racial and national privilege was a frequent topic of conversation with Mapuche respondents, as was the need for my research to be meaningful to them. Interviewing the racially dominant, to whom Mapuche researchers had less access, held the possibility of providing data and analysis that could be relevant to them. Despite their general openness, some local elites were also sensitive to the fact that a U.S. researcher was investigating their racial attitudes. They may have had power in the local context, but I exercised power by studying them, and several expressed discomfort with this. A few local elites, for example, wondered why I didn't study "my own Indians." All in all, interviews with local elites forced me to confront the fact that although my own race and nation may have given me access to certain types of people, this access came with some serious responsibilities. I hope to have written this book in a way that respects the humanity of all involved in the conflicts.

The conflicts were discussed everywhere in the Araucanía—in restaurants, at parties, in taxis, in hotel lobbies, in the city, and in the country—by

Mapuche and Chileans alike. I was often asked my opinion of the situation, particularly by non-Mapuche. Although I did have some thoughtful discussions, I quickly learned people were not usually looking for my opinion but rather a validation of their own. For example, Priscila Álamos, the middle-aged director of education in a Cautín comuna, asked me what researchers who come to the region thought about the Mapuche. I said it depends on what they are studying, but the general impression is that they are oppressed. She immediately looked offended and, turning to her Mapuche assistant, Lourdes Caifal, said in a high-pitched, innocent-sounding voice: "They aren't oppressed. They are the least oppressed here. Don't you think, Lourdes?" This left Lourdes to point out the many shortcomings of intercultural education as an example that might lead people to think the Mapuche were oppressed.

More often, non-Mapuche respondents sought to educate me. They claimed to know the Mapuche better than I did, saying that you could not "know" the Mapuche if you came from the outside. My first experience with this was with a Chilean professor at a U.S. university. He disputed my claims and maintained that Mapuche demands are really just about social class and then said: "Yes, we know our Indians, in all of their ugliness." Likewise, a hostel owner in Temuco told me: "You know, all the foreigners come and they are fascinated by the Mapuche, but they aren't well liked here in Chile," implying that Chileans knew better. A timber company lawyer claimed that foreign journalists, NGOs, and academics were actually dangerous because they came with preconceived notions and then filtered them to the outside world. Gonzalo suggested that I study Mapuche "responsibilities" rather than their "rights." At a birthday party one woman quizzed me about the basis for my knowledge, asserting: "I've lived my life surrounded by Mapuches. I know them." She proceeded to recite a variety of stereotypes. She asked how I got access because "they are very closed." I said it was difficult sometimes, but that mutual acquaintances helped, and once people understood my intentions, it was okay. "Yes, because they are very closed," she repeated, and then preceded to insist that all the Mapuche ate was meat and bread, which they made with lard, which was why they were so fat.

Social scientists are accustomed to a certain amount of reticence and mild suspicion on the part of potential research participants. As a qualitative sociologist, I recognize that social "truths" are in the eye of the beholder. My interest lies in how multiple truths contrast with one another and what that might say for living in a multicultural society in a global age. Nevertheless, in this study the suspicions went further than I was accustomed, largely because it took place in a context of serious conflict in which certain details could be dangerous for some respondents to address. One municipal employee in Malleco tried to hide the fact that she agreed to be interviewed by me from her boss, who, she said, did not like the topic of intercultural relations. On another occasion, when I learned that the wives of landowners had formed a group to support families who had experienced atentados, I telephoned the leader, thinking the group might be inclined to talk about these issues. Her terse response was that "the ladies have no interest in talking about the Mapuches." Certainly the context of the conflicts may have circumscribed my access to some potential respondents' versions of the truth.

On the Mapuche side of things, several respondents expressed apprehensions about spies and CIA agents. Although others laughed off such concerns, these worries speak to the legacy of U.S. intervention in Latin America as well as to the degree of state intervention and police violence that has occurred in Mapuche communities in the context of the conflicts. For instance, over the two days I spent touring a Malleco comuna with Hernán Curinao, a middle-aged Mapuche man, he expressed periodic concern that I might be a spy, or that people who saw me with him might think I was a spy, or that the military police in the area might think I was giving material support to the communities in conflict. (A number of foreigners had been arrested over the course of my fieldwork for doing just that.) Hernán talked about how spies were everywhere: in the communities, in the restaurants, on the buses. He mused about whether several young Mapuche and Chilean scholar-activists in Temuco might be "infiltrated" because they had access to so much information.

Hernán worried about spies in general, but others targeted researchers—and me—more specifically. Adriano, a young Mapuche activist who later became a friend, told me the first night I met him that all academic studies were good for was to inform the CIA. When Pato, who worked for Orígenes, wondered aloud if I were a CIA agent, he added that he knew he was paranoid, but the fact that the police searched his car almost every time he traveled into communities in conflict for work made him that way. One night, through Pato, I met a young man in a remote community, who, when I told him I was doing a study, looked completely stricken and said: "But you could be infiltrated!!!" He was likely on the lam, accused of terrorism, and though I never intended to interview him, he spent a long time testing my political positions. I responded to these situations by being as direct as possible about my intentions and the efforts I would undertake to protect the identities of participants. Having acquaintances who were well respected in the movement often helped smooth things over. But sometimes, after lengthy conversation, I just shrugged my shoulders, as if to say, believe what you want to believe. Such suspicions forced me to recognize the limits of what I could know in this context as well as the limits of what I needed to know as a sociologist (as opposed to a detective or journalist). I speak to this issue again in chapter 3.

My gendered embodiment—the social experience of being a woman in a female body—pervaded my experience in the field as well. Whenever gender appeared, its intersections with race and nation were also readily apparent. My access to colonos and local elites was facilitated not just by my whiteness but by the fact that, like Ruth Milkman (1997), I often seemed to be perceived as a harmless young woman. Sometimes this resulted in ostentatious displays of masculine superiority; other times, in enthusiastic efforts to help me out. For example, although Malleco lawyer Martin Rahm was reluctant to be interviewed and somewhat rude at first, in the end he arranged a meeting for me with another local elite, telling him by phone that I was a "very nice gringa." Other experiences, with local elites and Mapuche respondents alike, bordered on sexual harassment. Hernán Curinao grabbed my hand at one point, marveling at its paleness. He observed that I must be a romantic and exclaimed: "I'd like to take you to the mountains, far, far away, to live like they lived in the beginning. Would you like that?" Although I never felt threatened, this situation and others made me reflect on the ways harassment can be something women researchers simply deal with as part of fieldwork. Such harassment is indicative of the fact that power is not unidirectional in the relationship between the researcher and the researched. (Of course, my participants exercised power over the process in other ways too.)

I have done my best to represent the participants in this study accurately, with my ethical responsibilities as a scholar and respect for human dignity in mind and heart. Nevertheless, the story I tell is filtered not only through my respondents but through my own subjectivity as an author. It is a story of racism and social conflict, to be sure, but also of hope for a shared future of mutual respect, justice, and peace. After many years of travel back and forth to the Araucanía, it is my great desire to see such a future come to reality.

CHAPTER 2

CONTESTED MEMORIES, SYMBOLIC VIOLENCE, AND THE HISTORY OF THE ARAUCANÍA

History and memory alike are socially constructed. As Barry Schwartz (2007, 588) has defined it, "collective memory refers to the distribution throughout society of beliefs, feelings, moral judgments, and knowledge about the past." We say memory is socially constructed because, as Schwartz points out, while individuals may hold beliefs or draw judgments about the past, "they do not know (it) singly; they know it with and against other individuals situated in conflicting groups" (ibid.). Thus there is never complete consensus in collective memory. Memory is contentious, informed by social, political, economic, and cultural context and shaped by power and inequality (Stern 2004). Memory is also dynamic, as Nadje Sadig Al-Ali (2007, 2) has explained: "not static and frozen in time, but . . . alive, rooted in the present as much as in the past, and linked to aspirations as much as actual experiences." Groups that hold competing narratives about the past also are likely to possess distinct visions for the future (ibid.). The telling of history can be understood as one vehicle for the expression of collective memory (Schwartz 2007). Different versions of memory and history yield different versions of the truth, which may be wielded in defense of competing interests. Examining contentious narratives about the past can therefore provide important insights into the analysis of contemporary conflicts over rights and resources, such as those in the Araucanía.

In this chapter I address history and memory, first providing the background necessary to understand Mapuche-Chilean relations and then turning to the memories that *colonos*, other local elites, and Mapuche recount in the Araucanía today. Mapuche remembrances serve to maintain a continuity of struggle, whereas the memories of local Chilean elites often serve to justify their relative wealth and presence in the region. As Florencia Mallon (2005, 58) has observed, in the Araucanía there is "a selective amnesia around the origins of regional fortunes." Indeed, collective memory often involves the suppression of "memories of collective injustice" (Wolin 1989, 33) or "sustained collective forgetting" (Feagin 2006, 44). While Mapuche and local elites both used memories and historical narratives to justify contemporary positions vis-à-vis the conflicts and state-driven multiculturalism, local elites' relative economic and social power meant that the very act of relating their memories frequently entailed symbolic violence. The multiple and contradictory mobilizations of memory, this selective remembering and forgetting, are important because, as Juliet Hooker (2009, 112) has explained, they are central to struggles for racial justice: "What a political community chooses to remember about its past determines what it considers to be just or unjust in the present."

As theorized by Pierre Bourdieu, the concept of symbolic violence focuses on how power inequalities are sustained not just through physical violence and repression but also through social and cultural norms and practices (Caron 2003; Wolfreys 2000). Symbolic violence refers to the process by which economic domination comes to be masked as wealth, status, prestige, and taste (or symbolic and cultural capital) and thereby legitimized (Bourdieu and Wacquant 1992). This transformation leads members of society to see wealth and power, as well as poverty and exploitation, as deserved rather than built on a system of domination. In this way domination and power inequalities are disguised and legitimated by cultural values that are understood as universal but are in fact socially constructed (Wolfreys 2000). Individuals with symbolic and cultural capital exercise symbolic violence over others, often unconsciously. At the same time, the dominated frequently participate in their own domination, as they misrecognize the power wielded over them (C. Williams 2006). In this way social structures of domination—the bases of systemic racism—are reproduced. Symbolic violence also can allow direct violence to be avoided, although in the Araucanía, the two are sometimes used in tandem. It is those with symbolic capital who, in epistemological terms, are the "knowers," the subjects of the social world. By virtue of their cultural and economic power, they are able to establish the privileged version of history and the rules, regulations, and norms by which shared existence proceeds. Symbolic violence is reflected in how different groups in the Araucanía remember their collective past. But more important, memory does not just function as a form of symbolic violence; it is also a central element in Mapuche resistance.

A HISTORY OF THE ARAUCANÍA THROUGH THE EARLY TWENTIETH CENTURY

History is socially constructed and reflects systems of power. "Official" Chilean history has often relied on and perpetuated myths in order to tell a version of history that negates Mapuche identity and justifies Chile's actions toward them (Lewis 1994). Here I seek to tell a version that contextualizes contemporary events in southern Chile and lays bare the domination and exploitation that have shaped the relationship between Chile and the Mapuche. I recognize, of course, that the history I tell is partial in both senses of the word (see Mallon 2005); no telling of history is ever complete or completely disinterested.

The Mapuche are believed to have lived in what is today the Chilean South since 500–600 B.C. (Bengoa 2004). Before the arrival of the Spanish in the mid-1500s, the Mapuche relied mainly on hunting and gathering for sustenance, though chronicles from the era also record some plant domestication. The extended family served as the basis of political structure. Whereas the conquistadors subjugated the indigenous populations of central Chile (the historical heartland of the country), they were unable to conquer the Mapuche of the southern frontier.[1] Instead, the two parties established a series of more than thirty agreements at mass meetings called *parlamentos*, the most important of which came in 1641 (Parlamento de Quilin) and 1726 (Parlamento de Negrete), recognizing the Bío-Bío River as the border between Chile and Mapuche territory. The uniqueness of this situation must be stressed. Unlike the indigenous in other parts of the Americas, the Mapuche (or *araucanos*, as the Spanish called them) were not *indios cristianos* (tribute-paying indigenous communities subject to the crown) or *indios bravos* (those who remained outside settled areas and subject to Spanish punitive campaigns). Rather, they were people whose rights to independence, sovereign territory, and (albeit precarious) peace were officially recognized by the Spanish.

Still, contact with the Spanish provoked profound changes in Mapuche society. Raising livestock replaced hunting and gathering as the main source of subsistence. Trade with central Chile and the Argentine pampas was also prominent, leading to great wealth for some *lonkos* (leaders) (Aylwin 2002; Pinto 2003). Thus, even though peace with the Spanish was precarious, the parlamentos made prosperity possible in the Araucanía. Like their counterparts elsewhere, Chilean patriots symbolically incorporated the Mapuche in their struggle for independence from Spain (1810–18). Fernando Casanueva (1998, 58) has explained that for the patriot leaders "the rebel Indian represented love of the soil of the fatherland and irrevocable liberty, high values that had impelled them to fight victoriously during long centuries against the Hispanic conquistadors and against the royal army. Arauco constituted, then, an example to follow, a goal to be achieved."[2] Nevertheless, efforts to symbolically incorporate the Mapuche into the nation failed to garner their support for Chilean independence. Although there were important exceptions, most lonkos sided with Spain during the war of independence, largely because their treaties had generally been respected.

After independence was achieved, the new state maintained border relations with the Mapuche until 1862. Nevertheless, there is some dispute as to the character of the relationship between Chile and the Mapuche in these early years. José Bengoa (1985) has suggested that Chilean attitudes quickly changed with the Guerra a Muerte, a guerrilla war waged at the beginning of the 1820s by royalist officials, whom many Mapuche supported by pillaging, burning, robbing, and ambushing Chilean settlements. The Chileans won this war, which resulted in huge Mapuche losses in life and material goods. In 1825 the two sides held a parlamento that entailed the loss of some Mapuche land but maintained the border at the Bío-Bío River and allowed for increased Chilean (read: colonial) presence at certain outposts. For Bengoa (ibid.), the Guerra a Muerte traumatically contradicted the Chilean idealization of Mapuche as heroic defenders of liberty and contributed to the growth of the notion that the Mapuche were lazy, ruthless barbarians. Casanueva (1998) has agreed that the Guerra a Muerte, combined with some lonkos' sponsorship of organized banditry (committed by *winkas*), contributed to souring Chilean attitudes toward the Mapuche. He suggests that by the 1920s, many saw the Mapuche as barbarians who would have to be subjugated in the interest of progress and unifying the territory.

In contrast, Jorge Pinto (2003) has argued that the first half of the nineteenth century can be divided into two periods. From 1810 to 1830 the Chileans sought to include the Mapuche in their new nation, and then from 1830 to 1850, recognizing that the Mapuche would not be integrated, the Chileans engaged in diplomatic mechanisms similar to those of the Spanish: parlamentos and religious missions.[3] Pinto (2003, 87) maintains that the Chilean ruling class expressed admiration for the Mapuche and did not convey the intention to occupy their lands. Until midcentury, the dominant idea was that "the Araucanía formed part of the national territory and that the Mapuche, although they were a different nation, should form part of the great national brotherhood." Official documents such as the Constitution of 1833 portrayed the Mapuche as a neighboring nation, the residents of which, Pinto asserts, Chilean elites respected.[4]

In any case, the initial decades following Chilean Independence were relatively peaceful: there was ample commerce and Mapuche ranching prospered, allowing for the accumulation of wealth (Bengoa 1985). By the 1850s, however, economic and geopolitical interests led to a shift in discourse and policy toward the Mapuche (Pinto 2003). Chileans were no longer interested in the Mapuche as a labor force or as a people to be evangelized (Casanueva 1998). Rather, they were motivated to claim Mapuche territory because they wanted the land for agricultural production (Chilean imports at the time were exceeding exports), but also because they wanted to unify the Chilean territory, which, with the exception of the Araucanía, extended from the Atacama Desert to Cape Horn. This objective reflected the general belief that even though the Araucanía was in indigenous hands, it was part of Chilean territory (Pinto 2003). Thus began a slow process of penetration and usurpation of Mapuche lands through diverse methods, including fraudulent purchases and "spontaneous colonization," whereby private citizens simply encroached on Mapuche territory, a process facilitated by the fact that the Mapuche did not valorize land in monetary terms (Bengoa 1985, 2004). This took place especially in the northern part of Mapuche territory, between the Bío-Bío and Malleco Rivers. Cities and forts were founded, and in 1852 the administrative province of Arauco was established in what is today part of the Bío-Bío Region, just north of the Araucanía.

Chilean designs on Mapuche territory were justified by positivist logic and scientific racism. The Mapuche were portrayed by politicians and newspapers alike as barbarous, uncivilized beings whose conquest could no longer be delayed. For example, the historian Diego Barros Arana (1830–1907) argued that as a result of their barbarity, the Mapuche were unable to fully exploit their lands, and therefore it was in the interest of Chile to occupy them. Barros Arana believed that women's performance of "industrial and productive work"—such as agriculture, weaving, and pottery—was further proof of the "lazy and improvident" ways of the Indian (in Casanueva 1998, 70). His vision has much in common with stereotypes of today; he said the Mapuche were reserved, drunks, distrustful, and only showed creativity and intelligence in war. Politician and historian Benjamin Vicuña MacKenna (1831–86) held similar views. In 1868 he referred to the Mapuche as "enemies of our independence" and "disloyal by nature." He went so far as to deny any Mapuche roots to the Chilean nation: "Our people do not descend from the barbarian of Arauco, who has never wanted to submit himself to the foreigner nor ally with him." Instead, Vicuña MacKenna argued, any indigenous roots came from the Andean north (Casanueva 1998, 75–76). Anti-Mapuche sentiment was laced with sexualized fears; there was much apprehension about Chilean women being kidnapped by the "uncivilized" Mapuche.[5] There were some voices of dissent but only regarding the means by which conquest was to be achieved.

Political discourse regarding the Mapuche had transnational elements as well. In an 1868 debate in the House of Deputies regarding increasing troops at the border and financing military operations to occupy Mapuche territory, Minister of the Treasury Vicente Reyes supported waging war by citing the examples of Argentina and the United States as well as the dealings of the French in Algeria. Vicuña MacKenna also cited U.S. indigenous policy as a positive example (Casanueva 1998). Again, there was some dissent, but all sides saw the Mapuche as barbarians and the occupation of their territory, by violent or peaceful means, as necessary (ibid.).[6]

Press coverage was especially virulent. There were some defenders of the Mapuche, including sectors of the Catholic press, which maintained that the Mapuche had inalienable rights to their land, but these voices were a minority. Pinto (2003, 143) has asserted that the occupation of the Araucanía "was practically directed by El Mercurio de Valparaíso." In 1856 an editorial in El Mercurio actually aligned Chileans with the Spanish against the Mapuche: "[For] three centuries [the Mapuche] have mocked the power and force of the governments that have governed Chile and they still remain as in primitive times" (in Casanueva 1998, 92). The paper argued that the Araucanía was the "most beautiful and fertile part of our territory, inhabited by savage hordes" (1856, in Pinto 2003, 153), asserted it was time to use force, given that for three hundred years "they have refused civilization by peaceful means" (1859, in Casanueva 1998, 94), suggested that "nature had spent everything on the development of [the Mapuche's] body, while his intelligence has remained at the level of scavenging animals," and posited that the Mapuche "are nothing more than a wild horde, whom it is urgent to chain or destroy in the interest of humanity and for the good of society" (1859, in Pinto 2003, 154–55). Chileans were depicted as victims of the Mapuche "barbarians who invade us" (1859, in ibid., 156). Here the idea that the Mapuche were a different nation, not to mention uncivilized and antiprogress, was used to justify occupation.

Buttressed by this discourse, the state began a war of occupation, formally titled the Pacificación de la Araucanía.

Although there was little all-out opposition to occupation, there were debates about strategy. General José Manuel Pinto, for example, advocated total extermination. Nevertheless, the first occupation strategy was a plan Coronel Cornelio Saavedra presented to Congress in 1861. It involved shifting the border little by little. Rather than using only war and massacre, Saavedra engaged in trickery, took advantage of rivalries among Mapuche, and purported diplomacy (Bengoa 1985). He famously advocated achieving victory through "mucho mosto, mucha música y poca pólvora [a lot of alcohol and music, and little gunpowder]," and was named commanding general of the campaign in 1866. Already in 1859, in response to the increasing encroachment of the Chileans into their territory, the Mapuche attacked and destroyed most cities south of the Bío-Bío. But by 1866, Chile had advanced the border to the Malleco River (Bengoa 2004). Also in 1866 the state effectively declared itself owner of the lands of the Araucanía. In 1867 the Mapuche staged another significant military response, known as the General Uprising of the Arribanos.[7]

In 1869, Chile began a new phase of the Pacificación, referred to even at the time as a War of Extermination (Bengoa 1985). This war was waged against Mapuche warriors and civilians alike, a product of the scorched-earth policy favored by Pinto, whom Saavedra had put in charge of Malleco (Bengoa 1985). The Chileans burned *rukas* (Mapuche homes); killed and captured men, women, and children; stole animals; and destroyed crops. The Mapuche were obliged to flee further south or into Argentina. Simultaneously, though, Saavedra held his parlamentos with *mucho mosto y música* to more easily manipulate the Mapuche. By 1870 the Mapuche had lost many animals and were unable to plant crops. As a result, many of them starved to death. These dual strategies are reflected in the contemporary selective remembrances of local elites, who highlight the negotiations while eliding the massacres.

For most of the 1870s the situation remained relatively stable, with Mapuche territory to the Malleco River firmly occupied by the Chileans (Bengoa 1985). During this period the state began auctioning off land in the areas of the Araucanía that had been occupied (particularly in the north but also around Temuco) (Bengoa 2004). In addition, between 1873 and 1880 camps were created in the northern part of the region, to contain Mapuche who had already been displaced. But in 1879 the War of the Pacific between Chile, Bolivia, and Peru began, and most troops were sent north to fight. The war against the Mapuche was more or less put on hold. In the absence of the troops, a National Guard of sorts, made up of Chilean citizens from the forts and cities, terrorized the Mapuche with murders, lynchings, rapes, and other violence.

By the time the Chilean army returned south upon victory in the War of the Pacific, it had been transformed by modern techniques and weapons. The military's strategy vis-à-vis the Mapuche changed from one of gradual occupation to quick conquest and definitive occupation (Bengoa 1985). At this point a few lonkos, certain the Mapuche would lose, negotiated with the Chileans. Most, however, fought in a final attempt to defend their political and cultural sovereignty. Between November 3 and 9, 1881, the Mapuche staged a final general uprising, a *futa malón*, attacking Chilean forts and cities everywhere. By November 15 it was over and the Mapuche were defeated. Chilean military and civilians, who had already occupied much of the Araucanía, continued to attack and burn rukas, kill animals, and murder Mapuche people long after the uprising had finished. The town of Villarrica was refounded on January 1, 1883, after having been destroyed by the Mapuche more than three hundred years earlier. This event "marked the end of independent Mapuche life" (Bengoa 1985, 325). Dispossessed of their land, thousands of Mapuche died of starvation, epidemics, and lack of shelter after the war had ended. "Indigenous groups wandered around the outside of the forts and during almost twenty years, the army fed thousands of Mapuche who, defeated, could not procure their own sustenance" (Bengoa 1985, 329). The Mapuche population was around 150,000 before the war; it was diminished to around 111,000 in 1907, probably even less in the war's immediate aftermath (Bengoa 1985).

Mapuche survivors were relegated to three thousand small *reducciones,* which made up a little more than five hundred thousand hectares (Aylwin 2002). The deeds establishing the lands that would belong to the Mapuche were called *títulos de merced*. In the Araucanía alone, 71,253 people were assigned to reductions. (This represents 86.2 percent of the individuals accommodated under títulos de merced; the other 11,407 were placed on reductions in what are today the regions of Los Lagos, Los Rios, and Bío-Bío.) The average number of hectares per person was 8.56 in Malleco, 5.29 in Cautín, and 6.18 overall. Mapuche reductions made up 6 percent of the territory of Malleco, 17.7 percent of Cautín, and just 6.4 percent of the territory that had belonged to the Mapuche before their defeat (González 1986, cited in Aylwin 2002 and Correa, Molina, and Yáñez 2005). However, not all Mapuche were designated land. At least thirty thousand (almost a third of the surviving Mapuche) were left with nothing (Bengoa 2004). Much of the appropriated land was auctioned off to Chilean *latifundistas* (owners of large estates) and small-scale farmers or deeded to European immigrants. Ironically, these measures were backed by the promotion of a unitary national identity that once again incorporated images of the noble Mapuche warrior. Nevertheless, some schoolbooks to this day discuss the Pacificación as a victory of civilization over barbarity, disregarding Mapuche losses in human life, territory, and autonomy (Pinto 2003).

The reductions were a far cry from the expanses of land that the Mapuche had used for ranching horses, cows, and sheep and gathering provisions. They were forced to become peasants, a way of life to which they were unaccustomed. Forced to survive on small-scale agriculture on some of the worst land in the region, the Mapuche often lacked the background to make the best use of the little they had. Many attempted to continue ranching on these small plots, and few had enough land to be able to afford rotating crops and leave fields fallow (Bengoa 1985; Mallon 2005). As a result, soil degradation came on quick, and by the 1930s substantial numbers of Mapuche had begun to migrate elsewhere.[8] In establishing the reductions, the state did not respect the traditional basis for Mapuche social organization and often grouped more than one extended family in the same reduction. In many cases this resulted in internal conflicts. In this way the effects of the reductions were psychosocial as well as spatial. Destroying the family-based authority system by mixing families in a single reduction meant they did not have the mechanisms to distribute land, to work collectively, and so forth (Bengoa 1985). Reductions were often surrounded by private fundos, the owners of which would not let the Mapuche open a road or cross their land, thus isolating them completely (ibid.). Lynching, brandings, and other violence continued to be committed against the Mapuche well into the twentieth century (ibid.; León 2005). The loss of Mapuche patrimony and the injustice it perpetuated set the stage for conflicts that would unfold for over a century.

Although auctions to Chileans made up a much greater proportion of the land designated, it is worth giving some attention to the racist intentions of immigration policy. Europeans were sought not only to occupy the Frontera but to civilize it. Cecilia Díaz (1984) has cited the Ministry of Foreign Relations' records from 1892 and 1902 that make this mission explicit. She notes that the colonization laws only allowed for the entry of people from Europe and the United States, denying access to Asians and Africans. The idea of bringing European *colonos* to civilize the region was already introduced in Congress in 1823 (Pinto 2003). Vicuña MacKenna was a big proponent, to get rid of what he considered the lazy, drunk, lying, traitorous characteristics of the Mapuche (Pinto 2003). It goes without saying that the colonos recruited to the region received far more resources than did the Mapuche forced to reside in the reducciones; they also received more than most Chileans who acquired land in the region. Each colono family was granted sixty-two hectares, plus thirty more for each son older than ten years, free passage to Chile, boards, nails, a pair of oxen, a cow and calf (or a pregnant cow), a plow, a cart, a trunk-removing machine, a monthly pension for a year, and medical care for two years (Bengoa 2004).

As Sergio Caniuqueo (2006) has observed, there are few historical studies of relations between the Mapuche and the early colonos. Alberto Dufey (2000, cited in Caniuqueo 2006) has written that the earliest colonos viewed the Mapuche, through their Eurocentric optic, as wild and primitive. He also suggests that some colonos, particularly the Swiss, arrived at a more harmonious coexistence with the Mapuche, citing an 1885 Swiss consulate report: "The immigrants maintain very good relations with the Mapuche that still inhabit these districts" (in Caniuqueo 2006, 155). In contrast, the report deplored the banditry committed by Chilean peasants.[9] In their letters home the colonos in Dufey's study described the Mapuche as "lazy and distrustful" but also spoke of friendships among the children of the two groups. Dufey writes of commercial exchanges and notes that the Swiss used Mapuche medicine and attended Mapuche social and ceremonial events. Dufey's observations are made from the perspective of the colonos, however, and do not necessarily reflect Mapuche experiences of these encounters.

The history of the Pacificación and initial colonization exposes very direct and physical violence against the Mapuche. After colonization, physical violence persisted, but new forms of material and symbolic violence developed as well, pursued in local courthouses and everyday interactions. Almost as soon as the process of putting the Mapuche into reductions was finished, the state began to promote the division of Mapuche lands into individual parcels that could be sold to non-Mapuche (Aylwin 2002). This process was facilitated by a 1927 law permitting the legal division of Mapuche land titles. In subsequent years a complex series of laws addressed whether or not Mapuche lands could be divided and sold to others. The net effect was that between 1931 and 1971, 832 of almost 3,000 communities (as the reductions have come to be called) were divided, and at least a fifth of Mapuche lands were sold to nonindigenous people (ibid.). A host of extralegal practices also contributed to usurpation. Symbolic violence played a significant role in these processes, as they were continuously justified in the name of the supposed superiority of the colonizer over the colonized.

The history discussed here conditioned the Chilean response to the myth of mestizaje. In much of twentieth-century Latin America, mestizaje, or racial and cultural mixing, was a tool for assimilationists who sought to dissolve minority racial and ethnic identities into a homogeneous national citizenry (Gould 1998; Hale 2002). In the process claims to rights based on collective, indigenous identity were construed as unfair to other citizens. Once they were defined as citizens, regardless of whether they were actually granted the substantive rights associated with that status, indigenous peoples' rights and cultures were effectively suppressed. Chilean assimilationism diverged from this pattern. In the first half of the twentieth century, middle-class nationalists used figures from literary *criollismo* and Nicolás Palacio's (1904) writings on the "raza chilena" to define the essence of the nation (Barr-Melej 2001).[10] By the late 1930s images of Araucanian warriors from the time of the Spanish conquest were incorporated into school curricula that promoted a mestizo identity. But according to Patrick Barr-Melej, this ideology was principally directed at diluting class conflict in the cities and mining regions of the north. It was not developed to integrate the actual Mapuche subjects south of the border who had recently been defeated militarily and divested of their lands.[11] Although the Araucanos from the time of the Spanish arrival were incorporated into national imagery, the Mapuche who survived the war with Chile were excluded symbolically and materially, setting up their erasure throughout the remainder of the century. These trends contributed to the dichotomous understanding of identity predominant in the region today.

In central Chile the idea of the "Chilean race" built on but elided indigenousness. Maria Angelica Illanes (2003) has argued that while the "raza chilena" is not considered purely "white," mestizo identity is, to this day, taboo, and the mestizo is denied just as the Indian is. Maximiliano Salinas (2003) has explained that the oft-repeated descriptor "the English of Latin America" was taken on as evidence of Chilean civilization in comparison to neighboring countries with higher indigenous populations. And Leonardo León (2007, 335) quotes a 1905 Chilean yearbook: "No country in America possesses a more homogenous population than Chile," observing that this reflects not reality but elite desires. These desires reveal the symbolic violence that undergirds Chilean identity.

In contrast to central Chile, the historical existence of the border between Chile and the Araucanía uniquely shaped the discourse and experience of race in the Chilean South well after the Pacificación, allowing Mapuche-Chilean relations to be understood in dichotomous terms. First, the Mapuche were an external other, the enemy who threatened the integrity of the Chilean nation. Later, they became an internal other, either negated or set apart from Chileans. The relegation of the Mapuche to the reducciones shows the extent of their otherness; recruitment of European immigrants to the area further marginalized the Mapuche and privileged whiteness. While by the early twentieth century, images of the noble Araucano warrior were once again incorporated into national identity discourses, in everyday practice the

Mapuche were marginalized in their interactions with Chileans and colonos. Although authorities nominally expected the Mapuche to become "Chilean" like anyone else (Foerster 2001), daily life in the borderlands relentlessly underscored the Mapuche's purported racial and cultural inferiority.

CONTESTED MEMORIES OF THE ARAUCANÍA POST-PACIFICACIÓN

I now turn to the selective remembrances and contentious memories of Mapuche and local elite/colono respondents. I focus on their stories regarding the Pacificación and events of subsequent decades, blending respondents' memories with contributions from the historiography. Javier Auyero (2003) has described the importance of memory work, explaining that through the act of remembering, we make meaning. He cites Alessandro Portelli (1991), who writes that oral sources are compelling not because they adhere to fact but because they may depart from it. Such departures allow "imagination, symbolism, and desire [to] emerge" and lead us "beyond facts to their meanings" (Portelli 1991, in Auyero 2003, 184). Here I focus on respondents' memories in order to explore the contentious meanings Mapuche, local elites, and colonos associate with their collective past and to provide a sense of the ways this history continues to live on, retold in diverse ways and for diverse purposes.

An additional word on my respondents might be useful. The vast majority of Mapuche interviewees were involved in the collective struggle in some way, either now or in the past, as members of formal organizations, or communities in conflict or as state employees. Despite the discourses of resistance presented here, it is important to note that resistance has coexisted with assimilation in many ways—through the pressures of education, migration, everyday interactions, and intermarriage. Racial mestizaje is a reality even as the dominant discourse dichotomizes the population into Chileans and Mapuche and sometimes leads to the expression of internalized racism. Although Mapuche have generally not served as *inquilinos* (tenant farmers) in the traditional sense, communities frequently do have patron/client ties of a sort with their colono and Chilean neighbors—a relationship that leads to ambivalence for some Mapuche. There are political differences among the Mapuche, and some communities in the region consistently vote for the Right. While my Mapuche respondents tell a tale of resistance, their narratives must be contextualized with these subtleties and contradictions.

Mapuche views are contrasted here to those of local elites. I focus on local elites because of their role in conflicts with the Mapuche and because of the sway they continue to hold over public opinion. I did not systematically study other non-Mapuche social strata. However, the work of María Eugenia

Merino and her colleagues (2004; also Merino and Pilleux 2003) shows pervasive discrimination, antagonism, and stereotyping across all social classes in the region, although particular discursive strategies vary. My limited observations and conversations with non-Mapuche families who live in Mapuche communities and share their day-to-day existence suggest they have much in common with poor Mapuche families. Nevertheless, racial stereotyping emerges in their discussion of the conflicts and daily interchanges. Thus, despite the limited scope of my Chilean sample, there is evidence to suggest that many of the narratives here are shared, though not universally, throughout the regional population.

The stories passed down in Mapuche families about war and dispossession reveal a continuity of struggle. They show Mapuche land claims today are not only linked to contemporary political activism but rooted in collective memories of a shared history. Pepe Morales, a teacher at an intercultural school in Cautín and a onetime councilman in a nearby comuna, remarked that stories passed down by elders were essential for the survival of a collective Mapuche consciousness. He related a conversation he once had with a lonko who, when he heard Morales was a teacher, announced: "I am going to teach you the true story." Morales explained: "And he began to tell history as he saw it, and as his ancestors had told it to him. And he said, 'Diego de Almagro or Gregorio Urrutia: cattle rustlers and assassins, nothing more. From there to here, they crossed our lands, killing, raping. They stole our children; later, they sold them.'"[12] Morales concluded: "These are living memories."

I asked respondents what their parents and grandparents had told them about the Chilean invasion and its aftermath. In a Mapuche community in Malleco residents spoke of massacres and beheadings. In Cautín an elderly widow spoke of a colono man who would kill Mapuche who tried to cross his land. He had a well and would bury them there. "Who knows how many bodies?" she reflected. In Malleco older residents told of a man who refused to let Mapuche cross through his fields. The colonos did not greet the Mapuche. "It was as if we didn't exist," one said. The widow's mother also told her about the Anglicans, who hosted a big party and killed four horses for people to eat. They told the women to take their shirts off and fight over the intestines. They made a movie and took it back to England to show people what savages the Mapuche were, so they could get more money. These stories, handed down through generations, are important less for their infallible historical accuracy than for what Begoña Aretxaga (2000) would call their "truth effects"—how they shape Mapuche understandings of their history and contemporary reality. Regardless of whether the Anglicans staged a movie (which is not unimaginable), or whether the colono in Cautín dumped

Mapuche bodies down his well, these stories depict a violence perpetrated against Mapuche—physical as well as symbolic—that has been both severe and very real. The willingness to harm, to treat Mapuche as subhuman, and the desire to make them disappear by refusing to greet them or let them cross one's land—all of this reflects a continuity of mistreatment, and it is part of Mapuche collective memory. These stories are important both for the truth they tell and the continuity of struggle they inspire. While memory works as symbolic violence, it also is a force for resistance.

The sense of loss is palpable when Mapuche talk about their history: loss of land and territory as well as identity and the right to be a people. José Antiman, a member of the Coordinación de Identidades Territoriales Mapuche (CITEM, an organization that supported recuperation of territory-based Mapuche identities), was in his mid-forties. He was educated in the Mapuche language and worldview before being exposed to the Spanish language and Chilean ways. (He eventually received some religious training as well.) He spoke of the intense cultural loss that resulted from the wars not just with the Chileans but the Spanish before them who, he reminded me, continually broke the treaties and agreements they established with the Mapuche. "There wasn't even time, in the era of war, . . . to attend to the family. There wasn't time to educate the children. We lost [our form of] education. We lost the way of speaking, we lost the way of believing, we lost the way of respecting the universe. . . . We can say that we haven't lost it completely, but it has hurt us, it has hurt us a lot."

Mapuche memories of the territory have been passed down through generations. From early on, individuals, communities, and organizations waged efforts to reclaim their ancestral lands as well as their "reduced" land claims (Bengoa 2004; Foerster and Montecino 1988).[13] Members of communities that were making land claims when I spoke with them were especially clear about their ancestral rights. For example, in Malleco, I was told that colonos might say the land is theirs, "but we demand what they stole. They looked at us like savages. They are always going to deny that there was Mapuche land." Further south, on the island of Chiloe, I spoke with Doña Emiliana, an elderly woman who told of her mother's fight to prevent the government from usurping her land: "The injustice has been very hard, very strong with the poor campesino," she said, before describing how her mother tore down a fence the government had put up, restricting her access to her land. "Yes, my mom tore down the fence, because, my mom said, 'These lands do not belong to the rich man. These are our lands, of [our] ancestors. God left us the land. We are not foreigners. We haven't come from any [other] place. How could the rich man, the foreigner, kick us out of our own land that God gave us to live? We are born and raised, our grandparents raised, born on this land, and we are the owners of the land, and no one is going to take us out.'" Such stories demonstrate the historical basis of Mapuche claims and the role of collective memory in the struggle over time. Current conflicts are understood as part of the same continuous process of dispossession.

For some, dispossession was not a memory passed down through the generations, but something they learned about as adults. Andrés Lonkomilla, a development worker in Malleco, lamented that he was not taught Mapuche history in school: "They taught us the history of Chile beginning in 1810, I don't know, about [Bernardo] O'Higgins and his heroes . . . and that they little more than came to domesticate the Mapuche. But they didn't talk about how before the Spanish, the whole region, from here to the Bío-Bío was governed by different Mapuche tribes, and that they were rich, and . . . had a ton of animals. They didn't say that when they came, the Spanish came to rob them of their animals and leave them in poverty."[14] Learning these things—either as they were passed down by older family members, by participating in the movement, or through courses offered by NGOs, universities, or even Orígenes—left many Mapuche with a great sense of anger and injustice.

Chilean stories of conquest and settlement are quite different. As Hermes Peralta, head of a municipal department of culture in Malleco, told me: "The winners write history. . . . The Chileans won it and wrote it as they saw fit." Colonos spoke with pride of the hard work and sacrifice settling the land entailed. They saw this as contributing to the Chilean nation. Colonos and other local elites denied hearing about conflict with the Mapuche in their family lore, speaking instead of "a coexistence without tensions," as Esteban Marcial, who was involved with an early terrorism trial after fires were set on his fundo, put it. His perspective finds echo throughout this chapter. Although power differentials might indeed have meant that overt conflict was not prominent (especially given the physical violence to which Mapuche who stepped out of line were subjected), Mapuche memories cast doubt on the idea that there was no tension.

More interesting are the explanations local elites gave for the lack of conflict. Many had heard stories of how their grandparents worked to settle the land but claimed to have been told little about early interactions with the Mapuche. They said: "When my family came here, there was nothing! We made this what it is today." This discursive turn reflects the fantasy of terra nullius, which John Cash (2004) suggests involves the condensation of repressed memories and experiences of "conquest, violence, and appropriation" into "a specific mode of thinking, feeling and relating that eclipses the claims to recognition of the indigenous other." Focusing on the case of Australia, he argues that this fantasy "continues to organize the relations between indigenous and non-indigenous citizens within the discourse and practices of the nation."[15] I see a similar pattern in Chile, whereby the fantasy of terra nullius informs state discourse and practices as well as the selective remembrances and desires of local elites.[16]

This fantasy not only explains the supposed absence of conflict but serves to justify non-Mapuche presence in the region. Simon Baum, an elderly businessman and landowner in Malleco, was among those who suggested the Mapuche were simply not there:

> Why weren't there problems, in my judgment? . . . Because the lands they gave
> to colonos—and also to Chileans, because not only colonos arrived to colonize
> this, but also Chileans, Chileans who bought lands from the state, the govern-
> ment—were lands that had no people. They were bare, without cultivation,
> without anything. So they didn't displace anyone. They weren't facing an
> enemy, you understand. This is always being twisted, it's being told backwards,
> the Pacificación of the Araucanía, that the colonization was done [by] kicking
> the Mapuche out. No, . . . at least not in this corner. . . . No, there wasn't a bad
> relationship between the colonos and the Mapuche.

In Baum's estimation, there were no Indians on the land, but (paradoxically) the colonos still had a good relationship with them. He uses the notion that the Mapuche were not there to justify Chilean and colono possession of the land. Baum had written a short treatise on this issue, which he shared with me. His main point was that as a result of illnesses brought by the Spanish, war with the Spanish, internal fighting, migration, and mestizaje, the Mapuche went from an estimated one million at the time of the Spanish arrival to only sixty-five thousand people three hundred years later. (Actually, a census from 1907 estimated the Mapuche population in the region at 101,118, and this figure is thought to be underestimated by at least 10 percent [Bengoa 1985].) Baum argues that the existence of three-hundred-year-old trees at the time of the Pacificación proves that once-settled lands had been long abandoned. Absurdly, he contends that the only lands that ancestrally belonged to the Mapuche were those on which they lived around 1880 "in their reductions, as a meticulous map edited by the Chilean government at the beginning of the twentieth-century signals." He ends the document by asserting that purchasing lands on behalf of the Mapuche will lead to a drastic decrease in agricultural production "because those people do not have the technical capacity, the economic means, nor, oftentimes, the desire to work." Here we get a hint of the role history plays in the contemporary arguments of local elites who oppose the Mapuche struggle.

Others echoed Baum's views, insisting the land was empty or close to it. The zone was unsettled before the colonos arrived, Gastón Muñoz, a military man turned local historian in Malleco, insisted, and it is important not to walk away with the idea that Mapuche had lived there. "That smells more like myth, . . . it smells more like legend to me," he said. "The truth is that this zone was occupied by families of Mapuche origin, but the quantity wasn't such, wasn't so numerous." Chile had good reasons to "pacify" the area, he added, citing not economic and political objectives but the presence of French citizen Orélie-Antoine de Tounens, who declared himself king of the Araucanía in 1860 and was perceived as a threat by the state. Muñoz suggested that the Mapuche had done little to fight the Pacificación. "There wasn't much resistance by the Mapuche ethnic group because there weren't many inhabitants here, of course, in comparison with other places." Muñoz had "a discrepancy" with the Mapuche; that the state had conceded títulos de merced "to calm them down" did not mean the colonos and Chileans who came to reside in those areas had taken land from them, because "they were never the owners of these lands; rather, they only lived in an isolated way." His explanation is full of contradictions; it seems that for Muñoz the Mapuche were there—just not there *enough*.

I met with Franco LaPorte, a middle-aged agricultural businessman whose family has significant and diversified holdings in the region, at his office in Temuco. (LaPorte's ancestral home in Malleco, which he co-owned with his siblings, was burned down in 2001, purportedly by Mapuche, though responsibility was never determined.) LaPorte suggested it was because the land was relatively empty that it was occupied at all: "When they decided to colonize the area, it was because of the depopulation that existed. . . . The Mapuches had died, like, by thousands and thousands with all of the sicknesses that the Europeans brought. They were exterminated in such a way that when the Pacificación of the Araucanía happened, there were so few people living in the area." With this justification LaPorte used genocide to suit his own purposes. The notion that they were not there contradicts the Mapuche version of history. It also absolves colonos and local elites of blame for being in unjust possession of Mapuche lands. In effectively removing the Mapuche from the postoccupation history of the region, they exercised symbolic violence as they justified their own good fortune.

In addition to this view, others suggested that the Mapuche were not really native to the land and thus could not claim it was theirs. For example, a high authority in the Catholic Church contended that the Mapuche had originally invaded Chile from Argentina and "did the same with the Indians who were here before. . . . So it is not that they were original [peoples] and that they've been here in Chile for 10,000 years. No, that is idealism, idealization." Interestingly, there are scholars and laypeople in Argentina who contend the opposite: that the Mapuche originated in what is now Chile and later colonized (or "Araucanized") the Argentine pampas (Ray 2007; Warren 2009). On both sides of the cordillera, such contentions are used to delegitimate contemporary Mapuche claims for territory and other rights. In fact, there are centuries of evidence of Mapuche crossings of the cordillera to pasture animals, engage in trade, conduct ceremonies, and, later, escape persecution.

Questioning the authenticity of the Mapuche is not a practice unique to local elites. Sergio Villalobos, one of Chile's most esteemed historians, whose texts are the basis for schoolbooks throughout the country, has been at the center of a highly visible campaign in *El Mercurio* contending that, as a result of mestizaje dating back to the 1500s, the Mapuche no longer exist (Villalobos 2000a, 2000b). In a September 2008 interview in *El Mercurio* (Almendras 2008), Villalobos restated his argument: "There are not exactly indigenous people, but rather, simply mestizo groupings that formed on the old ethnic groups that existed in the country. So, for example, there are descendants of Aymaras in the north of the country; there are mestizo descendants of the Araucanos of the Araucanía. In Chile, exactly pure indigenous people don't exist." He contends: "The original peoples in Chile disappeared. The peoples there now are not the originals, but rather their descendants." Villalobos resurrects the myth of mestizaje precisely to deny the continuity of indigenousness. Drawing a distinction between Mapuche and their descendents is symbolic violence. Not only does it deny contemporary Mapuche the right to their identity but, as former director of CONADI (Corporación Nacional de Desarollo Indígena, National Indigenous Development Agency) Domingo Namuncura (2008) has pointed out, by asserting that the Mapuche stopped existing at some point, it also represents a denial of the "internal exile, cultural uprooting, poverty, and marginality" faced by the Mapuche for decades following their defeat.

Such symbolic violence is also reflected in Villalobos's academic writings on the Pacificación, in which he contends that the Mapuche proffered little resistance, their desire for Western goods meant they were active participants in their domination, and the whole thing was resolved with relatively little violence (Lewis 1994; Ray 2007).[17] Gastón Muñoz's rewriting of the Pacificación followed in this vein: "Now imagine, . . . to occupy these lands, do you think the army killed anyone? They didn't kill anyone, no." He clarified that he was talking about the entire Frontera, from Concepción in the north to Osorno in the south. He continued: "How many died when the pacifying forces arrived to occupy this whole zone with force? How many died? No one, . . . because they were so into eating and drinking that the army only with drinks and alcohol [defeated them] and they didn't spill a bit, not a drop of blood was spilled in all the Pacificación. Sure, they gave them wine, okay, they left them contented."

Muñoz here reproduces Saavedra's "mucho mosto y música" myth. He cited a soldier's report documenting an occasion when the army was having trouble crossing a river, then happened upon some Mapuche who offered their canoes in exchange for food and wine. Muñoz concluded, directing himself at the Mapuche: "If you were drunk or you were not drunk, if it was with wine, or without wine, or with food, you handed all of this over so that the forces passed through and conquered and pacified all of this. Come to your own conclusion." Muñoz went to great pains to argue that the Pacificación was peaceful, observing that colonos soon began to "relate sentimentally with the Mapuche," whenceforth "Mapuche with pretty eyes, with blue eyes, began to be born." He elided the process of eradication brought about by the war, which progressively forced the Mapuche further and further south. He also disregarded the violence that occurred, which many Mapuche have characterized as genocide, as well as the agency in Mapuche resistance.

Chilean denial of Mapuche history is not universal, however. Gonzalo Lara had taught in rural and urban schools for many years before becoming an administrator in a school system in Malleco. He was sympathetic with the Mapuche version of history, observing that non-Mapuches arrived after a "violent conquest" driven by weapons as well as religion, and their presence was "imposed" on the Mapuche. He added that Mapuche were taken advantage of in deals in which they sold their land "for a couple of coins," papers that were manipulated, and other abuses. But even as he acknowledged this, he worried that the educated Mapuche of today might propose "that all the Westerners leave here" so the land would again be their own.

In telling their history, Chilean and colono landowners insisted not just on peaceful coexistence (when they admitted the Mapuche had been there at all), but that their land was acquired legally. Helga Stein, an elderly colono descendant, said: "There was never any conflict. We always lived in harmony with them, always." After a series of bothersome events (missing animals, broken fences), she and her brother had decided to sell their family's fundo via CONADI.[18] The fundo was seventy-one hectares—hardly a huge spread. "Forty-five hectares belonged and always belonged to colonos, and twenty-three hectares my dad bought from the Mapuche, but he made the purchase the correct way": through the *juzgados de indios* (the special court system set up to deal with Mapuche land and property).

Martin Rahm was a forty-something member of the regional development council and a lawyer in Malleco. Fires had been set on his family's five-hundred-plus-hectare fundo on several occasions in the years before our interview, resulting in the loss of several hundred forested hectares and some storage barns. He acknowledged that his family did not know for certain whether their land had belonged to the Mapuche before they lived there. "I have no reason to [know], and if it was, . . . it doesn't seem to me that I have to pay the blame. . . . The people who arrived here bought the land and paid the [Chilean state], I don't know if it was a lot or a little, but there weren't gifts. It [was] a policy of a state that invited colonos to come and take charge of lands that weren't occupied." In fact, the initial colonos were given land as opposed to purchasing it, but Rahm's point is that if the land was acquired legally through the state, the Mapuche have no basis for objection.

Despite their insistence that their land was acquired legally, it is well documented that Chileans and colonos usurped Mapuche land through a variety of means long after the military invasion (see, among others, Bengoa 2004; Caniuqueo 2008; Pinto 2007). *Corridas de cercos* ("fence running," or shifting the location of a fence so as to appropriate part of a neighbor's property) are one example. Colonos generally denied corridas had occurred. Franco LaPorte said Mapuche had come to him saying somebody in his family ran a fence onto their property some time back. He responded that he was not saying it did not happen but asked if they thought their ancestors just sat there and let it happen. He said: "I think they knew how to defend themselves." LaPorte's answer denotes a lack of consideration of the power dynamics that allowed Chileans and colonos to carry out these practices with impunity. Claiming today that their ancestors "should have defended themselves," given what we know of the Pacificación and its aftermath, is another instance of symbolic violence; the claim naturalizes economic and political domination. By virtue of their relative power and status, local elites are able to exercise symbolic violence through their historical narratives, demonstrating the socially constructed and contentious character of memory.

Mapuche respondents recalled countless additional forms of usurpation and exploitation that were common practice in the Frontera. Hernán Curinao, a Mapuche man who advocates for communities in conflict in Malleco, asserted that the rich made usurpation legal; they would steal the land and then write up documentation that made it their own. Because they had friends or relatives in government, it was all quite easy. It was common practice for the *juzgados de indios* to revoke títulos de merced when nonindigenous individuals provided "proof" of prior title (Bengoa 2004). Land was also lost in taverns, where Mapuche and Chileans interchanged goods under the effects of alcohol, as well as jails, where Mapuche were forced to turn over their land as punishment or to pay fines (Le Bonniec 2009a). These practices were facilitated by the legal division of Mapuche land titles mentioned earlier.

Mediería (half-sharing of various sorts) was another form of exploitation, although local elites occasionally told me Mapuche engaged in it because they were lazy. For example, Raúl Burgos, a land and mill owner in Cautín, characterized the Mapuche as friendly and caring but also lazy, which is, he said, what led them to "*trabajar a medias*," whereby the Mapuche would supply the land and the Chilean would invest the labor and money for seeds or supplies. In actuality, most Mapuche who half-shared in this way did so because they lacked the resources to plant and frequently invested a fair amount of labor in the process. Mapuche stories about mediería contradicted Burgos's version. There was mediería of oxen, whereby a Chilean or colono would loan an ox to a Mapuche, who would use it to plow his fields. Not infrequently, according to Horacio Quilapan, a member of CITEM who was college-educated and continued to live in his home community in Cautín, the ox's owner would then hire someone to steal the animal and make the Mapuche pay for it. Díaz (1984) notes that up until the 1970s, some Mapuche in the area of Capitán Pastene in Malleco half-shared on Italian-owned lands, receiving only a small part of the production in exchange for their labor. Mallon (2005, 74) documents the inequities of mediería with a story related by Don Heriberto Ailío regarding his father's experience sharecropping with a Chilean smallholder: "This partner would charge their father for the use of his draft animals and agricultural tools, since their family had none, and even though their father did all the work during planting, weeding, and harvesting, at the end of the year he was left with almost nothing." Mallon (ibid., 76) documents other cases in which Mapuche worked for large- and medium-scale farmers because they "lacked tools, seed, animals, and capital to make (their) own land productive." Economic need led others to move to the cities or become day or migrant laborers, which, Mallon points out, made it even more difficult to work one's own land.

A related practice was known as *compra en hierba*. When a crop, say wheat, was planted, if the Mapuche needed money to buy seed or supplies, they would sell a winka five bags of wheat in advance. The winka would say fine, I'll buy five now, but when you harvest, you have to bring me ten. If the Mapuche farmer did not manage to harvest ten bags, the winka would take his sheep or other property, with the assistance of the police. Horacio Quilapan mentioned another practice, known by the saying, "Good sheep, good justice," meaning that if you brought the local judge a good sheep, you would get the justice you wanted, but if you did not have a sheep to give him, you were out of luck. He estimates that these practices were commonplace until the mid-1960s. Pinto (2007) has documented similar practices. Quilapan summed things up by saying, "In [my comuna], there is so much rage, so very, very much."

Cattle rustling, often attributed to the Mapuche but acknowledged by Chilean and Mapuche respondents alike to be driven by winka families, was also common in the region, particularly in one of my focus comunas in Cautín. Mapuche respondents identified nearly all of the comuna's elite families as somehow linked to the trade in stolen animals, some to this day. They hired Mapuche to steal the animals, but it was they who made the profit. As judges and other local lawmen, their friends and family members facilitated their illegal trade. Elites in this comuna displayed some sympathy with the Mapuche on this issue. On how rustling operated in the area, Raúl Burgos stated: "The Mapuche serves to be told what to do, to do it, but the brains [behind the operation] are Chileans." Billy Montoya, the middle-aged son of a European missionary, suggested that winka men in town were totally involved in the operation, financing it and buying the stolen animals. Despite this sympathy, cattle rustling was highly damaging to Mapuche, who were often its victims as well as the accused perpetrators. Rolf Foerster and Sonia Montecino (1988) have argued that throughout the 1930s and 1940s, rustling was a pretext used by elites and authorities to justify false accusations, murders, and other violence against the Mapuche. This practice fomented distrust of the police, who carried out searches and on-site punishment of the "guilty."

Narratives legitimating the exploitation of Mapuche labor and appropriation of their land accompanied practices like mediería and cattle rustling. Many local elites spoke with pride and nostalgia about their comunas as the "granary of Chile," the zone that fed a growing Chile as well as foreign markets. The notion of the pacified frontier as the granary of Chile was linked by local elites to a discourse of work. They spoke of the hard labor that went into "virgin lands" that had "never been cultivated." Ideas about "work" are an important means by which Chileans delegitimated Mapuche claims and objected to indigenous policy. But here work was used to legitimate colono presence on the frontier. Rene Ravinet, a store owner and former authority in a small town in Cautín, explained: "My grandparents were [European] colonos. . . . They had a restaurant and a bakery, but very rustic, because you will understand that the colonos arrived with little money. That is, they didn't come here from being rich. They came to work, and in general, the Swiss, German, French, Italian colonos came to work."

The topic of work also dominated a conversation about loss of Mapuche lands with two women descendants of Italian colonos in Malleco. When I asked what they had been told about relations between Mapuche and Italians in the early days, one said: "Well, what I knew was that they began to negotiate . . . with the Mapuche and they began to have more land." The other amplified this response but first cautioned, "Well, I don't know. You have to be very much on the inside," suggesting that I might not be able to fully comprehend what she was about to tell me and also, perhaps, warning me of its offensive character:

> I think the Mapuche, with their lands—they allege that their lands are theirs, isn't that right? But if we analyze the issue of the Mapuche lands in those years, the *nonos*, the grandparents of the Mapuche of today, they were the owners and sires of the lands, that's fine. . . . But what happened with that? The Mapuche didn't find a better economic situation than to go selling their lands, and in fact, they went on selling them. . . . They sold them for the price of an egg, as we say in Chile—"for the price of an egg" means that the Mapuche all his life has been very into [*muy bueno para*] drinking, into alcohol. . . . Now the Mapuche of today say that their grandfathers had one pulled over on them.

Although Mapuche today wanted the land back, on the basis that they were tricked or deceived, she felt that a deal was a deal. They sold because they wanted to sell, whether for alcohol or other goods: "Here each Mapuche handed over their land not because they were giving it away, nor because it was taken from them, simply because they made a deal. Now, if the deal was badly made, it is not the fault of the one who bought it. . . . In those years, Italians entered into negotiation, surely, with the Mapuches, . . . but there weren't conflicts between the Mapuche and them. Nothing was ever heard about having a conflict." The first woman agreed and clarified that the Italians were able to enter into these negotiations because they were hard workers and tight with their money, whereas "the Mapuche always needed money to drink, what do I know?" The other again: "The Mapuche, to this day, [is] the same." The first woman added that many have land and don't work it, and the second said:

> Now there are many Mapuche with a lot of culture, because now they have entered the University. They have a different social range, and are helping bring up those who have nothing, but the Mapuche to this day, the *campesino neto* [meaning the "true Mapuche"] comes to town in his cart, sells the firewood, and takes the cart [home]. He doesn't take it with flour, nor with merchandise. He takes it full of drink. That is what he takes to the countryside. He takes a quintal of flour and five crates of beer, and I don't know how many carafes of wine, you understand me. . . . But conflicts with the Italians, no. They didn't have them and I think, to this day, there have never been problems.

Here, Mapuche alcoholism and laziness is contrasted with Italian industriousness to justify increasing Italian landholdings. The second woman was particularly venomous in her portrayal of the Mapuche, and even though she saw "culture" as something you get by attending university, she seemed to suggest that those who had access to education were not "true" Mapuche—a discursive ploy that makes it impossible for "true" Mapuche to improve their position. Masking structural inequities by blaming them on faults in Mapuche character, the work narrative is a form of symbolic violence.

Given the level of inequality and the distinct relationship of Chileans and Mapuche to the territory, it is easy to imagine an Araucanía in which Mapuche and Chileans lived mostly segregated lives. And yet this was not the case. The border was never impermeable; there was cross-border trade since the time of the Spanish, and, as León (2007) has observed, there was a mestizo population in the Araucanía for three centuries before the Pacificación. Although historians have largely ignored the transitional years from 1900 to 1940, as León also notes, that work is beginning to take place. While the Mapuche resided mostly in the communities during those years, and were in some ways inward-looking and isolated (Bengoa 1985), there were also points of contact with Chileans. Not only did Mapuche often work for their Chilean or colono neighbors, or interact with them in the innumerable exploitative ways described earlier, but between 1884 and 1910 lonkos permitted a considerable number of poor Chileans, looking for refuge, fleeing *inquilinaje* (tenant farming) or the law, or for other reasons, to live in the communities (Caniuqueo 2008). Even before their military defeat, some lonkos hired Chileans as workers or translators.

Despite the marginalization documented here, a sort of partial, imposed integration did occur. Schools, the Catholic Church, the law, and the military were important agents of assimilation, of course, but there is even some record of Mapuche customs being integrated into the *fiestas patrias* (independence celebrations) (León 2007). In addition, the Mapuche had some allies in the church and the media who spoke up against their mistreatment in the early 1900s (Pinto 2007). Yet they were generally not viewed as a living people with specific concerns and rights. The contemporary memories of local elites hearken back to this form of symbolic violence; the forces of assimilation largely functioned to destroy Mapuche identity and lifeways, not maintain them on equal standing with Chilean ones. Although the Mapuche, colonos, and local elites share a territory, their memories of how that territory and the social relations within it came to be constructed are in contestation with one another. This contestation would become even more acute with the political upheaval of the mid-twentieth century.

AGRARIAN REFORM, THE UNIDAD POPULAR, AND DICTATORSHIP

Before addressing agrarian reform and the political upheaval of the 1970s, it is worth discussing a long-standing analogy that became dominant around the mid-1940s. Mapuche communities are known as the "suicide belt" that suffocates development in the region (Foerster and Montecino 1988). In 1946 the *Diario Austral* opined that the so-called suicide belt was "the barrier against greater progress in the regional economy" because the lands were in "lazy hands," where "work and progress do not flourish" (in Caniuqueo 2005). Foerster and Montecino (1988) have argued that the use of the word "suicide" as opposed to "assassin" is important, because it suggests a belief that colonos and Chileans were killing themselves by allowing the Mapuche to have land. As Otto Berg put it in the *Austral* in 1946: "How is it possible that it is permitted that the most fertile lands in these provinces, which are Chile's granary, remain in the hands of Indians and that they produce absolutely nothing?" (in Foerster and Montecino 1988, 278). Why were local elites not able to wield their political influence to do away with the "suicide belt"? The *Austral* attributed the Mapuches' ability to maintain control of their land to the activism of Venancio Coñoepan's Corporación Araucana, the most important Mapuche organization of the era (ibid.).

State agencies also expressed concern about the suicide belt. In a 1962 document, CORFO (Corporación de Fomento de la Producción, Economic Development Agency) lamented that the Mapuche "not only conserve that which legitimately belongs to them, like language and their typical dress . . . but, most gravely, they also conserve totally primitive ways of life, ceremonials, and work techniques." This was thought to be particularly serious because the Mapuche still possessed about four hundred thousand hectares. (in Caniuqueo 2005, 13). Local elites and state officials who espoused such opinions were unlikely to view favorably agrarian reforms that would put more land in Mapuche hands.

But the winds of change were in the air throughout Latin America in the second half of the twentieth century. Mestizo nationalism, which formed the basis for popular movements elsewhere in the region, was not prominent in Chile.[19] Instead, Chilean reformist and revolutionary movements privileged class ideology with little ethnic content. One such organization that had a huge impact in Mapuche territory was the Movimiento Campesino Revolucionario (MCR). The MCR was the peasant arm of the MIR (Movimiento de Izquierda Revolucionaria, a Marxist-Leninist revolutionary party founded in 1965). Although agrarian reform had begun under Presidents Jorge Alessandri (beginning in 1962) and Eduardo Frei Montalva

(1964–70), it intensified during Salvador Allende's Unidad Popular (Popular Unity) government. The Miristas (MIR members) headed south to mobilize poor Mapuche and Chilean peasants before Allende was elected. The MCR was formally organized after the election, sparking an intense period of fence running and land occupations. During January and February 1971, Minister of Agriculture Jacques Chonchol and the CORA (Corporación de Reforma Agraria, Agrarian Reform Agency) literally moved operations to Temuco to regulate and adjudicate the expropriations. This period became known as the Cautinazo.

It is worth stressing that Mapuche and Chilean peasants, though both poor, had a different relationship to the land. Only a small proportion of the Mapuche were *inquilinos* on the large estates in the region—a role more likely to have been filled by poor Chileans (Correa, Molina, and Yáñez 2005).[20] They were, nevertheless, a reserve labor force for the large estates (Mallon 2005). However, many Mapuche envisioned agrarian reform as a way not only to get land but to reclaim that which had been stolen from them. Yet Mapuche and Chileans worked side by side in the MCR for social change. The unified character of this movement was reflected in the name chosen to represent it. Mapuche MCR member Rafael Railaf explains that they chose "campesino" instead of "Mapuche" to inspire poor Chileans to join the organization. "We thought that if we struggled (alone) we would be weak, because we were very few, we weren't millions like the winka" (Carvajal, Peralta, and Ribera 2006, 61). Jose Peralta, a Chilean Mirista who helped form the MCR, echoes Railaf, noting that to successfully occupy fundos, the Mapuche needed alliances with the inquilinos, who were greater in number, mostly Chilean, and also exploited. In fact, this class-based focus was somewhat orchestrated from above, and as Mallon (2005) has noted, influenced by Marxist sociologist Alejandro Saavedra. Saavedra argued that dividing the rural poor by race only served the interests of the landowners by weakening the bases for collective struggle and providing them with a racial justification for subordination of the peasantry. He and others were "also convinced that the Mapuche had stopped being a separate culture, ethnic group, or race" (ibid., 82).

Certainly, as Mallon (ibid.) has pointed out, poor Mapuche and Chileans *did* share some class-based commonalities. Mapuche who joined the Far Left often explain their affinity with those groups in terms of their positions on poverty and social justice. Ernesto Manquecoy, who was a member of the Communist Youth and later played an important role in the antidictatorship organization Ad-Mapu, recalled reading Lenin at the library at a young age and listening to Fidel Castro on the radio. He explained what drew him to communist politics: "There was a lot of poverty in our own family. We were hungry, we didn't have anything to put in the pot, we would be waiting for the *digueñe* to appear, some mushrooms, to be able to nourish ourselves. So it was the social condition, the misery that we were living, that drew me to that." MCR member Victor Molfinqueo (in Carvajal, Peralta, and Ribera 2006) echoes this sentiment when he suggests that it was the extent of the misery in which people lived that motivated them to run fences and occupy fundos. Rosendo Huenuman, later a communist member of the national parliament, worked with a leftist politician in the 1960s to reclaim some of his community's usurped land: "For me, the injustice against our people was clear and I wasn't going to keep my mouth shut" (Cayuqueo 2008b). In rejecting exploitation and inequality, these Mapuche activists contributed to laying bare the economic and cultural privilege behind the symbolic violence that had for so long governed social interchange in the Chilean South.

Mapuche participation in leftist and campesino organizations in the 1960s and 1970s should not be read as purely instrumental. Many of the Mapuche involved in those organizations legitimately saw their interests as intersecting with those of poor, rural Chileans. Nor should it be understood as the only organizational strategy of the period. Respondents recalled individuals on the Mapuche Left who insisted, despite participating in class-based movements, on the importance of autonomous Mapuche organizing (see also Caniuqueo 2006, 194). Indeed, consistent with a long history of cultural and political mobilization, Mapuche continued organizing as Mapuche during this period. For instance, the National Mapuche Congresses held in 1969 and 1970 laid the groundwork for a new indigenous law.

The Mapuche benefited from agrarian reform. This is true of the Alessandri and Frei eras, but especially of the Allende years. In all, 163 properties, totaling more than 152,000 hectares, were expropriated in favor of the Mapuche between 1962 and 1973 (Correa, Molina and Yáñez 2005). Although the expropriations were not framed in these terms, some of these properties were ancestral lands; others were part of the títulos de merced. While the Alessandri and Frei administrations treated the Mapuche as peasants, like other rural Chileans, there was some movement toward recognizing the specificity of Mapuche claims under Allende. In 1972 parliament passed a modified version of a law that had been proposed in 1970 by indigenous organizations. This law represented the first time indigenous people were legally recognized as existing independent of their lands, created an Institute of Indigenous Development, and included a promise to restore to the Mapuche lands that had been usurped since the Pacificación (Comisión Asesora 1999; COM 2006). All of this became inoperable, however, upon the military coup the following year. Despite the 1972 law, the Allende administration has been criticized for forcing collective production practices on the Mapuche and failing to recognize their rights to participation and self-determination (Aylwin 2001; COM 2006).[21]

The symbolic violence exposed by the Unidad Popular and its supporters was soon replaced with the physical and psychological violence of the dictatorship. In the Araucanía the military takeover actually started before September 11, 1973 (the official day of the coup). For example, Rucalán, an appropriated fundo described by Mallon (2005), was invaded by the military at the end of August. With the onset of the coup and the ensuing counterreform, leaders of the appropriations as well as average community members were terrorized by torture and many were disappeared (Correa, Molina, and Yáñez 2005). Today, many at the grassroots feel they suffered more than the higher-ups (as well as wealthier participants) who had come to organize them and had access to networks that could lead them into exile. After the coup many felt they had been "tricked into believing that things really could have changed for the better" (Mallon 2005, 157). The material, psychological, and social consequences of the coup run deep in many Mapuche communities.

Much of the land that had been returned to the Mapuche under agrarian reform was restored to local farming elites, in accordance with the notion that it was the Mapuche who had usurped winka land, or deeded to corporations that would plant it with pine and eucalyptus, laying the bases for a lucrative logging industry in the region. In fact, the timber industry had long been fostered by the state, including the Popular Front in the 1940s, the Christian Democratic government of Frei Montalva, and the Unidad Popular (Klubock 2004). Between 1965 and 1973 the government planted pine on expropriated lands (McFall 2001). It was often Mapuche who worked on these plantations, but they were never given legal title to the land. By 1973, CORA, which maintained title to the lands, had more than 710,000 hectares of forested land in the provinces of Arauco, Malleco, and Cautín (ibid.). Many of these lands were returned to latifundistas under Pinochet, but more than four hundred thousand hectares were transferred from CORA to CONAF (Corporación Nacional Forestal, the semiprivate National Forestry Agency) and then auctioned off to timber companies at negligible prices (Aylwin 2002).[22] Timber companies burned down much of the native forest they purchased, replacing it with pine saplings (Klubock 2004).

Altogether, of the 163 properties expropriated in favor of the Mapuche through agrarian reform, 97 were returned to their previous owners, 3 were auctioned to other individuals or companies, and 63 were parceled out into small, individually owned plots (as opposed to communally or cooperatively owned lands). It is estimated that fewer than 50 percent of the plots in this final category stayed in Mapuche hands (Correa, Molina and Yáñez 2005). All told, by the end of the counterreform, Mapuche families retained only about 16 percent of the land they had recovered between 1962 and 1973. In addition to being expelled from their land, communities suffered abuses from the regime as well as local elites who supported it. One member of a community that lost land during the counterreform recalled Mapuche *comuneros* being tied up at gunpoint by elite farmers under suspicion of being Allende supporters, or shot at if they walked across their property. The redispossession of Mapuche communities under Pinochet's rule is the immediate antecedent of present-day conflicts among the communities, local farmers, timber companies, and the state.

In 1978 the regime enacted a decree law designed to facilitate the division of community lands, institute private ownership, and make it easier to sell these lands to nonindigenous individuals. The law stipulated that indigenous lands could be divided at the solicitation of just one community resident, regardless of whether he or she was Mapuche. Some Chilean families actually settled on community lands at this time to take advantage of the law of division, which recognized those who were present on the land as legitimate owners, independent of their ethnic origin.[23] Conversely, Mapuche people who had migrated for work and were not in the communities at the time of division lost legal right to their land. Community residents were frequently intimidated into agreeing to divide their lands. All told, the law resulted in the division of 1,739 Mapuche communities between 1979 and 1986 (Comisión Asesora 1999; Aylwin 2002 puts this number at nearly two thousand communities and notes that average plot size after division was 6.4 hectares per family). After division some plots ended up in non-Mapuche hands as the result of ninety-nine-year rentals and other types of contracts that became common during this period (Aylwin 2002). Diane Haughney (2006) has estimated that by 1990, Mapuche communities possessed around three hundred thousand hectares, signaling a loss of about 40 percent of the lands deeded to them in the títulos de merced.

The decree was also designed to obliterate indigenous identity; it mandated that "the parcels resulting from the division of the reserves will no longer be considered indigenous lands, nor indigenous their owners and residents" (in Comisión Asesora 1999). Upon division of their lands, the Mapuche would no longer be Mapuche; they would be campesinos like any other. Mapuche organizations believed this decree was an effort to pave the way to legally annihilate their people (Aylwin 1998). Many Mapuche organized in resistance to the decree, and the section regarding Mapuche identity was eventually modified. Most important among the organizations that emerged at this time were the Centros Culturales Mapuches (Mapuche Cultural Centers) and their successor Ad-Mapu. Ad-Mapu was the most broad-based Mapuche organization of all time, at one point representing fifteen hundred communities (Reuque Paillalef 2002). It was an active force in the movement against the dictatorship.[24]

The fallout from the dictatorship highlighted the difficulties of working together with Chileans.[25] Mapuche who participated in political parties during that era spoke about being used by the parties, noting that Mapuche issues were forced to the margins, dealt with only in "ethnic commissions." Mapuche were subordinated within the parties, and there was little room to propose political initiatives based on the principle that they were a people. Rosendo Huenuman complains that that the Communist Party tried to control him, which he resisted to the point that he rejected their help in finding refuge after the coup (Cayuqueo 2008b).[26] Huenuman's conflicts with the Chilean Left continued when he was in exile and a leader of the Comité Exterior Mapuche (Mapuche Committee Abroad), an organization of Mapuche exiles in Europe. He told Pedro Cayuqueo (ibid.): "We publicized the whole problematic, the policy applied against the Mapuche since this republican country was founded. That bothered the winka exiles, who only wanted to talk about Pinochet, but we Mapuche had more things to say." Similarly, today some MCR members, like Rudecino Quinchavil, suggest that it might have been preferable to create "a distinct consciousness" in the Mapuche, but that did not happen because they had the attitude that "we [were] all Chileans" and wanted everything to be "even" (Carvajal, Peralta, and Ribera 2006, 38–39).

Jose Peralta, the Chilean who helped form the MCR, likewise acknowledges in retrospect that despite the close relationship between Miristas and the Mapuche, "we didn't understand that the Mapuche were Mapuche. As a product of our Chilean condition, and at the same time with an artisanal Marxist-Leninist-Guevarist-Maoist ideology, we weren't capable of understanding a much denser, richer, and complex reality. . . . We maintained a vision where we Miristas were the only vanguard" (ibid., 87). Mallon (2005, 83) has argued that a lens, such as the MIR's, that focuses on social class alone overlooks "an entire fabric of social relations, a particular view of the world and of the land, and a system of labor organization that differentiated the Mapuche from other groups within the rural poor." Thus the dictatorship era found many Mapuche not only suffering severe repression but also beginning to question their alliances on the left.

Local elites' memories of these years are very different from those of the Mapuche. They tend to focus on the damage agrarian reform did to the social fabric of the region and see the dictatorship as a kind of salvation. Raúl Burgos, the land and mill owner from Cautín, called agrarian reform a "hateful system," a policy imposed by the United States through the Alliance for Progress that became especially "political" under Allende. In fact, he said, one of his own fundos was scheduled for appropriation, but the coup happened before the process could be completed. He insisted that the Mapuche did not take part in the occupations in the area, but rather, "political groups" were behind them.

Others acknowledged Mapuche participation but still placed the bulk of the blame on the Unidad Popular. Even though his family had been required to cede part of its fundo to its workers in the 1960s, Esteban Marcial cited 1970, when the Unidad Popular came to power, as the end point to their friendly relationship with their Mapuche neighbors. In Marcial's opinion the expectations opened by Allende led the Mapuche to be more aggressive, occupying land, and once even kidnapping his father. The Marcial fundo was scheduled for expropriation under Allende, although they were able to delay it in court until after the coup. Marcial said the situation remained tense until the coup, when the military applied "an iron fist," and "for seventeen more years, we lived an era, let's say, of tranquility." Local elites contended that the Mapuche only destroyed the property they recovered through agrarian reform. Marcos Rohrer, who was a regional authority in Malleco under Frei Montalva and had a role in administering some of the expropriations, conceded that some of them were called for.[27] Nevertheless, he felt the beneficiaries of the expropriations did not know what to do with the land when they got it. Several respondents related stories about Mapuche who ruined the houses on the expropriated properties by setting hearth fires on the floor (as they would in a ruka) or using them as barns. Others noted that they simply did not know how to make good use of the land, tractors, and fertilizer they were given. These stories presage local elites' objections to giving the Mapuche land today. In suggesting that the inequities of the era were somehow deserved, they also contribute to symbolic violence.

Local elites tended to evaluate the contemporary conflicts, as well as the state's response, through the lens of the turbulent 1970s. Guillermo Hanssen was a middle-aged agricultural businessman very involved in regional development associations. At the end of the 1990s he faced atentados on one of his former fundos in Malleco.[28] He met with me at his office in Temuco, where he suggested there is a "political cycle" in which at certain times there is "a softness, a permissiveness, an authorization to do things" that violates the normally symbiotic and "very intimate relationship between the landowner and the worker" in the countryside. Similarly, the tranquility Marcial so appreciated about the dictatorship ended in the 1990s, he said, with the creation of the Indigenous Law and global "effervescence" around indigenous rights. Colono Iván Isler, who also has faced atentados on his property, similarly reminisced: "The military government arrived, and there was peace. We could work tranquilly during 17 years. . . . Well, it ended, and democracy returned. I don't know, for me, Pinochet was more democratic than today's government, because I am more suppressed [*sometido*] today than before. I am more suppressed because today I am accosted by the illicit ones, because today, terrorism is protected, delinquency is protected." Memories surrounding agrarian reform, the Unidad Popular, and the dictatorship are deeply contested, reflecting class positions and revealing fissures that continued to shape intercultural relationships in the region for years to come.

MEMORIES OF DISCRIMINATION, MEMORIES OF SAMENESS

The differences in how Mapuche and local elites talk about the past are crucial to contextualizing their competing views on the conflicts and policies of the Concertación years. In addition to stories about dispossession and exploitation, Mapuche respondents related painful memories of discrimination. Schooling was perhaps the most common arena that came up in these conversations. This was as true of respondents in their seventies as it was of those in their thirties. Mapuche often struggled to get access to education, but when they achieved it, the experience was not always positive. Discrimination at school was often compounded by poverty; Mapuche students frequently did not have adequate supplies, clothing, or shoes (Mallon 2005). Other students made fun of them for their accents, grammatical mistakes, and last names, taunting them for "smelling like smoke" because they lived in rukas. Teachers punished them, often physically, for speaking Mapudungun, the Mapuche language. The teachers who meted out these punishments were sometimes Mapuche themselves (Caniuqueo 2008). The sanctions they experienced for speaking Mapudungun led many parents to refuse to teach it to their children, in the hopes that they would not experience the same kind of discrimination. In this way education played an assimilationist role. Today many Mapuche blame the educational system for the endangered status of their language.

Angélica Antillan, a woman in her sixties who participated in a regional Mapuche women's organization, spoke extensively about being discriminated against in school. When she and her sister were school-aged, their father paid for them to stay in a pension, so they could attend school in the town nearest to their community. It was there, isolated from the support of her family and community, that she first felt rejected for being Mapuche.

Other students made fun of her name, and a teacher once insisted on know-ing where she got her nice shoes and clothes (which her father had purchased) because she assumed that if Mapuche had anything nice, it must have been provided through charity or stolen. The discrimination was so great that at times, Doña Angélica remembered, she did not want to be Mapuche. She only studied through sixth grade. She became ill around that time, which she now interprets as psychosomatic, "as if I didn't dare to arrive to other parts [i.e., to achieve more] because the discrimination had been so strong." An-gélica's experiences contrast greatly with the anecdote told to me by Nilda, the non-Mapuche wife of a dictatorship-era mayor in Malleco. She grew up in the same comuna as Angélica. She told of the "feroza" (ferocious or savage one) who sat next to her in school, who "even dressed Mapuche." "The *feroza* loved the *inferoza*," she said, and hugged and doted on her. Nilda laughed as she related this memory; perhaps not recognizing the way she robbed her Mapuche classmate of her humanity, it was a source of bemusement for her.

Discrimination led many Mapuche to rely on their families for emotional support and protection. But family could not always fully protect them and sometimes was itself a source of discrimination. Several respondents spoke of horrendous treatment at the hands of non-Mapuche relatives. The workplace was another site of discrimination. Respondents cited domestic service and the marketplace, where Mapuche women, more visible because they dressed in traditional clothing, were made fun of, ripped off, and treated like they were stupid, as particularly forceful examples. Younger respondents reported labor force discrimination even today. Trained in social work, Millaray Ca-trillanca was born in the region and spent her early years there. She returned in 2001 to work for the regional government. She was surprised by the con-tinued pervasiveness of racism, concluding: "[This] is a region that doesn't want to be indigenous, that denies the indigenous, . . . [and] only makes it visible for commercial effects, in terms of tourism, craftwork, and nothing else. For everything else, it is ballast." Discrimination is important because of its social and psychological effects on individuals and communities, but also because of its role in justifying systemic inequality and exploitation.

In contrast to Mapuche memories of discrimination and exploitation, colono and Chilean respondents were more likely to say relations had always been fine. Negating Mapuche claims of discrimination is, of course, symbolic violence, concealing what many Mapuche have recognized as domination.[29] In this way colonos denied any historical basis to the present conflicts. The erasure of past conflict led many colonos and local elites to blame current conflicts on outsiders. I do not wish to suggest that they necessarily were being consciously disingenuous to justify their positions. Rather, beyond the fantasy of terra nullius, for the colonos what existed before *was* a good relationship, from their point of view; this is how they understood the region's collective past. Most colonos were stupefied by the conflicts. They remembered a peaceful, happy coexistence and expressed a desire to go back to the way things used to be. Hernán Rohrer, the adult son of Marcos, who had recently run for mayor in his Malleco comuna, put it this way: "This situation is producing a rejection of the indigenous people. . . . But in the old days, we all shared together, and we didn't have any problems, *we were the same.*"

Local elites made frequent assertions of sameness to explain the absence of conflict as well as to negate Mapuche assertions of discrimination. For example, in an informal conversation with a group of Rohrer's family members and friends, a woman suddenly exclaimed: "We've always been the same, and all of the sudden, they [the Mapuche] say, 'we're different.'" The frequency with which comments like this emerged over the course of my fieldwork has led me to believe they represent an underlying fear of what recognizing Mapuche culture and rights might mean in material terms and a wish that difference could simply be willed away. Ultimately, assertions of sameness imply a number of things: the Mapuche do not have a historical basis for animosity toward the colonos, their demands for the land are illegitimate, they were never culturally different or treated unequally, and those who are currently making claims for territory and rights are not "real" Mapuche.

Although respondents did not necessarily explicitly use the word "mestizaje," references to racial and cultural mixing were often part of these assertions of sameness and the absence of past conflict. Rene Ravinet related the opinion of a Mapuche friend of his who contended that the Mapuche in Chile were lucky compared with indigenous peoples in the United States and Argentina, where they were mostly killed. "Here the Spanish with the Mapuchitas and the Mapuchitas with the Spanish integrated. Here, right away, there was a fusion of blood. The one who considered himself pure, of special race . . . , was never lacking, but a great percentage fused."[30] Ravinet insisted that Chileans were conscious of this mixture, but it is telling that he related this story from a Mapuche person, because it seems to me that Mapuche were more willing to acknowledge mestizaje than were most non-Mapuche. (Ravinet himself identifies as a descendant of Swiss-French colonos.) He argued that, as a result, at least in his comuna in Cautín, the situation is different from parts of Malleco, where there is greater differentiation and "open, face-to-face racism like you had there [in the United States]."

In addition, the assertion of sameness was often contradicted within the same conversation. For example, Hernán Rohrer referred to the Mapuche as a "race" even as he asserted: "We were all the same." Similarly, when asked about intercultural relations in his comuna, Billy Montoya painted a picture of mixture and coexistence that was imbued with hierarchy, inequality, and difference. He insisted relationships between Mapuche and non-Mapuche in the area had not changed much over time because they have always been "mixed," but he also resented his Mapuche farmhands for using the informal Spanish term for "you" (*tú*) rather than the formal (*usted*). Although not all colonos asserted sameness, and many contradicted themselves in their narratives, it is important to note the role that power—the cultural and economic resources that allow one to be the subject of the social world rather than its object—has in this construction. Local elites can assert that the "mixedness" of their region makes everyone the same, and they might even believe it, but as Horacio Quilapan pointed out, the Mapuche's lived experience of this mixedness—understood in biological or sociocultural terms—is quite different. While not without contradictory effects, for the Mapuche that mixing of cultures, those social interactions, formed the basis of the initial dispossession and genocide as well as ongoing discriminatory practices, not to mention that it was premised on the rape of indigenous women. Narratives of sameness erased these experiences, contributing to the symbolic violence that sustains inequality and misrecognition in the region.

Somewhat in contrast to the notion of sameness, colonos also fondly recounted paternalistic moments when they "helped" Mapuche—by driving someone to the hospital, teaching them about cleanliness, or lending them money that was never repaid. Helga Stein, for example, said her family never had conflicts with their Mapuche neighbors, and in fact, "my father taught them to cultivate the land." Daniel Hauri, of Swiss-German and French descent (his grandfather arrived right around 1900, after the original wave of colonos, but did not get the oxen and other benefits), similarly spoke about how his mother founded a school for Mapuche kids and taught families how to get rid of lice. Hauri recalled going to school with Mapuche kids and playing soccer with them. "There was never any problem." Here Mapuche existence is recognized and provides convenient evidence for the European farmers' benevolent superiority.

In a sense, we see sameness and difference operating simultaneously and reinforcing one another in the colonos' discourse; everybody was the "same" and everybody got along. This could be believed because Mapuche claims were not interfering with the colonos' daily lives and demonstrating that not everyone experienced the situation similarly. But still, the Mapuche were "different" to the extent that they needed to be helped and civilized by the colonos. In both cases this is reality as constructed by the colonos, and this is the reality on which dominant understandings of the contemporary conflicts are built. We see how local elites' and colonos' recollections function as symbolic violence. Mapuche land claims, demands, and activism are seen as illegitimate because they have no historical basis in the eyes of the dominant. This is what makes the contemporary Mapuche movement so frightening— these Mapuche, so long treated as objects for the consumption of the Chileans and colonos (through their territory, their labor, and so on), are forcing themselves onto the social stage as subjects and demanding to be taken into account.

Clearly, Mapuche activists did not share this fantasy of sameness and benevolence. For example, Ramiro Raipillan, a resident of the community with which Hauri has a territorial conflict, reflected on reading a news interview in which Hauri's wife talked about the school Hauri's mother had established in the community. "My mom's only memory," he said, "is that they whipped her because she didn't know Spanish. She only spoke Mapudungun." I asked him if it was true, though, that Hauri's father was well liked by many in the community. "Sure," he responded, "I've also heard that. The people in some parts say, 'No, that man was good.' But, does it make him good that he gave a gift, or paid for a job with a kilo of wheat? . . . Those were forms of power, to manipulate the people." Hernán Curinao agreed that few Mapuche share colono memories. He said it was true that he and other Mapuche kids played with the sons of the rich, but as soon as they became adults, it became apparent who had power over whom. It was also true, he said, that Hauri's father was "much loved" by the Mapuche, but it was the love of a patron, not an equal. In response to the assertion that the colonos treated the Mapuche well, he too spoke of the patronage system. Sure, he said, they paid a sack of flour and two pieces of bread for sunup to sundown work, always just enough to survive, never enough to save a little or live a little better, while they made tons of money. Although it may be true for the colonos that everything was great before, their Mapuche neighbors do not share those memories.

Local elites and Mapuche remember their shared histories quite differently. In justifying inequality and oppression, memory can function as symbolic violence but also as resistance. Competing memories and histories are a central part of contemporary conflicts over rights and resources and are used to justify a diversity of positions. This analysis is important because, as Hooker (2009, 106) has pointed out, it indicates that racial justice will require changing how the "political community as a whole understands itself and remembers its past." Indeed, many local elites are very resentful of academic interest in the Mapuche. This has a lot to do with their desire for *their* version of history to remain the hegemonic one. Malleco landowner and businessman

Simón Baum, while very cordial to me during our interview, was clearly ir-ritated by academic and social concern for the Mapuche. He told me the story of a professor he met in the 1950s, who insisted on asking questions about the Mapuche. A friend of his asked the professor why he was not talking about Peru, where there was actually a major indigenous population, instead of Chile. This question caused some conflict with the professor, who didn't think it was legitimate. But Baum did and repeated to me: "They're barely 4 percent of the population here!"

This was the final thought he left me with when he dropped me off at the bus station for my return trip to Temuco. His point: Why bother with the Mapuche, when they are such an insignificant sector of the population? This attitude reflects a desire to eliminate the Mapuche from the social imaginary. Such willed invisibilization functions as symbolic violence and sustains sys-temic racism, justifying the material dispossession of the Mapuche and colo-nial presence in their territory. At the same time, it also informs the memories Mapuche carry with them. This subjugated version of history, the Mapuche version, has not been forgotten. As shall be seen, it was an important factor in the mobilization of Mapuche communities under the Concertación.

CHAPTER 3

NEOLIBERALISM AND THE CONFLICTS
UNDER THE CONCERTACIÓN

Neoliberal economic policies extended upon the legacy of racism and inequality to create a situation in which conflicts over land, resources, and indigenous rights thrived throughout the 1990s and early 2000s. This chapter examines these neoliberal roots as well as how Mapuche and local elites explained the conflicts, paying special attention to how the concepts of law and legitimacy inform these differing explanations. I make two interrelated arguments. First, the conflicts exemplify how, vis-à-vis the Mapuche, neoliberal policies—as the foundation of Chilean national development—represent the continuity of the colonial condition. Second, the distinct ways Mapuche and local elites understand law and legitimacy reflect a struggle over epistemic privilege, a struggle grounded in the original colonial assault and central to the perpetuation of systemic racism. Epistemic privilege not only makes local elites' claims more "believable" than those of the Mapuche in the context of particular conflicts; it also facilitates the imposition of neoliberal development in ancestral Mapuche territory. As Nancy Grey Postero (2007, 24–25) puts it: "Domination of Indians did not only happen through massacres, but also through the establishment of regimes of social order that naturalized such domination. These regimes laid out categories of belonging and Otherness that continue to operate today." This chapter shows how racist and colonialist systems are perpetuated, even as they change in form.

THE PINOCHET LEGACY AND CONTINUITY UNDER THE CONCERTACIÓN

"Neoliberalism" refers to a form of socioeconomic governance broadly characterized by an export-based economic strategy, opening of the economy to international investment, elimination of trade barriers, decentralization, privatization, and the elimination of universal social services. In many parts of the world, neoliberal reforms were instituted as a result of the 1980s debt crisis, driven in large part by such transnational entities as the World Bank, the International Monetary Fund, and the World Trade Organization. In Chile neoliberal development has a somewhat different history. Around 1975 the "Chicago Boys," a group of economists trained under Milton Friedman at the University of Chicago, convinced Pinochet to adopt an economic model featuring a "rightist shrunken state and extreme free market capitalism." Thus began a process of neoliberal reform that was both prior to and more severe than that implemented elsewhere in Latin America (Winn 2004, 25).

Neoliberalism has shaped the content of Chilean democracy; the Concertación governments maintained many of Pinochet's economic policies, even as they made efforts to reduce poverty (Paley 2001). Thus it is not just the Mapuche but all Chilean citizens who are affected by neoliberalism. In the Araucanía, for example, neoliberalism has meant an increased focus on farming for export and greater competition from foreign agricultural products; these trends negatively affect Mapuche communities as well as small- and medium-scale nonindigenous farmers. The drive to increase exports has led the state to promote the timber industry; this has had negative impacts on indigenous and nonindigenous small landowners alike. The strategic goals of the democratic Chilean state cohere comfortably with global neoliberal agendas.

To understand the impacts of neoliberalism on the Araucanía, it is worth looking at the timber and agricultural industries in some detail. As Thomas Miller Klubock (2006) has pointed out, the development of the timber industry was a product not just of Pinochet but of a series of policies dating back to the 1930s and championed by socialists and reformists. The dictator's specific policies contributed significantly to the current conflict-laden context. Decree Law 701 from the Pinochet era provided subsidies covering 75 percent of the costs of planting, pruning, and administering timber plantations. This measure supplemented a 1930 law that already exempted plantations on land apt for timber production from taxes (Haughney 2006). At one point in the 1980s, subsidies for timber plantations rose to almost 90 percent (ibid.). Between 1976 and 1992 the state (through the Corporación Nacional Forestal [CONAF], the semiprivate National Forestry Agency housed within the Ministry of Agriculture) gave timber companies US$110 million, including US$29.6 million in the Araucanía alone (Seguel 2002). These subsidies starkly contradicted the regime's rhetorical commitment to free-market enterprise.

Klubock (2004) has explained that in the early 1980s, three financial groups (Cruzat-Larraín, Matte-Alessandri, and Vial) dominated the industry. Two companies—Copec (then controlled by Cruzat-Larraín) and CMPC (then controlled by Matte-Alessandri)—owned 50 percent of pine plantations and 100 percent of the wood pulp industry. The three combined owned 75 percent of plantations, 78 percent of industrial production, and 73 percent of exports. They received 85 percent of state subsidies and credits. Nevertheless, those paper and pulp plants had actually been set up under state direction in the 1960s and 1970s, and the wood harvested in the 1970s and 1980s had been planted earlier under those same state programs. So not only did these companies receive huge subsidies, but they did not have to invest the cash to set up the industry in the first place. The Cruzat-Larraín and Vial groups went bankrupt in 1983 and 1984, and shortly thereafter Matte and Alessandri solidified their dominance in the industry.[1] Today, the main corporations are Empresas Arauco, CMPC, and Terranova/MASISA. Empresas Arauco is part of Copec, controlled by Angelini. (Copec also includes Chile's major petroleum company.) Empresas Arauco includes various timber companies whose holdings total more than nine hundred thousand hectares in Chile as well as pulp and paper plants and other related enterprises. The well-known Celco (Celulosa Arauco y Constitución), a major wood pulp and timber company, is part of Empresas Arauco. CMPC is controlled by the Matte family and includes Forestal Mininco, which has approximately five hundred thousand hectares, in addition to pulp and paper plants. In 2005, Swiss-owned Terranova, less significant in holdings than the other two, merged with MASISA, a wood products company with holdings throughout Latin America. Controlled by the Swiss firm GrupoNueva, MASISA owns Forestal Millalemu, which comprises more than 120,000 hectares (Seguel 2003a).

By the late 1980s the timber industry ranked third (behind mining and agriculture) in Chilean export revenues (Haughney 2007). Today most timber plantations in the country are located in the Maule Region, and especially the Bío-Bío and Araucanía Regions, both of which include important parts of ancestral Mapuche territory. Together, the Maule, Bío-Bío, and Araucanía Regions contain 80 percent of Chile's total hectares occupied by timber plantations (INE 2007a, 44). The number of hectares planted with timber in Bío-Bío and the Araucanía increased dramatically between 1997 and 2007, even as the number of hectares planted with timber in the country as a whole decreased by 3.4 percent (INE 2007a, 30). In the Araucanía, Malleco is the more affected province; 32.5 percent of the "exploited" land there is planted with timber. In Cautín the figure is 18.9 percent. In some *comunas* in the Araucanía, such as Lumaco and Collipulli, timber plantations make up more than 60 percent of the total land being used for timber, agricultural, and livestock purposes; in the four comunas I focused on, the percent ranged between 17 and 42 percent. (These are my calculations based on INE 2007b, Table 1.) After the dictatorship the Concertación continued to heavily subsidize the timber companies, and the three big conglomerates controlled most subsidiaries and subcontractors as well (Haughney 2007).

The industry is accompanied by a communication campaign called Bosques para Chile (Forests for Chile), which was started around 2000 and promotes the idea that plantations are forests. Among the members of the Bosques para Chile coalition are timber companies, paper mills, municipalities, universities, and state agencies, including CONADI (the Corporación Nacional de Desarollo Indígena, the National Indigenous Development Agency). There are some environmental goals among Bosques para Chile's organizational principles, but the reason-for-being of the association is to promote the timber industry. For example, the association seeks to promote environmental education and the creation of protected natural areas, but the first two principles listed on its website are to promote "the creation of new forests to re-green the country" and "the prompt forestation of eroded lands" (Bosques para Chile 2010). Ads show images of pine plantations and refer to them as if they were forests. Environmental and Mapuche activists argue that the use of the term "forests" to describe timber plantations is deliberately deceptive, defying the rightful perception of many citizens that Chile's forests are disappearing (Liberona 2000). The discourse of Bosques para Chile is consistent with the broader regional trend of repackaging resource extraction as environmentally sustainable (e.g., Gedicks 1993).

In the agricultural sector wheat remains the most important nontimber product in the region. Nevertheless, small- and medium-scale farming is on the downswing, largely as a result of neoliberal policy decisions. Not all Chilean farmers whose land was expropriated during agrarian reform got it back in Pinochet's counterreform, which sought to dedicate more land to timber and cultivation of monocrops. Many farmers, beginning under Pinochet, sold their estates to timber companies because of the falling value of their products (Haughney 2006) or simply because their plots were surrounded by timberlands. Under the Concertación this situation was aggravated by free-trade agreements, which have made it difficult for regional farmers of wheat, beef, dairy, sugar beets, and other products to compete with cheaper imports. This led Manuel Borja, head of an important agricultural association in the Araucanía, to argue that not just Mapuche farmers but anyone with fewer than five hundred hectares was destined to go under.

These conditions set the immediate context for conflicts. Although it negatively affects other subordinated groups as well, vis-à-vis the Mapuche, neoliberalism represents a continuation of coloniality and systemic racism. Indeed, in the Araucanía the neoliberal development that enriches the state and elites is built on the appropriation of Mapuche lands and resources, facilitated by the Pacificación and laws and policies instituted since then. These circumstances require that we examine how Mapuche interests are fundamentally racialized and distinct from those of Chileans, even as they may overlap in some circumstances with those of working class and poor Chileans.

MAPUCHE DEMANDS, THE INDIGENOUS LAW, AND GROWING CONFLICTS

The dominant model of indigenous policy, which, following Postero (2004), Hale (2006), and others, I call "neoliberal multiculturalism," is not a preordained set of policies and discourses. Rather, it has developed over time, shaped in part by processes of negotiation and conflict between Mapuche organizations and communities and the state, and in part by the economic development priorities of the state and elites. Here I address how the Concertación responded to Mapuche demands in the early years after the return to democracy. The response was inadequate to the growing conflicts in the region, which were fueled by the very development policies advocated by the state as well as by the historical legacy of inequality and racism. Neoliberal development can be understood as the contemporary manifestation of historical practices and policies that have long left Mapuche demands for land and other rights and resources unaddressed.

Mapuche activism against the dictatorship led to hope that their claims would be addressed upon the return to democracy. In the early 1990s movement demands focused mostly on constitutional recognition, land, education, healthcare and other social services, and participation in the creation and implementation of indigenous development policies. It is important to acknowledge, nonetheless, that there has always been a diversity of voices and demands in the Mapuche movement. Demands rooted in material need (for social services, economic development, and so forth) and those rooted in autonomy (such as territory and self-government) have a long presence among Mapuche claims. The first group addresses socioeconomic rights with some cultural elements mixed in, as in the case of "development with identity" or intercultural education and healthcare. The second group encompasses collective political rights—that is, they involve the right of indigenous peoples to be understood as a collective political subject. Although there is sometimes conflict among proponents of the two types of demands, they are frequently hard to separate out. This is because often the same people make both types of demands, and especially because Mapuche poverty is ultimately the product of a legacy of colonialism and denial of their right to autonomy and self-determination. In this sense, even demands that seem palliative are related to the need for recognition of Mapuche status as a people (Richards 2004).

In 1993 a new Indigenous Law was passed, in partial satisfaction of promises made by President Patricio Aylwin to indigenous peoples upon the return to democracy. A Special Commission for Indigenous Peoples (Comisión Especial de Pueblos Indígenas, CEPI) created the initial proposal for the law. Although some organizations, most importantly the Consejo de Todas las Tierras (which was a new organization with a significant grassroots base), chose to not participate in the process, the writing of the proposal involved significant participation, consultation, and debate among indigenous actors (Haughney 2006; Richards 2004). Even before it made it to Congress, however, representatives from the armed forces and several ministries made adjustments to the proposal that reflected nationalist and neoliberal concerns, especially relating to the concepts of territory and peoples (Haughney 2006). For example, the proposed law set up Indigenous Development Areas (Áreas de Desarrollo Indígena, ADIs) as instances of indigenous territoriality that would be co-governed and managed. Even though the ADIs were not suggestive of self-governance per se, the word "territory" was entirely taken out of the law and substituted with "areas" by these early reviewers and conservative sectors of Congress, for fear that it would result in the fragmentation of the Chilean nation-state (Aylwin 2001; Haughney 2006). Today the ADIs are simply zones with high indigenous populations that are targeted with special socioeconomic programs.

Also removed from the proposed law were provisions for indigenous consultation in private investment projects impacting their communities, as well as ones recognizing their right to share in profits from natural resource extraction within their communities (Haughney 2006). Lawmakers were also concerned that "indigenous peoples" implied a collective subject, the recognition of which could have grave geopolitical and economic consequences, and thus eliminated it in favor of "indigenous" or "indigenous ethnic groups" in the final law (ibid.). Efforts to incorporate procedures to maximize the participation of indigenous organizations and communities in CONADI's ongoing work were also severely curtailed.

So what did the law accomplish? It established means for protecting and expanding land and water rights and created CONADI to administer these policies, a development fund, and other programs (including the ADIs). CONADI is also responsible for coordinating social, economic, and cultural programs with the various ministries. CONADI is not a ministry but an agency within MIDEPLAN (the Ministerio de Planificación, Ministry of Planning), a step that limited its power from the start. The aspects of the law that focus on land are perhaps the most important. The law stipulates that indigenous land cannot be sold to nonindigenous parties, and communities can only be divided by solicitation of an absolute majority of titleholders. It establishes a fund that provides subsidies for individuals and communities wishing to purchase additional land and also finances the direct purchase of lands in conflict. Between 1994 and 2004 more than 416,000 hectares were transferred to indigenous families nationwide (MIDEPLAN 2006a). Nevertheless, the law has serious limitations. It does not restore usurped lands on a comprehensive basis but rather case-by-case (Haughney 2007). Much of what has been transferred were previously public lands, of which there is a finite supply (112,000 of 170,000 hectares transferred between 1994 and 2000 were publicly owned, according to Aylwin [2002]). And, significantly, the law deems "indigenous" only lands deeded to the Mapuche since the Pacificación, thus excluding *tierras antiguas* (ancestral lands) (FIDH 2006). In general, the law falls short of international standards for the recognition of indigenous rights and fails to consider indigenous peoples as possessors of collective rights (Aylwin 2002; Haughney 2006).

Despite (and reflected in the creation of) the 1993 law, conflicts over national identity and development have colored the relationship between the Mapuche, the Concertación, and other social actors since the return to democracy. The privileged status of neoliberal development over indigenous rights was an important source of the conflicts. In addition to the timber industry and large-scale agriculture, hydroelectric dams, airports, highways, corporate fisheries, and garbage dumps were among the initiatives Mapuche communities found themselves struggling against, usually losing the battle.[2] When it comes to development, to many Chileans the Mapuche seem anachronistic. Government representatives and elites talk about how it is necessary to "integrate" and "develop" the Mapuche, as if they were somehow opposed to development. To many Mapuche, however, the question is not one of re-jecting development but of resisting a model in which they always seem to lose. Time and again, I witnessed Mapuche leaders speaking of the contra-dictions between the development they seek for their communities and that promoted by the state. The most profound example was Ralco, a controver-sial dam project in the Upper Bío-Bío. The dam's construction violated not only internationally recognized indigenous rights, but Chile's own Indige-nous Law (Richards 2004). It was forcefully opposed by the local Pewenche (Mapuche of the cordillera), who were portrayed by government agents and the media as a threat to national development and prosperity. President Ri-cardo Lagos (2000–2006) himself declared that development could not be hindered by small groups of people (Haughney 2006). The dam was even-tually constructed and most of the local Pewenche relocated to other lands.

There are many other examples. Celco, the pulp plant owned by Angelini in the Región de los Lagos (to the south of the Araucanía), is threatening the environment and survival of Mapuche and poor Chilean communities in the region. For several years Celco had sought to build a waste-drainage duct to the sea, an objective that was met when regional authorities (including some appointed by President Michelle Bachelet) approved its construction just days before Bachelet left office in 2010. Mapuche and environmentalists had long argued that construction of the duct would destroy the local aquatic envi-ronment. At a conference I attended on the issue, one leader from an affected community said that as they mobilized against it, the people from the munic-ipality treated them "like Indians," asking: "Don't you want development?" He reflected that it is lovely to have development plans, and some commu-nities in the region had even worked with the indigenous development pro-gram Orígenes to establish their own goals and strategies for development. But if a bigger foot comes from above to flatten everything, Mapuche devel-opment plans are worth very little.

Gabriel Ancamil, a member of CITEM (the Coordinación de Identidades Territoriales Mapuche, the Mapuche Territorial Identities Coordinating Or-ganization) in his early forties, had a ninth-grade education and lived in his community of origin, although for financial reasons he worked in Temuco. He observed that such conflicts over development demonstrate that "the sur-vival of the people is not in the hands of the Mapuche themselves," but rather it depends on the disposition of the government. This is the key problem: state actors spoke of the importance of indigenous development, but it was consistently either sacrificed to or defined in terms of national development priorities. Mapuche definitions of development, in contrast, tend to focus on having enough to get by and ideally to move forward in life.[3] Some refer to

the concept of *ta in kumeletwaim*, which means "to return to being well"—
a concept that stands in stark contrast to the mega-development projects in-
vading their lands. The contradictions between the promises the Concertación made to the Mapuche and its dedication to neoliberal development at
their expense were a significant factor in the radicalization of the movement
(Haughney 2006).

Chilean development policies have also threatened Mapuche rights to
natural resources. In ancestral Mapuche territory, national and foreign timber companies own three times more land than the Mapuche (Aylwin 2002).
Pine and eucalyptus plantations surround Mapuche communities. The government and timber companies have told Mapuche communities that the
plantations do not cause environmental problems and actually improve the
soil, which has been degraded by intensive farming (Reiman 2001). This discourse is misleading. Klubock (2004, 355) has discussed the effects the plantations were having already in the 1980s:

> Pine plantations' corrosive effects on the regional rural ecology undermined
> the viability of campesino agricultural production. The extensive planta-
> tions caused the desiccation of topsoil and diminished the amount of water in
> the valleys at the feet of planted hillsides, leading to the deterioration of the
> conditions of agricultural production upon which peasants depended for their
> subsistence. Pine trees retain water in their needles, facilitating evaporation be-
> fore water hits the soil, and pine plantations lack the low plants and bushes that
> grow in Chile's native forests and that help to conserve rainwater and humidity
> in the soil. In addition the very concentrated nature of pine plantations—their
> biomass—means that they absorb several times the amount of water consumed
> by native forests.

So severe are the desert conditions produced by the plantations that in the
summer months the government actually has to ship water into some Mapuche communities. In addition, Klubock (2004, 356) notes, pine plantations "prevent the formation of a layer of nutrient-rich humus" and create
"excessive soil acidity, contaminating groundwater and poisoning wells
and streams used for irrigation." The pesticides and fungicides used by the
timber companies contaminate streams and groundwater. These conditions
make even subsistence agriculture untenable. Communities have witnessed
the disappearance of medicinal plants, birds and other wildlife, as well as the
genko de agua (owners or spirits of the water) and other "forces that maintain
equilibrium in the universe" (McFall 2001, 53). Diane Haughney (2006) has
emphasized that the loss of biodiversity is also a cultural loss: when plants
and wildlife die off, specific knowledge and practices die with them. Timber

companies also restrict access to the plantations, making collecting firewood and the few medicinal plants that still exist extremely difficult, and access to sacred places that are now within the plantations near impossible. A leader of Temulemu, a Mapuche community, explained the ongoing effects of the timber companies there: "When the logging companies first arrived, they hired us to do the planting but the work lasted only a few days. After about four years, the companies applied pesticides by plane, and then our animals died, our cattle were poisoned. . . . Then we were left without water. . . . Now we don't even have firewood. The guards don't let us onto the logging plantations. . . . Now the plantation guards are armed with rifles. They threaten even the children" (Castro et al. 1999, in Haughney 2006).

A CONAF executive I spoke with acknowledged that the plantations have contributed to water problems in the region but, in contrast to Klubock (2004) and evidence cited by Haughney (2006, 178, 263n73), including one study cosponsored by CONAF itself, he maintained that there have not been rigorous studies to measure the problem. The state and the timber companies, it seems, do not have an interest in acknowledging the full extent of the problem. On top of this, the state owns subsoil resources to water and minerals in the name of the nation but can sell the rights to explore and exploit them, even in and near Mapuche communities (Haughney 2007).

Lack of access to natural resources is also apparent in Ralco, where there is no public access to the dam without prior appointment. ("It's private property now," a friend wryly observed.) And it became an issue in 2005 for Mapuche communities in the comuna of Curarrehue, when SERNATUR (the Servicio Nacional de Turismo, the National Tourism Service) and CONAF solicited proposals from the private sector to implement ecotourism projects in Villarrica National Park, which they neighbor. (Applications were solicited for nearly fifty other national parks, reserves, monuments, and protected areas as well.) Although the communities would be allowed to compete with other postulants, the call for applications was sent out without first conferring with the communities—a violation of their right to be consulted as codified in the Indigenous Law and in international documents.[4] Development interventions not only cause environmental harm but also extract wealth from Mapuche territory. The Mapuche themselves not only usually remain poor; they may become resource-poorer. They also disproportionately suffer the environmental consequences.

In addition to factors directly associated with neoliberal policies, the legacy of racism and dispossession contributes to the conflicts. As in previous decades, Mapuche and local elites come into contact with one another in myriad ways. As neighbors in the countryside, they may participate in *mediería*. Mapuche may work for a *fundo* owner in various capacities, often seasonally.[5] Mapuche and Chileans of all sorts interact in towns and cities—in shops, mills, hospitals, markets, law offices, and banks. While some Mapuche and Chileans counted one another among their friends and relatives, these everyday relationships tended to be understood differently by local elites and Mapuche. Whereas local elites emphasized the long-standing symbiotic character of their relationship with Mapuche neighbors, Mapuche emphasized how exploitation and discrimination continue to color these interactions. For example, Celestino Huentequeo, who ran a Mapuche school in Cautín, had been active in Mapuche politics around the return to democracy. He related a story told to him by a woman who could not afford seed to plant potatoes on her land. She contracted with a man to provide her with seed potatoes and agreed to give him part of the crop in return. At harvest, she told Celestino, the man hauled away a truck full of big, beautiful potatoes and left her with two sacks of the smallest, most inferior ones. Celestino observed: "I don't know if it is racism, shamelessness, or robbery."

Unsatisfied claims on usurped portions of the *títulos de merced* as well as *tierras antiguas* also inform the conflicts. Anger about the injustice of usurpation was common among Mapuche of all persuasions. Many Mapuche respondents indicated that they were seeking not just land but usurped territory.[6] All told, the sources of the conflicts are both contemporary, involving increasing pressures on the land as a result of neoliberal policy and exploitation of natural resources, and historical, given the continuity of racism, dispossession, and unsatisfied Mapuche demands. Although the creation of the Indigenous Law did respond to some Mapuche demands, it only did so to the extent that they did not threaten national development goals. As a result, the law did not respond to the root causes of the conflicts.

UNDERSTANDING THE CONFLICTS

With more than three thousand communities and over two hundred associations of various sorts, Mapuche priorities and demands are very diverse (Richards 2004). Some continue to focus on issues related to development with identity, microenterprise, and access to healthcare, education, and other social services. As the conflicts between indigenous rights and national development have become more acute, many organizations and communities have shifted to focus more forcefully (though certainly not exclusively) on political rights to territory, self-determination, and autonomy. At the return to democracy the most prominent organization making such claims was the Consejo de Todas las Tierras (from 1990 to the present). Over time a range of organizations began making these demands, from a variety of perspectives. Some rooted claims for territory, autonomy, and self-government in traditional notions of territorial identities, as was the case with the Identidad Lafkenche (from the mid-1990s to the present) and the Coordinación de Identidades Territoriales Mapuches (from 2002 through 2007). Others have focused on asserting a collective political identity, as was the case with the Coordinación de Organizaciones Mapuches (in 2006) and Wallmapuwen (from 2005 to the present). These organizations are discussed in more detail in chapter 6.

While Mapuche organizations worked on a variety of issues, specific conflicts, and political goals, the most emblematic conflicts have centered on the construction of Ralco and the timber industry. Timber plantations have been a major target of Mapuche protests, including land occupations, fires, and equipment sabotage. Mapuche have also been accused of committing arson on fundos that were once part of Mapuche territory but now belong to colono farmers. The conflicts have been particularly intense in the provinces that have been most deeply affected by timber plantations: Arauco (in the Bío-Bío Region) and Malleco (in the Araucanía), although some parts of Cautín are affected as well. Most observers cite December 1997, when three logging trucks were set on fire in the comuna of Lumaco (Malleco province), as the beginning of the contemporary conflicts. One organization in particular has been deemed responsible for most (though not all) of the most violent actions: the Coordinadora Arauko Malleko (CAM, from 1999 through the present). The CAM seeks to establish "territorial control" to reconstruct "the Mapuche nation." Its occupation of disputed lands is "intended to be permanent, rather than symbolic," meaning that they do not just walk onto the lands and leave willingly when the police come (as other organizations have) but rather attempt to remain on the lands to work them (HRW and ODPI 2004, 18). Although a small number of communities (2.4 percent) are estimated to be involved in the more extreme forms of protest, most Mapuche share the general grievances (ibid.).

Next I delineate the details of some of the conflicts and explore how Mapuche as well as local elites and colono farmers, some of whom are victims of the alleged *atentados* (attacks), talk about the conflicts. My objective is to begin exploring the content of contemporary social relations in the region and how they inform, intertwine with, or diverge from state policy decisions. The Concertación's tendency to privilege national development over indigenous rights was an important immediate factor that set the stage for the conflicts. Tensions also reemerged between colono farmers and other local elites and the Mapuche. This suggests that it is not just neoliberalism and the incursion of global capital into Mapuche territory that is informing the conflicts.

It is also shared history. While many of these farmers are also suffering the consequences of free trade, they remain symbols of dispossession for the Mapuche—and not just symbols, either. Colono farmers or their families were the *agents* of dispossession shortly after the Pacificación and later by running fences and illegally acquiring Mapuche land in other ways, by exploiting Mapuche labor, and in their opposition to agrarian reform. Moreover, they still have relative wealth compared to most Mapuche.

By the return to democracy, the Mapuche had lost as much as 40 percent of the land deeded to them in the títulos de merced. This situation contributed to growing pressure on the land, high outmigration, and the conflicts. Although some of the land has been returned to the communities through CONADI's land fund, the Mapuche still have disproportionately little land. According to the Agricultural Census in 2007, rural Mapuche in the Araucanía held about 12 hectares per household—9.8 in Cautín and 24.7 in Malleco (INE 2007b, Chart 14). Based on my fieldwork, these figures seem inflated, and in any case, looking at averages alone is somewhat misleading. The largest Mapuche landholdings are extremely mountainous and therefore not apt for agriculture. This, as well as other limitations on agricultural use—such as severe erosion and lack of irrigation—should be taken into account when estimating Mapuche holdings (Haughney 2006). Nor do the census figures account for household size or the many Mapuche who live *allegados* (transitorily) on the property of relatives, perhaps informally receiving a half-hectare to farm for personal use. In fact, many Mapuche plots remain in the one-to-five hectare range (ibid.). In general, property ownership is skewed in the region. Agricultural households with fewer than twenty hectares represent 73 percent of all agricultural properties (a category that includes timber properties); they hold 14.3 percent of the land. Landowners with between two hundred and five hundred hectares (a category that includes several of the landowners I interviewed, although some had more and a couple less) represent 1.8 percent of all agricultural properties; they own 15.8 percent of the agricultural land. Landowners with more than five hundred hectares represent under 1 percent of all agricultural properties in the region; these properties total over 34 percent of the hectares dedicated to agriculture and timber in the region (INE 2007b, Table 3). When we take into consideration that the Mapuche represent more than 50 percent of the rural population in the Araucanía (INE and Programa Orígenes 2005), the injustice becomes even more apparent.

The radicalization of the Mapuche movement has occurred in part because spaces opened, due to the return of democracy and the emergence of indigenous rights as a transnational struggle, and in part because the situation faced by Mapuche communities is extreme, given the invasion of global capital into their territory.[7] But the Mapuche are also making claims that are historical in nature, similar to ones they have been making for more than a hundred years, even if they now use different terminology to explain them (see LeBonniec 2009b). The fundo owners, on the other hand, are just trying to defend property that, from their point of view and according to Chilean laws, they have legitimately acquired. Frequently they defend themselves with racist rhetoric, which makes them easy to despise. Their viewpoints are important if we are to understand the conflicts and point a way forward.

In many ways it is the violence—both material and symbolic—of the state and Chilean civil society that has led to the most extreme conflicts. Institutional and interpersonal discrimination, a dispossession that continues to this day, the stripping of the land of natural resources, the privileging of national development over indigenous rights, the repression of nonviolent forms of protest—the list goes on. Mapuche organizations and communities have responded to this situation with violent and nonviolent actions and protests. It is important, though, to see Mapuche protest not just as reaction but also as action. Even as their options are extremely limited, Mapuche communities and organizations have chosen strategies; they have made decisions and asserted their agency. Doing so has frequently led to being labeled terrorists by the state. A vast majority of local elites in the Araucanía supports state violence against the Mapuche. This is an important part of the story because it indicates that they consent to the oppression of the Mapuche. (They have also lobbied for it by demanding the application of antiterrorist legislation.) Rather than opposing state violence against their fellow (Mapuche) citizens, local elites benefit from it because it allows them to maintain their place at the top of the social hierarchy.

But local elites—and colono farmers in particular—have also been the victims of violence perpetrated by Mapuche actors. Perhaps they are easier targets than the state and timber companies and thus find themselves caught in a cycle they have contributed to as minor players (but often as major players in the lives of particular communities). Nevertheless, that they are beneficiaries of state violence does not mean they have not been victimized by Mapuche in particular conflicts, or that the failure of the state to resolve the conflicts does not also victimize them in some respects. Although a few atentado victims spoke of feeling abandoned not just by the government but also by their peers, in reality most had pretty substantial networks. They were often members of national and regional agricultural associations such as the Sociedad Nacional Agrícola (National Agricultural Society) and the Sociedad de Fomento Agrícola de Temuco (Agricultural Promotion Society of Temuco), both of which pushed forcefully for state action against Mapuche purportedly involved in the conflicts. Many were members of regional development boards, and a couple were directly involved in national politics. In general, atentado victims had the ear and support of centrist and rightist politicians at the national level, as evidenced in 2002 by Senate hearings held on the issue and an ad taken out by fundo owners and timber companies in *El Mercurio*, demanding the application of antiterrorism legislation against the Mapuche.[8] In general, local elites are not passive participants in the conflicts; they have committed symbolic and material violence historically but also contemporarily, by supporting state violence, organizing paramilitary brigades, and according to some Mapuche sources, staging crimes blamed on the Mapuche.

The multiple perspectives of my respondents have forced me to deal with the limits of my own access to truthfulness. Qualitative researchers often measure validity by the extent to which we are able to access respondents' true feelings and impressions. Yet in times of conflict, it can be extremely difficult to ascertain this kind of truthfulness. Carolijn Terwindt (2004a) has discussed such difficulties, noting that Mapuche, timber company representatives, and fundo owners involved in the conflicts all seemed less than forthright in their responses sometimes. In my experience, too, there are contradictions within and among the stories of Mapuche and fundo owners. These contradictions bring home the postmodernist position that there is no absolute truth but only multiple truths. Even more important, though, the contradictions are part of the substance of this story, a story fraught with distrust and feelings of betrayal on all sides. Thus my goal is not to ascertain or reflect the absolute "truth" of the situation but to describe how actors' explanations of the conflicts differ and then to suggest how these differences have informed the Chilean policy response and ascertain what they might mean for continued turmoil in the region.

Conflicts between Mapuche communities and colonos or other local elites have sometimes involved mobilizing efforts by organizations like the CAM or the Consejo de Todas las Tierras, and they usually involve long-standing disputes over parcels of land that belonged to the Mapuche ancestrally or as part of the títulos de merced. Sometimes these lands had been returned to the Mapuche communities during agrarian reform. This chapter describes four of the most visible and ongoing conflicts.[9] First is the conflict between the communities of Temulemu, Didaico, and Pantano and Forestal Mininco. In 1997 the communities began a long process of occupying land belonging to Mininco, in particular a large fundo called Santa Rosa de Colpi. The fundo, part of their *tierras antiguas*, had been expropriated in August 1973, when it belonged to Cardenio Lavín, but the expropriation was nullified after the coup and the fundo later sold to Mininco (Correa and Mella 2010). (Note that 52.5 hectares of this fundo already had been returned to Temulemu in 1972. This portion, part of their título de merced, was also lost shortly after the coup [Correa, Molina, and Yáñez 2005].)

By the late 1990s conditions were especially harsh in these communities: they faced drought, aggravated by the plantations, and the population pressure on their land was tremendous (Castro et al. 1999). According to Lonko Pascual Pichun, in Temulemu alone 170 families were living on only 770 hectares (in Correa and Mella 2010).[10] Community members literally fought with Special Forces police in reclaiming the land. In 1999, CONADI acquired and returned to Temulemu 58.4 hectares of Santa Rosa de Colpi that belonged to the community according to its título de merced. That same year the communities had what Lonko Pichun called "a tremendous fight" when they occupied the lands in order to prevent Mininco from felling trees there before turning it over (in Correa and Mella 2010, 222). Members of the community had planted the trees in the 1970s.[11] Special Forces were sent in to defend Mininco. The direct altercations over the course of these conflicts were extremely imbalanced. The police had arms, tear gas, helmets, and shields as well as tanks that shot birdshot or rubber bullets. A particularly evocative scene in footage available from these conflicts shows a large group of Special Forces in riot gear hovering together in the middle of a huge open field, throwing tear gas at Mapuche in everyday clothes, some with their faces covered with T-shirts or ski masks, throwing stones with *boleadoras* (Mapuche slingshots).

A conflict between Temulemu and Didaico and Juan Agustín Figueroa began a couple of years later. A lawyer with important political connections in Santiago, Figueroa was minister of agriculture in Patricio Aylwin's government. His family has a long presence as landowners in the region. They bought the land in question, an eighteen-hundred-hectare fundo called Nancahue, in 1950. CORA (Corporación de Reforma Agraria, the Agrarian Reform Agency) expropriated the fundo in July 1971 (Castro et al. 1999). Figueroa told me that the expropriation was "declared but never materialized," although Milka Castro and her colleagues have written that residents of Temulemu used the fundo for pasture, making carbon, and other tasks. In 2001 forested land and a house on Figueroa's fundo were set ablaze. The lonkos and other members of Temulemu and Didaico, who were thought to be members of the CAM, were blamed for the fires. The lonkos, Aniceto Norin and Pascual Pichun, and another individual, Patricia Troncoso, were tried for terrorism in this case.

Aside from the particularities of the case, Figueroa maintained that the

Mapuche had no rightful claim on this land, particularly because before the Pacificación they were not farmers, but hunters and gatherers. This position is suggestive of the fantasy of terra nullius. In fact, the Mapuche adopted ranching long before the Pacificación. Moreover, Le Bonniec (2009a), citing Sara McFall (2002), has pointed out that chronicles from the sixteenth and seventeenth centuries show the Mapuche also cultivated plants—including corn, potatoes, and beans—for consumption. This work was often done by women, which Le Bonniec suggests may contribute to why the Spanish and Chileans did not see it as legitimate development of agriculture.

Jorge Luchsinger was the sixty-six-year-old owner of the Fundo Santa Margarita, which comprised 238 hectares in the comuna of Vilcún in Cautín when I interviewed him in 2004. According to Martin Correa (n.d.; also see Leiva 2008), other members of the Luchsinger clan owned about a thousand additional nearby hectares. The Luchsinger family arrived in Chile from Switzerland in 1883 and came to Vilcún in 1906, right around the time the Mapuche there were given their títulos de merced. Correa reports that neighboring Mapuche communities complained from early on that the land the family occupied was usurped, part of their tierras antiguas. Although Luchsinger told me he voluntarily regularized his property during agrarian reform and gave up eighty hectares found to be part of the títulos de merced, Correa reports that he turned over fifty-six hectares only after four trials had taken place. An occupation of his land occurred in 1999, orchestrated by an organization called Ayjarewe Wenteche de Truf Truf. In 2000 more violent incidents began to occur.

By the time I interviewed him, Luchsinger reported that three houses on his property had been burned down (on separate occasions) as well as four storage barns filled with hay, in addition to fences being damaged and other more minor complaints. To bar Mapuche and their animals from accessing his land, Luchsinger dug a deep canal, dividing his property from that of his neighbors. Several animals and one man have fallen into this ditch and died. It also cut off the flow of water to some communities. In 2005, Luchsinger and his wife were forcibly removed from their home in the middle of the night, his nose broken, and the house set on fire. No individuals were found responsible for the incidents, but as of 2005, the fundo had permanent police protection. Luchsinger repeatedly insisted that no one had made a demand on his land, that they were just trying to scare him off. According to Correa, however, a community had filed a formal claim via CONADI. Luchsinger's land was transferred to the community of Juan Catrilaf II in January 2010.

During the dictatorship the community of Temucuicui (Ignacio Queipul) in Ercilla (Malleco province) lost possession of the Fundo Alaska, which had been returned to them under agrarian reform and on which they had an ancestral claim. Upon the return to democracy, the community possessed about 250 hectares, split among nearly two hundred families. In 1997 they began a struggle with Mininco, which had taken possession of the Fundo Alaska in the meantime. In 2003 the government purchased the fundo and returned it to the community, thus expanding their lands by about eighteen hundred hectares. Nevertheless, when returned the land was full of stumps, unsuitable for agriculture. The community neighbors the land of Rene Urban, descendant of Swiss colonos who arrived in Chile around 1900. Urban owns over three hundred hectares. One young resident of Temucuicui related a childhood memory of Urban as a cruel neighbor, who once beat him for collecting mushrooms on his property. He claimed the community had documentation proving that one of Urban's fundos was theirs historically and at one point were close to an agreement with Urban's father to have it returned, but this did not come to pass.

The manor on one of Urban's fundos was burned down in 2002, and five storage barns were set on fire in 2003. In addition, mature crops and timber plantations have been set ablaze on his land, and numerous fences have been damaged. The family counted fourteen atentados as of 2005, and there have been many more since. There have been physical injuries on both sides of this conflict. Urban was hospitalized with light burns after a 2006 atentado, and in 2011 a sixteen-year-old boy from Temucuicui was shot in the leg, apparently by Urban's son. The Urbans have permanent police protection on their land. The ongoing conflict has contributed to internal conflicts over strategy and land within Temucuicui such that some members have divided off to form a new community called Comunidad Autónoma de Temucuicui (Autonomous Community of Temucuicui). In the early years Temucuicui worked with the support of the Consejo de Todas las Tierras; they were never associated with the CAM. However, several people have been charged, some under the anti-terrorism law, related to these events.

How did Mapuche and local elites explain the conflicts? The Mapuche referred to structural and historical issues as the causes of the conflicts: the original dispossession, ongoing incursions onto their lands, poisoning of their environment, and discrimination. CITEM member José Antiman saw a clear link between the initial loss of Mapuche territory, encoded in Chilean laws, and contemporary institutionalized racism: "Today the municipalities, each one of those authorities, dedicate themselves to continue changing us, to continue the work [of the Pacificación] so that we, in one way or another, . . . disappear. That is also the reason why today . . . there are brothers detained with the antiterrorist law." Understanding contemporary conflicts as continuous with historical losses, coloniality, and systemic racism led respondents like Antiman to see the actions of communities in conflict as justified, even if they were not personally involved.

Local elites likewise mentioned some structural causes for the conflicts, but in contrast to the Mapuche, they tended to attribute the radicalization of the movement to the intervention of outsiders, delinquents, and terrorists. These differences demonstrate how a given social context may in fact contain more than one social reality. They also suggest the persistence of historical animosities and the difficulties entailed in resolving the conflicts on a social level, beyond the developmentalist interventions of the state and private corporations.

In terms of structural factors, some local elites saw agrarian reform as the root of the conflicts, because it gave Mapuche the idea that occupying and reclaiming land was acceptable. Others, both on the right and left, blamed poverty but declined to acknowledge the particular factors that contributed to poverty among the Mapuche. They also frequently blamed the Indigenous Law. For example, Carla Becker, who was from the region and wrote on Mapuche issues for a rightist think tank (and later became involved in national politics), sustained that the good relationship colono and Chilean landowners always had with the Mapuche was undermined by the Indigenous Law, which provided incentives to violently take over fundos (because lands in conflict were often prioritized) and by transferring communities to new areas, where they did not have relationships with the area's farmers. Others suggested the law was paternalistic, preventing Mapuche from selling their land as they like. This accusation is particularly striking in combination with the narrative of the "good" relationship that used to exist in the campo, which itself hinges on paternalism and is remembered quite differently by fundo owners and Mapuche.

Others offered a more subtle analysis, focusing on the changes wrought by the timber industry. Franco LaPorte (the agricultural businessman whose family lost its ancestral home to arson in 2001) criticized the Indigenous Law but also passed judgment on timber policy, arguing that if the regime had incentivized timber planting in Mapuche communities, rather than favoring big corporations so heavily, "it is possible we would be living another reality." Guillermo Hanssen, an agricultural businessman who faced atentados in the late 1990s, blamed the timber companies as well as the collapse of traditional agriculture. He explained that when agriculture began to fall apart in his part of Malleco in the early 1980s (as a result of neoliberal reforms in the sector), people fell into debt and were forced to sell their land. Timber companies bought it up. Families that remained in the countryside were not only more likely to be surrounded by timberlands but became more and more socially isolated: "The rural schools closed, the rural health posts closed, a lot of roads went to ruin." Timber companies, in his view, had not lived up to their social responsibility. Gonzalo Lara, an administrator in a municipal department of education in Malleco, emphasized that timber plantations had exacerbated outmigration. He viewed the timber companies as outsiders that cut down all the native trees, plant their pine and eucalyptus, but do little to support local communities. Towns in Malleco do not benefit from their presence, he felt, and in fact may suffer. Haughney (2006) confirms the sale of fundos as a result of neoliberal trade policies as well as the increase in outmigration associated with the expansion of the timber industry in the region.

But despite the focus of a few on structural factors, many respondents I interviewed shared the perspective of Hernán Rohrer, son of an elderly couple who had a fire set on their property in the middle of the night and who had recently run for mayor of his town: "The problems started since democracy returned." This position is reflected in Iván Isler and Esteban Marcial's reminiscences about the dictatorship discussed in chapter 2. Others simply argued that democracy logically meant there would be more social protest. For instance, Miguel Angel Carrizo, head of rural development in a Malleco municipality, suggested that after the dictatorship ended, people began to make demands because they could do so without being repressed. Rohrer seemed to agree, adding that the freedom associated with democracy allowed subversives to return to the country.

Almost all colonos and local elites asserted that outside influence was driving the conflicts, although the source and shape of that influence varied among respondents. At the same time, they frequently insisted that most Mapuche are not in favor of the conflicts, even within the communities most directly involved. The minority who do participate, they said, are ideologically motivated or manipulated by leaders or outsiders. As Daniel Hauri, a colono with a long-standing conflict with a Mapuche community in Malleco, put it: "Someone is sending them. Someone is making them commit these acts." This assertion galled Mapuche activists, who felt it was typical of elites' paternalism that they could not fathom the possibility that the Mapuche, who grew up in extreme poverty, have the capacity to see the problems, suffering, and inequality around them and decide to do something about it. It is true that Mapuche communities and organizations have had the support of outside actors at various stages in their history. (Indeed, although Chile has far fewer NGOs than its poorer Latin American counterparts, the Araucanía is home to a number of NGOs—foreign, national, religious, secular, Mupuche- and winka-run—focusing on issues related to indigenous development and rights. Some of them have played an important support role in the context of the conflicts.) It is also true that not all Mapuche support the most extreme tactics. But local elites implied that this makes Mapuche claims on the territory somehow less legitimate—as if it were not still Mapuche making them and as if they had no historical justification.

Some linked the contemporary Mapuche movement to the international indigenous movement—to the Zapatistas in particular. Others said donors from developed countries funded the organizations and communities involved in the conflicts. Franco LaPorte, who was on the board of an NGO promoting Mapuche development, explained that the organization had lost much of the funding it once received from European NGOs. He suspected that as a result of "ingenuousness or bad intentions," those NGOs were now funding some of the more radical Mapuche organizations. He felt such funders should be pursued as terrorists along with the Mapuche organizations themselves. Malleco lawyer Martin Rahm (whose family had lost several hundred forested hectares to fire) remarked that for a minority of Mapuche, the conflicts were "good business," insinuating that leaders could grow rich through dealings with European funders. When asked why Europeans would fund these organizations, Rahm surmised that they wanted to "expiate their own guilt because during many years they did exploit the colonies they had, and Europe today has a great wealth in part because of the American gold that . . . flowed freely to Europe." The conflicts, Rahm suggested, were not just funded but organized by outsiders. Máximo Ordóñez, a prominent businessman who held a high-ranking position in a national political party, had experienced arson and other atentados on a property he was planning to use for tourism. He claimed to have done research showing plans for the conflicts were put together mostly in France and Holland in coordination with "members of Chilean subversive organizations." Several respondents mentioned the presence of foreigners or other outsiders in the communities as proof of such intervention.

Others identified the remnants of Marxist or leftist groups from decades past as the instigators of the conflicts. For example, Daniel Hauri identified "extremists" from the MIR and the Frente Patriótico Manuel Rodriguez (a leftist guerrilla group founded in the early 1980s) as "the same terrorists of today." The Catholic Church also fomented the conflicts, he alleged, presumably through liberation theology, which was prominent in those years. Colonos and elites who faced atentados had good reason to feel aggrieved. Yet through their explanations it became clear that many resented not only the atentados but also Mapuche intentions to defend their interests in general as well as efforts on the part of others to empower Mapuche to do so.

For Ordóñez, though, the domestic influence went beyond militants to include those with left-leanings in general. Because of the example of how indigenous peoples were treated in Canada and the United States, he explained, there was a sense of historical guilt in Latin America today, a feeling that a "social debt" must be paid to the "descendants of the original [peoples]." As a result of this and the growing power of a Mapuche intellectual elite, the Concertación was captive to Mapuche interests. "I believe the Left in general has a sinister relationship with terrorism," he asserted, adding that the groups behind the atentados had likely received "direct and indirect financing" from state agencies. Implicitly referring to 1970s leftists and some sectors of the resistance to the dictatorship, Ordóñez said: "It has to be remembered that this government of the Concertación has within its branches leftist parties that were supporters or in the end friends [of] subversive groups that operated in the environment of terrorism." He insisted on a "deep link" between the "authors of the terrorist attacks" and leftists in the Concertación, ranging from financial support to legal and political assistance. So here, the "outsider" was within the Concertación itself, indicating the continued relevance of the political upheaval and divisive politics of years past. Often, respondents identified the "outsiders" as Mapuche themselves—in particular, the college-educated, returned exiles and intellectuals writing about nationhood and autonomy. Guillermo Hanssen identified another Mapuche outsider: "The immense quantity of Mapuches who live in Santiago and are discriminated against [there] much more than . . . here." These individuals came back to the communities "very bad off psychologically, very violent, very radicalized," he said, and they then instigated the conflicts.

Why were elites so eager to blame outsiders? Antonio Queipul, a college-educated former member of the CAM who now disavows their methods, has written on the goal of Mapuche autonomy. He cited a historical reference point for elite apprehension about the intervention of foreigners: Orélie-Antoine de Tounens, the Frenchman who came to Chile and named himself king of the Mapuche in the 1860s, with whom some lonkos were eager to align in the hope that he could help them resist the Chileans. But these apprehensions are also related to local elites' collective remembrance that there was no conflict in the past. Indeed, the erasure of past conflict may facilitate blaming the current conflicts on outsiders. For example, Margarita Leal, the now elderly former director of education in a Malleco municipality, was sure the problems were coming from the outside, because before, she told me, "the Mapuche was tranquil. He lived working his little piece of land and nothing else." The region was a peaceful place where people worked together and helped each other. Insisting that the Mapuche were happy with the previous state of things allowed local elites to dismiss the validity of their claims. It also signals a refusal to believe the Mapuche themselves are capable of rising up and rejecting the condition in which they have been forced to live. Thus, even when local elites admitted Mapuche were the central actors planning and theorizing their own resistance, it had to be pointed out that these were educated Mapuche, they had been influenced by political ideals, or they had spent time in the exterior—outsiders and in some sense not authentic Mapuche. If they admitted the Mapuche who were rising up were also "authentic," they might have to consider the legitimacy of their claims.[12]

The role of outsiders is where the "global" seemed to come into play in the minds of local elites, and it was perceived as a threat. They saw Mapuche empowerment as a result of their global connections, and they resented it. Their insistence on "sameness" and the absence of conflict in the past, as well as the role of outsiders in the conflicts, must be understood as an effort, conscious or not, to maintain their local privilege in the face of a changing transnational scenario. Indeed, colono farmers and other local elites were confronted with a free-market system that seemed destined to marginalize many of them and make their local power irrelevant. As the region faced competition from foreign grain and dairy producers, wealthier agrobusinessmen with large landholdings and diversified investments would survive, but small- and medium-scale farmers' livelihoods were threatened. While a sensible option for Mapuche and these colono farmers might be to form alliances as a manner of protecting themselves from the impacts of neoliberal agricultural policies, the entrenched racial ideologies in the region seemingly made it impossible for most colonos to identify their interests with those of the Mapuche.

LAW, LEGITIMACY, AND EPISTEMIC PRIVILEGE

Underlying the conflicts was a deeper debate about legitimacy and law. Local elites spoke extensively about the illegitimacy of Mapuche claims. Their first line of defense was to dispute the notion that the lands ever belonged to the Mapuche on the basis that the Mapuche were simply not there, were few in number, or had no legitimate claim to the land given their patterns of land use. Fundo owners, timber representatives, and their advocates insisted their land had been acquired legally, their papers were in order, and they had the right to use their land as they saw fit. They questioned the motives behind Mapuche land claims.

Antonio Grass (2001), a representative of CORMA (Corporación Chilena de la Madera, the Chilean Wood Association), feels Mapuche are scapegoating the companies and people who own the land. Ulises Ibáñez, a lawyer for one of the timber companies, is fine with the Mapuche saying the land is theirs, but when it changes from words to actions, he said, there is a difference. He told a common joke: "There's no land more sacred than land with fat trees." This is an insinuation that Mapuche assert ancestral claims on pine and eucalyptus plantations that are close to maturation in an attempt to profit from the sale of the timber. Grass (ibid., 64) was adamant that the Mapuche cannot "demand the forests planted on those lands because they are fruit of the effort invested by other people during many years, on lands that legally belong to them." This position is suspect for a number of reasons, not least of which is the notion that the corporations own the land legitimately and that the plantations on it are the fruits of their labor. (In many cases they were initially set up by the state under earlier governments, often relying on Mapuche labor.) Others simply said they owned the land and could use it as they saw fit. For instance, a representative of Forestal Valdivia said the law does not prevent them from planting water-greedy trees near Mapuche communities, completely disregarding the negative impact of the plantations on their neighbors (in Terwindt 2004b). The preeminence of neoliberal values of private property and unfettered choice are clear in these attitudes.

In general, the colonos, local elites, and timber companies had the law behind them. In contrast, many Mapuche disregarded the law as being written for and by Chileans, a perspective perhaps all the more understandable given the multitude of ways in which they had been bilked out of their land. The argument here is not simply about what the law "says," because the law is written based on particular ideas about what entails legitimate land ownership and use. From the start the political-economic system was built on knowledge claims that marginalized indigenous ways of knowing (Quijano 2000). This gives Chileans the upper hand epistemologically; as the subjects of the social world, it is their knowledge and forms of acting that are considered logical and correct. Epistemic privilege benefits elites and colonos in local conflicts and, to the extent that elites' positions cohere with state and industry interests in the global economy, their exclusionary tactics facilitate the imposition of neoliberal policies in ancestral Mapuche territory and reinforce state disciplining of Mapuche subjects. Epistemic privilege both justifies and perpetuates historical inequalities; it is essential to communicating and engraining racial hierarchies in Chile.

In addition to the work of Anibal Quijano (2000, 2007), my analysis is guided in this regard by the work of feminist sociologist Dorothy Smith (1979) and Maori education scholar Linda Tuhiwai Smith (1999). Dorothy Smith's work focuses on women but can be extended to understand the experiences of other subjugated groups in society. (Doing so, however, requires that we not draw a direct parallel; after all, the experiences of women are not analogous to those of indigenous peoples, and women from colonizing societies certainly have contributed to the subjugation of indigenous women and men.) Dorothy Smith (1979, 141) identifies a "line of fault" between "the world as it is known directly in women's experience and as it is shared with others, and the ideas and images fabricated externally to that everyday world and provided as a means to think and imagine it." The line of fault comes to exist because "the forms of thought, the means of expression, which we had available to us to formulate our experience were made or controlled by men. From that center women appeared as objects. In relation to men (of the ruling class) women's consciousness did not, and most probably generally still does not, appear as an autonomous source of knowledge, experience, relevance, and imagination" (ibid., 137).

The power of this epistemic privilege, which we can also understand as a form of symbolic violence, is not only that it often goes misrecognized but that it leaves women (or any other subordinated group) in a situation in which their main means "to reflect upon themselves is a reflection from outside themselves, the structuring of themselves not as subjects, but as other" (ibid., 138). The subordinated are forced to step outside of themselves in order to understand themselves—and even then, they are understanding themselves as "other," as objects, not as subjects of the social world. They are not considered the creators of the social world or its objective knowers. Their knowledge is considered subjective, and their "subjectivity does not draw upon the implicit authority of the generalizing impersonal mode," whereas (ruling class) men's knowledge does (ibid., 139). This situation has important consequences in terms of justifying social inequality. I observe a similar pattern in the Chilean South, whereby the Mapuche are not considered legitimate knowers, and their claims about social reality are tossed aside as subjective and illegitimate. In contrast, even given that their power is often limited to the local or regional level, the claims of local elites generally are those of the makers of the social world. Local elites and Mapuche activists and community members exist in a world that has defined elites as the legitimate landowners, whereas the Mapuche are dismissed as radicals when they claim to be the rightful owners of the ancestral lands. Local elites have epistemic privilege, even as this would be challenged in some ways by state-driven multicultural projects.

But we cannot understand the epistemic privilege of local elites simply in terms of a line of fault in a given system of knowledge. Before the invasion of the Spanish and the Chileans, it was, of course, Mapuche ways of knowing that organized daily life in their territory. Mapuche ways of knowing did not stop existing all together, and even today survive, although in some communities more forcefully than in others. However, colonialism did much to marginalize them (Bacigalupo 2007). The work of Tuhiwai Smith (1999) is essential in this sense because it elucidates the relationship between dominant epistemologies and colonialism.[13] She writes in the context of decolonizing research methodologies, but her discussion of colonialism can be extended to the analysis here. As she points out, the very notion of a Western "discovery" of the "new world" is rooted in an epistemology that privileges Western ways of knowing over non-Western ones. Colonialism rests on the notion that the colonists are the "knowers" and the indigenous that which is to be known, the objects of colonial knowledge, not knowers in their own right. The dominant system comes to be built on colonial knowledge—so Euro-Chilean knowledge about everything from how to set up governance and a legal system, to property ownership, to the relationship between humans and the environment, to religion, language, cultural practices, education, and healthcare—all is privileged as "correct" ways of knowing. Indigenous knowledge in these same areas is marginalized (often to the point of disappearance) or viewed as suspect and subjective.

Because Chilean customs, laws, and knowledge are considered "correct" ways of knowing, local elites were able to project the need for change onto the Mapuche. For example, timber company lawyer Ulises Ibáñez claimed to have a "pragmatic vision": people had to learn to live together. It was clear he meant the Mapuche needed to learn to live with Chileans, but all the same, I asked if to do so, the farmers and timber companies would have to cede something as well. He looked a little startled and very dubious and said he was not sure, explaining that it is hard to know who to go to the table with and what to cede (he was referring to the diffuseness of the movement). This seemed like a poor excuse, given that the conflicts generally involve particular communities, landowners, and corporations. This interchange demonstrates the extent to which the elite perspective is about maintaining power, and how doing so is contingent on disregarding other forms of being and knowledge.

Timber representatives and latifundistas contended that the Mapuche could not take justice into their own hands (Terwindt 2004a). Mapuche, in contrast, frequently suggested that at least some of the occurrences blamed on them were in fact *auto-atentados* ("self-attacks"). That is, they suggested that the fires were set or fences destroyed by colonos or timber guards, who then blamed Mapuche. In at least two cases there is substantial evidence to support this claim. In 1999 the main house on a plantation owned by the Mininco timber corporation in Collipulli was set ablaze; the fire was blamed on Mapuche. In 2000 a twenty-year-old man who had been a guard there committed suicide. The guard's mother, after her son's death, handed over evidence showing that the guards had in fact set the fire. The man's brother, also a guard, revealed that they were required to harass Mapuche communities in order to produce conflicts and influence public opinion against them. He admitted they set fires, blocked roads, blocked canals to flood Mapuche crops, and cut down *rewes* (wooden altars belonging to *machi*, Mapuche shamans), among other measures (Seguel 2002). All of this was revealed in the media but never went anywhere legally. Likewise, in 2009 six policemen were suspended for stealing timber from a plantation owned by the Arauco timber corporation—another act that had been attributed to Mapuche ("6 Carabineros" 2009). As Lonko Venancio Coñuepan Arcos (2009) expressed after the latter incident came to light, such revelations force the question of how many other "atentados" had actually been carried out by agents of the state or corporations.

Some Mapuche argued that the victims exaggerated the number of attacks or the extent of the damage. This tendency was corroborated by my interviews with some colonos, who after fires on their property retrospectively included other events, such as fences being broken or animals gone missing, as atentados. Some Mapuche respondents suggested they might do so to exaggerate the extent of an existing conflict with a community, because they felt threatened and wanted to rally support. But more likely, these Mapuche respondents suggested, given the economic situation facing small- and medium-sized farms, they actually want to sell and figure that if they can sell to CONADI, they will get higher-than-market prices for their land. Ramiro Raipillan, a member of the community in conflict with Daniel Hauri, maintained that since agriculture is not very profitable anymore, the Mapuche are useful to the farmers, because they can say they are being attacked daily and demand a solution from the government. Rather than selling right away, they can resist, saying, "I will never leave," thus gradually increasing the price the government will offer.

Meanwhile, Raipillan claimed, they stage attacks in order to add urgency, so the government will keep pressuring them to sell, offering more and more money just to end the conflict. Even individuals who had nothing to do with the conflicts were sometimes suspicious about the authorship of the atentados. Ramón Mariñan, a municipal worker in Cautín who was running for town council, pointed out that in most cases "they never find out who were the authors," and that "in Chile, the big agriculturalists have everything insured . . . so in case a fundo is burned, the state has to pay him, so . . . sometimes [they] send someone to burn it." Mariñan insisted that landowners who sell to CONADI are the biggest beneficiaries of the land policy (and, it seems, of the conflicts) because they overcharge for the lands (which belonged to the Mapuche in the first place) and then buy better properties elsewhere. Such explanations demonstrate the extent to which Mapuche believed the state continued to benefit winkas at their expense, something that certainly has been true historically.

Some Chileans were more generous than others in their assessment of Mapuche claims. This was particularly true among respondents who worked in local and regional government, either as elected officials or as workers. Oscar Arias, son of a local elite family and a councilman in a Cautín comuna, objected to the use of violence on the part of some Mapuche but felt the government had done little to resolve the conflicts. Like many Mapuche, some Chileans suggested that people automatically blamed the Mapuche, even when there was no proof. Vicente Cisternas, a doctor who worked with the intercultural health program in Malleco, added that the media intensifies the situation because it is so one-sided. Ximena Ortíz, who worked for INDAP (the Instituto Nacional de Desarrollo Agropecuario, the National Agricultural Development Agency) in Malleco, said it was "good that they fight for their rights" because before, they were "too oppressed" and people took advantage of them, "made them work without paying them, some even were like slaves, they even marked them, to that level." Still, like the *ladinos* in Charles Hale's study of Guatemala (2006), she was apprehensive about what this change signaled, suggesting that things had gone to the opposite extreme.

In contrast to local elites' portrayals of Mapuche as delinquents or terrorists, Mapuche respondents insisted their struggle is legitimate. Ramiro Raipillan explained that his community was claiming Daniel Hauri's fundos because the land belonged to them. It was not a crime but, rather, their right. My conversations with other Mapuche show the continuity in claims for territory over time. I met one young man from Malleco at an indigenous rights NGO when he came to Temuco to file charges against police who had been harassing children in his community. He explained that his original community, called Pillan, was already trying to reclaim about seven hundred hectares in 1933.[14] This went on until 1966, when some of their land was returned through agrarian reform. In 2000 they started the process of recuperation again, this time focusing on twelve hundred hectares. Today the community is surrounded by three timber plantations and seven farmers with smaller amounts of land. The original lands of the lonko, this man claims, consisted of between ten thousand and eleven thousand hectares. My discussions with him and others made clear that from their point of view these communities were making claims and taking actions that were legitimate. They were not, as many colonos and the media would assert, demanding the land because they were no-good degenerates, cheats, and rogues but, rather, because based on the history of their people, the land legitimately belongs to them. From this perspective it is Chilean law that is not legitimate.

Mapuche who were not directly involved in the conflicts again reinforced this view. For example, Victorino Manque, an important leader from the Unidad Popular era who now works in intercultural health in Cautín, related a conversation he had with the MIDEPLAN (Ministry of Planning) minister, in which he objected to the treatment of the Mapuche who had been imprisoned in association with the conflicts. He told the minister that *peñi* (brothers) were being imprisoned for demanding their legitimate right to their land, of which so little remains in their hands. "I would do the same thing," he said. A colleague who was present during the interview added: "And on top of that, they label them 'extremists!'" Horacio Quilapan, a member of CITEM from Cautín, echoed this view: "They took what is ours, not the opposite. The Mapuche aren't a warlike people, we've always been peaceful, but we defend our land." Along similar lines, at an event in Villarrica, a Mapuche woman observed that Mapuche could end up in prison for fifteen years "for defending a little piece of land" while the owners of the big businesses that wreak havoc on Mapuche lands remain free. "Who is the real terrorist here?" she asked. Such observations get at the core of epistemological privilege.

It is hard to portray this position as ideologically driven, as even Mapuche interviewees who repudiated the tactics of the CAM and other radical groups said their objective was just. This was true of an elderly Mapuche man I spoke with in Ercilla, for example, who opposed the more extreme tactics and sympathized with his neighbors, the Rohrers. These views did not necessarily reflect the political parties of respondents, either. Christian Democrat Ramón Mariñan observed that elites "see us as a problem, and it's logical we are a problem because we, what are we doing? We are trying to recuperate what is ours. We are not asking something that has never been ours, of course. What is it that we want? That they return what they stole from us, that they return what they usurped." Linguist Llanka Mariluan summed everything up when she said the debate surrounding the conflicts should not be about what is legal or illegal (Chilean land titles, militant Mapuche actions) but what is legitimate. That is, not only have Mapuche rights been violated through the application of special laws and double jeopardy, but the law itself, since before the Pacificación, has been systematically designed to benefit Chileans at the expense of the Mapuche. In this sense Mapuche respondents' view of legitimacy was the polar opposite of that of most local elites.

In chapter 2, Mapuche respondents spoke about interpersonal experiences of discrimination. The question of law versus legitimacy, however, points to the issue of institutionalized discrimination—racism built into the laws and policies of the state. Indeed, when we talked about discrimination, Mapuche respondents—particularly those most intimately involved with the conflicts—emphasized its institutionalized or systemic aspects. This was probably because these individuals and communities were most directly experiencing the brute force of the state for refusing to consent to discriminatory policies and laws. Ramiro Raipillan cited numerous examples in which the word of a Chilean is enough to jail a Mapuche, but Mapuche complaints are thrown out of court. Raipillan himself was on the lam when I interviewed him, accused of having committed arson at a time when he claims to have been working in another part of the region. The feeling that they were unlikely to be guaranteed a fair trial led others to run from the law as well.

The fact that discrimination is manifest in this way is, of course, related to epistemic privilege, including who has the power to create the system that will define what is legal and legitimate—a central element of systemic racism and the persistence of coloniality. Angélica Antillan, a Malleco woman who participated in a Mapuche women's organization as well as events for the elderly organized by her municipality, reflected on this when she described a land conflict in her area. The parents of the colono currently in possession of the land, it seems, had built an evangelical church on Mapuche land, with the cooperation of the Mapuche to whom the land belonged. Later the church was closed down, but the colonos did not return the land. When the Mapuche complained and sought to recover it, the colono, who was quite wealthy in Antillan's estimation, received the support of rightist politicians in Santiago and was provided police guards for three months. The problem, said Doña Angélica, is that "those lands really were Mapuche." Nevertheless, backed by official legitimating procedures, the Chilean remained in possession of the land.

The logic behind the radical strategies used by some organizations and communities is outside the traditional state-citizen relationship: they are acting as a distinct nation/people and being judged as citizens. I do not say this to excuse the use of violence by some groups but rather to point out that they are acting against the laws of a system that has historically disenfranchised them, and which they do not consider legitimate.

It is not only the contemporary neoliberal context that has shaped the conflicts. The imposition of neoliberal development in ancestral Mapuche territory and the attendant conflicts represent the continuation of a long history of depredation, systemic racism, and coloniality. Mapuche respondents were conscious of that continuity and also saw continuity in how the state and elites responded to Mapuche activism. Antonio Queipul, for example, argued that the Mapuche's legacy of independence contributed to heightened levels of fear and consequently a particularly harsh response against their claims. Horacio Quilapan pointed out the continuity in the image of Mapuche as violent warriors, observing that the image justified the Pacificación, just as it justifies police violence and antiterrorist legislation today. While Mapuche respondents did not ignore the political-economic issues fueling the conflicts, they also acknowledged the role of racial-ethnic-nationalist fear in shaping elite Chilean responses to the movement. This stands in contrast to local elites, who tended to argue that Mapuche leaders were motivated by the money they could make by selling their cause to NGOs, discrediting the possibility that their claims were based in a history of oppression and dispossession. If elites truly saw things in this light, it should come as little surprise that they considered Mapuche claims illegitimate; at the same time, their views reinforced their own positions of relative privilege. Mapuche who claimed the right to resist, the right to be subjects of the social world in their own right and not merely subjectified, faced swift and harsh discipline on the part of the state.

Mapuche land was originally usurped through the Pacificación. Then, through a variety of means and over the course of many years, Chileans and colonos usurped portions of the small parcels of land granted to the Mapuche after their defeat. When the Mapuche were able to recover some land through agrarian reform, it was again usurped through counterreform. For many elites it is the Mapuche who are now trying to usurp land, which they consider both illegal and illegitimate. Part of their objective, it seems, is to put the Mapuche, who once again are stepping out of line (having done so before with agrarian reform), back in their place. Although elite positions are not identical to those of the state, their epistemic privilege legitimates their claims. At the state level epistemic privilege allows neoliberal development to proceed without taking Mapuche concerns into consideration, demonstrating the continued relevance of coloniality to daily life in the region.

CHAPTER 4

CONSTRUCTING NEOLIBERAL MULTICULTURALISM IN CHILE

The Concertación responded to the conflicts with a dual approach. On the one hand, it created programs and policies that responded positively to Mapuche demands that could be construed as related to development or diversity. On the other, it harshly penalized Mapuche actions that favored principles of autonomy, self-governance, and territorial control. This policy response coheres to some degree—although it also diverges in important ways—with what other scholars of indigenous politics in Latin America have dubbed "neoliberal multiculturalism" (Hale 2002, 2004, 2006; Horton 2006; Laurie, Andolina, and Radcliffe 2003; Postero 2004, 2007). Throughout Latin America the shift toward multiculturalism took place as neoliberalism became hegemonic. Indigenous movements are among the strongest social movements in the region, and their goals and logic often directly contrast with those of the neoliberal project. As a result, multiculturalism has become an important means of generating consent for neoliberalism. Still, rights and recognition are granted to the indigenous only insofar as they do not threaten state goals in the global economy. Multicultural policies work well with the neoliberal agenda because they promote cultural recognition without the economic and political redistribution that would lead to greater equality (Hale 2006). All told, neoliberal multiculturalism represents a racial project that does little to challenge racial dominance or neocolonialism as manifest in the political-economic agenda of the state.

But neoliberal multiculturalism is about more than a policy agenda. Charles Hale (2004, 17) has linked it to "the creation of subjects who govern themselves in accordance with the logic of globalized capitalism." One subject position created through neoliberal multiculturalism is the *indio permitido*, or "authorized Indian"—a term coined by Silvia Rivera Cusicanqui (Hale and Millaman 2006). Hale (2004, 19) notes that, in dialectical fashion, neoliberal multiculturalism constructs another subject position as well: "Governance proactively creates and rewards the *indio permitido*, while condemning its Other to the racialized spaces of poverty and social exclusion." Hale (2006) calls this "Other" the *insurrecto,* or "insurrectionary Indian." While the "authorized" Indian readily embraces integrationist policies and participates unquestioningly in government programs, the "insurrectionary" defies the principles of neoliberal multiculturalism by pursuing recognition of ancestral rights and redistribution of power and resources. These subject positions are a resource that allows the state to constrain indigenous behavior; communities or individuals who do not adhere to the "authorized" model are marginalized at best or subjected to state violence at worst. These positions do not capture the full range of behaviors and attitudes of indigenous peoples, of course, but their dichotomous character is part of their power; individuals and communities who seek inclusion while also making ancestral claims walk a fine line between acceptance and marginalization (Park and Richards 2007).

As the Concertación was committed to promoting democracy and human rights as well as neoliberal growth, the years it held the presidency present a unique opportunity to observe the contradictions inherent in the neoliberal multicultural model. In Chile the "authorized" position describes an ideal Mapuche subject who accepts his or her role in fostering diversity and appreciation for Chile's folkloric past, does not make demands that exceed state-sponsored multiculturalism, and actively promotes the intercultural policies it entails. The authorized Indian serves to reinforce what the insurrectionary is not, prescribes what she or he should be, and denies the possibility that an individual could embody aspects of both—for example, participating in cultural initiatives and taking advantage of government programs while simultaneously supporting autonomist efforts (Richards 2007).

The transnationally informed set of discourses and practices that we call neoliberal multiculturalism became the prevailing form of governmentality under the Concertación. However, its scope was somewhat more limited than elsewhere in Latin America. The contours of neoliberal multiculturalism under the Concertación responded to the particularities of Chilean history, demands made by the Mapuche movement since the return to democracy, and the conflicts that brewed from the mid-1990s forward. Here I delineate the Concertación's response to the conflicts, which involved repression on the one hand, and addressing in a limited fashion some indigenous demands on the other. The punitive aspect of this response involved actively constructing the Mapuche not just as insurrectionists but as terrorists. The indigenous policies implemented by the Concertación over the twenty years it was in power included growing attention to interculturality and multiculturality, and were often put into practice at the local level with the involvement of municipal governments. These policies demonstrate the dualistic character of neoliberal multiculturalism theorized by Hale. I show that, in the Chilean case, the subject-formation aspect of the neoliberal multicultural agenda leaves little room for the indigenous to negotiate as valid interlocutors with the state.

NEOLIBERAL MULTICULTURALISM AS DISCIPLINE

In the face of land occupations, plantation fires, and other protests, the Concertación responded with punitive policies. These policies were an integral part of the neoliberal multicultural paradigm. Mapuche demands and actions perceived to threaten national development and identity were defined as illegitimate or illegal. Concertación authorities referred to the conflicts as "isolated incidents" but at the same time reacted forcefully against them. In the case of the Frei administration, this involved invoking the concept of rule of law and the National Security Law. Beginning with the Lagos administration, the strategy centered on constructing the Mapuche as terrorists, including the active use of an antiterrorism law originally established to control leftists under Pinochet.

It is difficult to assess with exactitude how many Mapuche individuals were arrested, incarcerated, and/or prosecuted in association with the conflicts during the entire Concertación period.[1] During the Lagos government alone, thirty-one individuals, mostly members of the Coordinadora Arauko Malleko (CAM), were accused of violating the antiterrorist law. (Hundreds more were detained and/or prosecuted under "normal" laws.) There were four antiterrorism "processes" initiated under Lagos but more trials, because all the accused were not tried at the same time.[2] The first occurred in 2003 and was known as the Trial of the Lonkos, because two of the three defendants were the heads (*lonkos*) of Mapuche communities (Aniceto Norin of Didaico and Pascual Pichun of Temulemu). The third defendant was Patricia Troncoso, a non-Mapuche sympathizer. The three were accused of committing terrorist threats and arson on the property of Juan Agustín Figueroa, a former minister of agriculture, and that of Juan Sagredo, another nearby landowner. They were found not guilty, but the Supreme Court declared a mistrial in response to a petition from the plaintiffs (which included the state).[3] They were retried and Troncoso was absolved, but the lonkos were each convicted to five years.[4]

The second case was that of Victor Ancalaf, who in 2004 was sentenced to five years for throwing an incendiary device at a truck during the construction of the Ralco hydroelectric dam. The third was the Poluco-Pidenco trial, in which five members of the CAM, including Troncoso, were charged with terrorist arson in association with fires on a pine plantation owned by Mininco. A lower court judge found the terrorist charges inappropriate before the trial began, but the Supreme Court removed her from the case, and in August 2004 all five were found guilty and sentenced to ten years. The final case focused on charges of illicit terrorist association brought against sixteen alleged members of the CAM. At least five of the sixteen had "already been convicted on a different charge for the same underlying acts" (HRW and ODPI 2004, 37). In November 2004 eight were tried and found not guilty.[5] The Supreme Court also overturned that acquittal; six were retried, and again there was insufficient evidence to convict them.

The terrorist construction has important legal implications, delineated in HRW and ODPI (2004, 20): "Under the anti-terrorism law, the public prosecutor is allowed to conduct criminal investigations in secret for long periods; pretrial release is usually denied for months, sometimes for longer than the eventual sentence received; defendants are not allowed to know the names of many of their accusers; and judges are given wider powers to allow prosecutors to intercept their correspondence, inspect their computers, and tap their phones than in normal criminal investigations." The law also authorizes sentences longer than those for similar violations of the criminal code. In addition, most of the crimes committed by Mapuche have been crimes against property, which do not qualify as terrorism as defined in international treaties (HRW and ODPI 2004).[6] Moreover, the legal artifice conceals the politics behind the use of the law: the Lagos administration repeatedly insisted that the conflicts were an issue for the courts to deal with but sponsored an intelligence operation called Operation Patience to substantiate charges against the CAM.[7] Although Bachelet promised during her campaign that her government would not apply the antiterrorism law, it was invoked numerous times during her presidency.

The application of the terrorist label also appears to have legitimated the use of state violence, including frequent and violent police raids on Mapuche communities, often in the middle of the night. Torture is reported to have taken place during interrogations (ibid.). Three young Mapuche protesters were shot dead by police under the Concertación: Alex Lemun in 2002, Matias Catrileo in 2008, and Jaime Mendoza Collio in 2009.[8] It is notable that two of these killings took place during Bachelet's government, just as multiculturalism was gaining prominence in state discourse. Communities in conflict have also faced psychological violence through constant police presence at the borders of their communities. When I visited one community in Malleco, for instance, the police were not stopping people or searching cars but registered people's comings and goings with cameras.[9]

Constructing the Mapuche as terrorists obscures their legitimate rights claims. Before their conflict with Figueroa, Temulemu and Didaico (along with Pantano) had occupied Santa Rosa de Colpi, the large fundo that had been returned to them right at the end of Allende's government and then lost again during the counterreform and later sold to Mininco. These were long-standing claims; the communities considered the land part of their *tierras antiguas*, and some of it was originally part of Temulemu's *título de merced* (Castro et al. 1999). A Mapuche interviewee who worked for a state agricultural program added that poverty played a role in the demands of these communities. In his work in Didaico and Temulemu, he had observed "the desperation of not having anything to eat." His remarks echo those of Lonko Pichun (in Correa and Mella 2010, 222): "[Those early occupations] were understandable because of the needs the people had, the poverty, the deterioration of the environment. . . . And obviously, the people had to rise up, so the claim [*reivindicación*] there is just. . . . We could no longer endure the scarcity, we no longer fit in the community, and aside from that, the timber company dried up all the water." Social inequality and ancestral claims both have a role in these conflicts, and the two cannot be easily separated out. Calling these conflicts "terrorism" only adds to the injustice that has been faced by these communities.

To protest the use of the antiterrorist law against them, Mapuche prisoners have undertaken several hunger strikes, including one initiated in October 2007 by Patricia Troncoso and four others. While the other four ended their efforts earlier because of health problems, Troncoso's strike was the longest in Chilean history. In January 2008, when the strike reached 112 days and Troncoso was near death, the government finally acceded to her request for herself and two others to be allowed weekend leaves and transfers to an alternative prison that would give them access to the rural outdoors.

The Concertación was not the only force shaping neoliberal multiculturalism from above. For a complete picture, it is necessary to explore the views promoted by the political right and the mass media as well. During the Concertación years the political right tended to reject Mapuche claims for territory and recognition while simultaneously critiquing the Concertación for failing to contain the conflicts. Libertad y Desarrollo (LYD) is a conservative think tank that issues reports, essays, and surveys on the conflicts. They were already calling Mapuche land recoveries "terrorist attacks" in 1999, and in September 2001 they published an essay lamenting the attacks on Washington and New York. The essay discursively linked Mapuche activism to the U.S. attacks by identifying the "indigenous issue" in Chile as a "risky situation" needing attention in the new global terrorist context. The use of "terrorism" to describe Mapuche land claims thus reflects global discursive flows. It also demonstrates historical continuity with the Southern Cone dictatorships (as well as the Guatemalan civil war), during which civilians were labeled terrorists to justify the state violence used against them (NSA "On the 30th Anniversary" and "Case against Pinochet"; Ross 1999; Taylor 1997).

Other rightist responses to the conflicts echoed these concerns about terrorism. In 2002 the Senate's Constitution, Legislation, and Justice Commission emitted a 160-page report on the "Mapuche conflict." The report was initiated by Senator Alberto Espina, who accused Mapuche of threatening the physical integrity and way of life of farmers, campesinos, and lumber transporters, and seeking not only to recover land but to make their own autonomous nation state. Another report, this one issued by a group of lawyers, exposed what they called "cybernetic terrorism," websites they said advocated Mapuche violence. These included several academic, advocacy, and human rights organizations. And in 2009, during a campaign stop in Temuco, then-presidential candidate Sebastian Piñera called for a second Pacificación of the Araucanía, observing: "I am convinced that in the Araucanía, the principle of authority is lost. The rule of law is broken" (in Gil 2009). Similar to representations of the Mapuche in the mid-to-late 1800s, during the Concertación years the Right represented Mapuche claims as illegitimate, dangerous, and in need of being contained.[10]

This tendency was clear in the print media as well. The media has played an important role in shaping notions of legitimacy in the conflicts. Although some outlets provided alternative voices, the daily print news that was most widely accessible in Chile over the course of my fieldwork leaned almost exclusively to the right. Mapuche activist Alfredo Seguel (2003a) has documented political-economic links between timber company owners and the mainstream media. For instance, the Matte family has a controlling interest in CMPC (Compañía Manufacturera de Papeles y Cartones, Paper and Cardboard Manufacturing Company), the parent company of the Mininco Timber Company. Bernardo Matte, a director of CMPC, has served on the board of directors for Televisión Nacional de Chile. His sister, Patricia, has served on the advisory board for the Catholic University channel. Members of the family, including brother Eliodoro, are also involved in various capacities in rightist think tanks and private foundations. Along with the Edwards family, which owns *El Mercurio*, the Mattes were deeply involved in efforts to prevent Allende from winning the presidency and later actively promoted his overthrow (Zeitlin and Ratcliff 1988). These links are important, contends Seguel, because they explain in part why the mass media so consistently defend the interests of the timber companies, present Mapuche actions as violent, terrorist, or illegal, and fail to examine the historical roots of the conflicts. In turn, these representations helped shape the general public's views on Mapuche claims.

By far the majority of articles about the Mapuche and the conflicts emphasized that Mapuche activism caused a lack of security in the region. Indicative headlines include: "Alert in Arauco, Fearing Wave of Mapuche Violence," "The Mapuche Intifada: The Indigenous Uprising Worsens," "Mapuches Threaten," and "Indigenous Communities on the War Path." One article read in part: "The kindling is there and the matches available—the indigenous conflict [could] end up becoming a little Chiapas."[11] In the print media the dichotomy between good and bad Mapuche was so strong that one article was titled "The Other Mapuches" (Zúñiga 2001). In bold type, a summary appears at the top of the article: "These don't shout, they don't march, they don't attack with *boleadoras*, they don't set fire or occupy *fundos*. They are tranquil and hard working. They live behind Temuco's airport . . . [and] send their products, of the highest quality, to England. What an example!" The presentation of "good" Mapuche as a discrete category serves to reinforce the notion that "bad" ones actually exist. That *these* Mapuche can manage to thrive with so little bolsters the idea that the demands and tactics of the *others* are illegitimate.

Of course, there is a global context to all of this, marked by the United States' "War on Terror" that began in September 2001. Many of the steps that the Concertación and the Chilean courts took, including all applications of the antiterrorism law, followed September 11, 2001, and can be read as part of a general context in which the label "terrorist" is used to delegitimate subaltern struggles much as the term "communist" was used during the Cold War.

As Human Rights Watch and Observatorio de los Derechos de los Pueblos Indígenas (2004, 5) put it: "The U.S.-led campaign against terrorism has, unfortunately, become a cover for governments who want to deflect attention away from their heavy-handed treatment of internal dissidents." Before Chile signed its Free Trade Agreement with the United States in 2003, it was widely rumored that the United States set getting the Mapuche movement under control as a precondition. More interesting than whether this rumor is "true" are its "truth effects" (Aretxaga 2000). It is illustrative of a political reality in which September 11, 2001, made it possible to use antiterrorism laws against the Mapuche without invoking substantial moral opposition among the Chilean public. In addition, the U.S. State Department (2007) acknowledged that Chile requested FBI support in their continuing efforts against the CAM. And in 2009 it was reported that the FBI was advising Chile in its efforts to collect DNA samples from Mapuche political prisoners (Cayuqueo 2009). Construing the Mapuche as terrorists was facilitated by this global context as well as historical representations of the Mapuche as a threat to the Chilean nation. The terrorist construction is a key element of subject formation in Chile—one that is held in contrast to the "good" Indian, the permitido, who is expected to gladly accept that which the state offers in the line of indigenous policy.

INDIGENOUS POLICY: DELINEATING THE SCOPE OF MULTICULTURALISM

Over the years it was in power, the Concertación developed a range of indigenous, intercultural, and multicultural policies. The content of these policies reflected the historical dynamic between the state and the Mapuche and, to the extent that they fit with neoliberal development goals, responded to some Mapuche demands. The historical context—the existence of the border, the relegation of the Mapuche to reductions even as the *araucano* was incorporated into imagery aimed at generating cross-class unity, and the belief that the indigenous were largely irrelevant or nonexistent—contributed to a situation in which, particularly at first, politicians in democratic Chile were reticent to endorse policies involving recognition. The specific character of conflicts in the south also shaped Chile's version of neoliberal multiculturalism, as did the centralization that continued to dominate the policy arena. All told, while Chile was the first Latin American state to embrace neoliberalism, it has been one of the last to embrace multiculturalism.

In this section I delineate the policies that made up the "permitido" side of neoliberal multiculturalism in Chile. In the early years indigenous policy under the Concertación focused principally on poverty alleviation and some light attention to diversity. Unlike others in the region, the Chilean state shied away from promoting recognition, even if it was unaccompanied by the substantive redistribution that would make it meaningful. Later, particularly in the latter years of the Lagos administration and throughout the Bachelet one, indigenous policy more directly promoted the concepts of interculturality and multiculturality. Nevertheless, even then the scope of these policies did not approximate that documented elsewhere by Hale, Nancy Grey Postero, and others, particularly in terms of opening spaces for autonomy and access to decision making. I focus on laying out the policies that were developed, but I also give some consideration to the question of whether the Concertación's policies—intentionally or not—created openings for the expression of any kind of alternative politics.

Mapuche demands have long encompassed concerns related to material need as well as collective and cultural rights, and different organizations and communities prioritize different demands. The range includes land, better access to education, healthcare, and other social services, creation of intercultural programs, participation in policy creation and implementation, consultation on decisions that affect them, constitutional recognition, self-government, and autonomous territory. In general, the Concertación's indigenous policies addressed socioeconomic claims when it was possible to do so without acknowledging historically based collective rights. Thus land subsidies, scholarships, housing grants, and agricultural training were established, but political demands for autonomous territory, self-government, or even collective representation were left by the wayside. The Concertación also reframed some recognition claims as demands for diversity and declared illegal or unreasonable claims that challenged the state's ideological and economic goals (Richards 2004). In this way the Concertación responded to Mapuche claims but removed their political content.

The tendency to construe Mapuche demands as socioeconomic problems that could be resolved with development-oriented solutions, particularly dominant during the first three administrations, is likely related to the historical tendency on the Chilean center-left to view the Mapuche through the lens of social class rather than ethnicity. It is suggestive of the ways that Mapuche ethnic difference continued to be denied in the Chilean collective imaginary. In this sense the Concertación, particularly in its earlier stages, differed from other Latin American governments by privileging a degree of redistribution over recognition. The policies tended to be ameliorative, however, and did not change the distribution of racialized power in Chilean society (Richards 2004).

Nevertheless, as Diane Haughney (2008) has observed, there were some differences among the four administrations. Under Aylwin the focus was on development with identity, and establishing CONADI (the Corporación Nacional de Desarollo Indígena, the National Indigenous Development Agency) and passing the Indigenous Law his major achievements. Still, CONADI was unable to fully satisfy indigenous demands, and in fact, the land program frequently brought about new conflicts within and among communities. In the face of growing conflicts during his administration, Frei's focus was on law and order and national security. Lagos emphasized a "new deal" for the indigenous (accompanied by the application of the antiterrorism law), and Bachelet's focus was multiculturalism directly. These shifts respond to several factors: the need to provide an answer to Mapuche mobilization and pacify the conflicts, the desire for transnational legitimacy in the arena of indigenous rights, pressures from the Right for a stronger punitive response, and some subtle differences in the priorities of the four governments.

Indeed, in Chile the word "multicultural" only became prevalent in state parlance under Bachelet. "Interculturality" gained prominence earlier, particularly in reference to education and healthcare. When I talk about Chile's version of neoliberal multiculturalism, however, I am referring to the indigenous policies and accompanying discourses that expanded over the course of the Concertación's tenure, recognizing that compared to other countries in the region, indigenous policy throughout much of the Concertación period was more assimilationist than multicultural (Burguete 2008; Hale and Millaman 2006). While Postero (2007, 13) differentiates between interculturality as an "interactive process of mutual influence among bearers of cultural and especially linguistic difference," and multiculturalism as implying "recognition and respect of numerous cultures," in Chile both terms carry multiple meanings and are frequently used interchangeably without a great deal of clarification. Thus, like Hale (2006), I use the terms interchangeably. For the purposes of this analysis, I view all of the indigenous, intercultural, and multicultural laws, policies, and programs instituted since the return to democracy as part of the movement toward neoliberal multiculturalism.

The creation of CONADI and the new indigenous law under Aylwin laid the bases for what would become the neoliberal multicultural paradigm. The Aylwin period also marked the initial absorption of many Mapuche leaders and NGO workers from the dictatorship era into the state apparatus—a tendency many have come to lament as "cutting off the head" of the movement. Some of the programs that came to be implemented by the Concertación (not necessarily under Aylwin), such as intercultural education and healthcare, were originally NGO projects initiated during the dictatorship, representing instances of what Verónica Schild (1998) has called "selective appropriation," whereby the state appropriates elements of movement activism that fit well with the neoliberal agenda as a means of generating consent.

While critics like Hale and Postero argue that neoliberal multiculturalism consists of symbolic recognition with little redistributive substance, recognition itself is a limited and highly controlled aspect of neoliberal multiculturalism in Chile. Concertación policies that recognized Mapuche culture to some extent, such as intercultural health or education programs, were limited in scope and focused on integrating the Mapuche into the Chilean whole. Intercultural education programs were only directed at the Mapuche, for example. Rhetoric presenting the Mapuche as part of Chile's folkloric past was also common (Richards 2004). Despite repeated attempts, Chile has failed to recognize the Mapuche in its Constitution. Only in 2008 did Chile ratify International Labor Organization Convention 169, which recognizes indigenous rights to consultation, territory, and self-governance. These have long been central elements of the multicultural agenda throughout the region, but while generally supported by the executive branch, they were repeatedly blocked by rightists—and some within the Concertación—concerned with the implications of recognizing more than one "people" for the Chilean nation.

To the extent that the Mapuche were recognized in indigenous policies, it was as potential neoliberal citizens rather than a sovereign people. Under Frei as well as Lagos and Bachelet, many specific indigenous policies linked directly into neoliberal values, emphasizing increasing indigenous individuals' access to the market. The market focus is a central component of social policy in Chile more generally (Schild 2000). Citizen participation may be integrated into these policies, but it usually takes the form of responsibility for carrying out projects, thus amounting to a form of free labor. Citizen groups also have the opportunity to receive government funding if they propose a "project" to one of a multitude of small "competitive funds" available at all levels of government. In the case of the Mapuche, the state (through CONADI as well as municipalities) sponsors programs through which elements of Mapuche culture can be exploited in the global marketplace. Examples include "ethnotourism" projects and marketing handicrafts.

The policies of the Frei and early Lagos administrations in particular reflected reluctance to understand Mapuche claims as political, cultural, and collective. In 1999, near the end of his presidency, Frei sponsored a polemical series of "communal dialogues," in which government officials met with more than a thousand Mapuche communities to assess their demands. The government presented the results proportionally, suggesting that while only

15 percent of the demands were sociopolitical, 40 percent focused on infrastructure and services, 32 percent on economic and productive issues, and 12 percent on land (MIDEPLAN in Lavanchy 1999). Compiling the data in this regard allowed the government to ignore the fact that the different types of demands are not mutually exclusive and that the same communities may be making all of them (Valdés 2000 in Richards 2004). Indeed, the government asserted that the results of the dialogues showed Mapuche demands were not generally political in nature, but instead focused on social services and economic production, conveniently areas in which the administration had already developed policies. Frei announced a series of measures, including infrastructural improvements, technical support, housing subsidies, improvements in land buybacks and dispute resolution, more land subsidies for young families, more scholarships, wider-reaching intercultural health and education programs, and the establishment of two new Indigenous Development Areas—all development-oriented solutions, most of the funds for which had already been designated before the dialogues.

Rather than communal dialogues, in March 2000, Lagos created a Working Group for Indigenous Peoples, incorporating representatives from indigenous organizations, business, and the government. Nevertheless, the results were fairly similar. After a final report was issued, Lagos announced sixteen measures addressing demands in the areas of land, training, intercultural education and healthcare, and constitutional recognition. The list notably did not include demands for autonomous territory, self-government, or collective representation. Both of these processes show that invoking participation and dialogue was no guarantee Mapuche political claims would be heard.

Perhaps the most significant step taken under Lagos was the creation of Orígenes. An indigenous development program, Orígenes was established in 2001 through a US$180 million Inter-American Development Bank (IDB) loan and $53 million Chilean counterpart.[12] Orígenes funded projects related to production, health, education, and community and institutional strengthening.[13] The program was designed entirely without indigenous input and was interpreted among indigenous leaders as a strategy to pacify the conflicts by throwing money at the communities.[14] Even the program's motto—"Look to the future from your origins" (Mira el futuro desde tu orígen)—seemed to encourage the indigenous to keep their traditions but forget their ancestral claims.

Orígenes was designed as a decentralized program with five coexecutors: the ministries of education and health, CONADI, INDAP (Instituto Nacional de Desarrollo Agropecuario, the National Agricultural Development Agency), and CONAF (Corporación Nacional Forestal, the National Forestry Agency), all under the supervision of MIDEPLAN (Ministerio de Plan-ificación, the Ministry of Planning). The program was purportedly carried out in a decentralized manner as well, because it involved the participation of indigenous communities in deciding what types of programs they wanted. "Promoters" were assigned to go into the communities and help them estab-lish priorities and lines of action. Together with their promoter, communities developed a Community Development Plan and CONADI-approved con-sultants came in to work on the different projects.[15]

Communities and promoters were limited in the particular projects they were allowed to undertake, however. Their plans could not go beyond the established Orígenes areas of health, education, productive development, and community strengthening, and even within these areas some communities' proposals were rejected. Thus, despite the involvement of multiple minis-tries and multiple local actors, Orígenes was definitely not decentralized in terms of who structured the available options among which indigenous actors were able to engage in "decision making." As a form of indigenous participation, this one was highly managed from above. Moreover, as Álvaro Bello (2007) has observed, by not giving CONADI—the official indigenous agency—authority over the program, the state sent a message about its lim-ited role and simultaneously demonstrated that it wanted to politically con-trol the conflicts. In practice, Orígenes became a way to provide funds while keeping important decisions out of indigenous hands and political claims off the table. Bello (ibid.) asserts that the program continued the state's ten-dency of delivering superficial, welfare-oriented programs "with identity" rather than responding to evolving indigenous rights claims. That is, even though the program was well-received in many sectors, it did not address the structural issues behind the conflicts, much less claims for collective political rights. Because Orígenes was born of the conflicts, it also had the flavor of trying to contain them.

In fact, some communities directly involved in the conflicts benefited from the program. After a lengthy decision-making process, the embattled community of Jorge Millan, the twenty-something son of an imprisoned leader, decided to participate in the program. I asked Millan what he thought the effects of state programs had been. He moved his head back and forth thoughtfully, as if there might be some positive effects as well as negative ones. Finally he said that programs like Orígenes only serve to keep leaders busy. Indeed, at the moment of our interview, he was in Temuco filling out paperwork for the community, which, he lamented, took away time, energy, and thought from the real issue: the land. The danger, he said, 'is that people stop thinking about what is at the root of things.'[16] On the other hand, he reflected, 'the state has two policies: they either throw money at the communities or give them the nightstick; you can participate or you can be repressed.' So, to participate was not just to take advantage of state resources; it was a strategy to avoid repression. I asked if some communities had opted not to participate, and he said yes and shrugged, observing that they end up with nothing. I asked where he thought things would be after another three years of Orígenes. He shrugged again, and said there would always be programs like this—trivial provisions to pacify them and distract from the struggle. Millan's comments suggest that some Mapuche were not unaware of the dualistic character of Concertación policy but, under threat of state violence, saw little option other than to participate, thereby consenting to the neoliberal multicultural project.

At the beginning of 2001, Lagos established the Comisión de Verdad Histórica y Nuevo Trato (Historical Truth and New Deal Commission). The commission was charged with writing a historical report and coming up with proposals and recommendations for policies that would contribute to a new relationship between the state, indigenous peoples, and Chilean society (Aylwin 2007). The commission submitted its report in October 2003. In April 2004, Lagos announced the measures he would take in response. Aside from proposing to give urgency to the ratification of ILO Convention 169, he did not take up the commission's recommendations regarding the recognition of indigenous peoples, the demarcation of their territories, or their rights to natural resources. Nor did he take up its recommendation to establish indigenous representation in Congress and regional and municipal governments. Instead, he focused on strengthening the existing law and on "development with identity" in the areas of education, production, and restitution of land and water rights. Once again, these measures amounted to strengthening programs already administered by CONADI and Orígenes, and doing little to respond to the issues that triggered Mapuche protests in the first place (Aylwin 2007). A Nuevo Trato report (MIDEPLAN 2006b) lauds the steps taken by the Lagos administration as acknowledging the "multicultural character of Chilean society." Yet, more than anything, the Lagos approach demonstrated persistence in insisting that the "Mapuche problem" was poverty-based and should be addressed with development policies, albeit with some symbolic recognition of their identity attached. Still, the mention of multiculturalism and interculturality became more common with the Lagos administration.

The explicit focus on interculturality and multiculturality solidified under President Michelle Bachelet (2006–10). While her government continued to promote Orígenes, the land fund, and other policies established during previous administrations, in 2007, Chile voted in favor of the UN Declaration on the Rights of Indigenous Peoples and in 2008 finally ratified ILO 169. The ratification process was not without controversy, however. In early 2008 the Senate approved the convention with the addition of an "interpretive declaration" limiting its scope. Indigenous organizations protested, and Bachelet waited several months to ratify it. When the official decree of promulgation was made in October 2008, there was no mention of the interpretive clause. In addition, in April 2008 the Bachelet government released a document called *Reconocer: Pacto social por la multiculturalidad*, summarizing plans for indigenous policy in the second half of her administration. The document recognized the persistence of indigenous poverty and unmet demands and outlined a plan of action related to the political system, rights, institutions, development, multiculturalism, and diversity.

Some of the proposals not taken up before included indigenous participation in parliament, regional and communal councils, institutionalization of the right to participation, construction of a multicultural policy, promulgation of the Verdad Histórica report, and passage of an antidiscrimination law. However, the document lacked specific details on how these changes would be put into effect and what they would consist of in practice. While these steps would bring Chile more in line with neoliberal multiculturalism elsewhere, the two years remaining in Bachelet's presidency were too few to put many of them into place. Finally, as of March 2009, the Senate was again debating Constitutional recognition. The bill, for the first time promoted largely by rightist politicians, was very problematic. It referred to the Chilean nation as "one, indivisible, and multicultural," recognized indigenous peoples but made clear that their communities, organizations, and members—not the peoples per se—were subjects of rights, and insisted that indigenous ways of life must not contradict Chilean law (Marín 2009).

In October 2009, well after my fieldwork was completed, almost two months after the death of Mendoza Collio, and in the context of a new round of land occupations led by an alliance of lonkos, the Bachelet administration announced an extraordinary step: it would purchase and hand over to Mapuche communities several of the most emblematic fundos in conflict, including those of Jorge Luchsinger (in benefit of Juan Catrilaf community), Rene Urban (in benefit of Temucuicui Autónomo), and two belonging to Mininco, including Santa Rosa de Colpi (in benefit of Pantano, Didaico, and Temulemu). The Concertación committed unprecedented funds to paying for these lands. It seemed the Concertación was finally willing to take major steps to resolve the most extreme conflicts, steps that did not involve criminalizing the Mapuche struggle. But at the same time, the purchases of these lands, which were expected to take place by January 2010, before Bachelet left office, did not stray far from what the Concertación had been doing all along. That is, while these purchases would be a step forward and would hopefully end the suffering faced by the communities as well as the *winka* farmers involved, they still did not entail any substantive recognition of Mapuche collective rights to territory and autonomy. This is particularly so given that the farmers and timber companies involved, by virtue of the huge sums they would be paid, would turn out to be important beneficiaries of the conflicts.

Moreover, this commitment was not accompanied by an end to state violence. Several major incidents of police repression occurred in the same month the purchases were announced. These included several occasions in which Mapuche children were shot with pellets or rubber bullets, and one in which a fourteen-year-old boy was shot in the leg with pellets by GOPE (Grupo de Operaciones Policiales Especiales, Special Forces police) agents while looking for medicinal plants for a treatment he was to receive from a *machi* (Mapuche shaman/healer). After fleeing, he was pursued by a low-flying helicopter for three kilometers. When caught, he was beaten and his head was dunked repeatedly in a nearby stream. The boy was then taken up in the helicopter, held with his head hanging out of it, and threatened with being thrown to the ground below if he did not reveal the names of participants in a land occupation occurring nearby (Acevedo 2009). That these events could occur in the same month demonstrates the dualistic nature of the state's dealings with the Mapuche. It also shows ongoing low regard for Mapuche lives.

After years of disillusionment with the Concertación, before the very competitive 2009 presidential elections, some Mapuche groups were calling on people to "vote null" or to vote for one of the non-Concertación leftist candidates. Thus the proposed purchases could also be read as a cynical effort on the part of the Concertación to win Mapuche votes, much as Frei's communal dialogues took place right before another very competitive election in 1999. In the end, rightist candidate Sebastian Piñera won the election in the second round of voting. Only some of the lands, including Jorge Luchsinger's, were purchased and handed over to Mapuche communities before Bachelet left office. The Mininco fundos, together comprising more than twenty-five hundred hectares, were turned over to Temulemu, Didaico, and Pantano in 2011. The Urban/Temucuicui Autónomo deal remained under negotiation at the end of Bachelet's government, and in February 2012 the community decided to withdraw their demand, to allow the traditional community of Temucuicui to pursue recuperation of the land (Tauran 2012).

Before moving on, I want to reflect on a suggestion made to me by two respondents—one Mapuche and one a local elite—that the conflicts, and the region itself, were really not much of a priority for the Concertación. Young Mapuche scholar Eugenio Huentelican spoke of the "economy of the conflicts" and took the position that they were necessary for the survival of the region. The conflicts themselves were the main thing that brought state resources into the regional economy, through land purchases as well as programs like Orígenes. Without the conflicts some income from the timber industry might flow out, but very little would flow in. Maintaining the conflicts was advantageous, he felt, to the economy of the region, and hardware store owners, animal sellers, elites, and even Mapuche leaders benefited from maintaining it. That the latter group actively participated in this economy and benefited from it is unarguably true, and it is a matter of grave concern. In addition to being bought into the hegemonic project in this way, Huentelican argued, most "movement elites" lacked a systematic political proposal of their own; they merely functioned in response to the Concertación's initiatives. Proposing and carrying out "projects" consumed much of their time, and a coherent political discourse was left behind in the process.

Armando Torres, a former rightist deputy and university administrator, similarly observed that although the conflicts were very visible, they were not very relevant. He referred to the marginal position of the Mapuche as well as medium-scale farmers in the regional and national economy. The idea that the conflicts are really not all that relevant suggests that these proposed land purchases may have been the product of a cost-benefit analysis on the part of the Concertación, a wager that they might finally be able to wash their hands of the region. Yet Huentelican's observations suggest that the Concertación's approach was having the desired effect: creating a situation in which indios permitidos are consumed by the projects of the state, leaders are bought in to the neoliberal hegemonic project, and the development of a coherent alternative project on the part of the movement is left by the wayside.

MUNICIPALITIES' ROLE IN IMPLEMENTING NEOLIBERAL MULTICULTURALISM

While municipal governments were not centrally involved in the conflicts, they were important policy deliverers under the Concertación.[17] It is worth emphasizing that the conflicts are exacerbated by the Chilean state's continued centralized character. In Chile no money generated in the regions stays there; all tax monies go to the central state. Policies and programs are usually designed centrally, then implemented locally, often through subcontractors. (The subcontracting of public labor is one area in which decentralization has occurred, but notably it does not affect decision making.) *Intendentes* (the top regional authorities) as well as provincial governors are appointed, not elected. Municipal mayors and *consejeros* (councilpersons) are elected (although they were appointed during the dictatorship). The limited autonomy associated with decentralization elsewhere in Latin America is not afforded to the Mapuche.

Relying on the municipalities to deliver social policies is thus one of the few ways in which the Chilean state is actually decentralized. For example, INDAP has a local development program (Programa de Desarollo Local, or PRODESAL) that funds programs at the municipal level. For PRODESAL to operate in a given comuna, INDAP and the municipal government create a formal agreement whereby INDAP finances the agricultural experts and technicians, and the municipality provides social workers, accountants, and other services. Another type of decentralization involved creating competitive funds that encouraged municipal departments to apply to state agencies, including INDAP, CONADI, and the Ministry of Education, for project financing. This type of decentralization kept decision making, and the purse, at the central level.

But as the level of government that often worked most closely with Mapuche communities and through which many policies were implemented, the municipalities are worth examining as an arena of indigenous policy. As they were somewhat free to innovate, the municipalities held potential to be liberatory. Conversely, they also held potential to even more intensively reflect the deep-seated inequalities that predominated in the region. I want to mention two particularly problematic issues. Perhaps the most controversial program involving the Mapuche was the Programa de Forestación para Pequeños y Medianos Propietarios (Forestation Program for Small and Medium Landowners). Run through CONAF, the semiprivate forestry agency within the Ministry of Agriculture, this program was an example of how municipalities can serve not to empower but to support the neoliberal multicultural objectives of the central state and elites. In the program, CONAF gives money to INDAP. INDAP gives small- and medium-scale farmers credit to plant seedlings, and the municipality provides training and some initial labor to properly set up the area that will be planted. (Individuals who participate provide the ongoing labor and care of the growing trees.) CONAF projected that this program could eventually access two million hectares suitable for timber plantations that are in the hands of small landowners (Seguel 2005). Seguel sees this as a new strategy on the part of the industry; instead of acquiring large expanses of land that are prone to conflicts, they were buying-in small landowners, including the Mapuche, making them complicit in the industry. Because the big timber conglomerates controlled most of the industry, it is likely that Mapuche who harvest timber would have to sell their product to them.

A CONAF representative explained that the program was important for the region because of the large number of *minifundios* (very small rural properties) there. Planting timber would contribute income to these households. Moreover, he said, these lands were highly degraded as a result of intensive subsistence agriculture but would be productive if planted with timber. Including timber in the campesino economy was desirable, he asserted, in order to improve the soil. He admitted the ideal would be to plant native trees but insisted this was an extreme situation, and planting pine and eucalyptus was better than nothing. This assertion flies in the face of evidence that pine and eucalyptus plantations contribute to degradation of the soil and water table (Haughney 2006; Klubock 2004) and disregards other possibilities for improving the soil. Altogether, 25 to 30 percent of timber plantations in the region are in the hands of small and medium landowners, although the CONAF/INDAP/municipal agreement accounts for less than 25 percent of the small- to medium-scale hectares that are planted. This program implicates municipalities and Mapuche campesinos who participate in the industry that has most threatened Mapuche communities in recent years.

The program was strong in one of the Cautín municipalities I studied, where I saw a poster that asked: "Will our children see the forest? Where did the forest go?" There I found a pamphlet about forest maintenance, which stated that in Chile in such and such a year, so many trees were cut down but so many more were planted. Like the Bosques para Chile campaign, these materials confounded forests with plantations. They represent an effort to get common people involved not in forest preservation but in the timber industry, through an emotional pull regarding future generations. In the process they contributed to the creation of neoliberal subjects whose duties as citizens were confounded with those of small-scale producers for international markets.

I spoke with Mario Crespo, who had worked for this municipality for many years, about how the forestation program operated. At the time of our interview, the program was two years old there, and thus far they had planted a total of 140 hectares. Most people who participated in the program only planted one or two hectares, in heavily eroded areas.[18] Participants were offered a range of trees, including pine, eucalyptus, and native species. Almost everyone opted for eucalyptus, a few for pine, and almost no one for native species. Crespo explained this was because eucalyptus grows more quickly, has greater commercial value, and automatically resprouts after harvest. (This final factor makes it preferable even over pine.)

I visited the field with Elisa Chodiman, a young Mapuche agronomist who worked for the program. On the way to visit some of the Mapuche who had decided to plant, she explained that much of their land was depleted and no longer of any agricultural use: 'The municipality has an interest in foresting the land because having anything planted is better than nothing,' in terms of erosion. 'Sure,' she said, 'Native trees would be better but pine and eucalyptus are better than nothing.' She repeated what I heard often—that people do not want to plant native trees because they grow slowly and would not generate profit anytime soon. As we made our rounds, in her discussions with Mapuche farmers, Chodiman reiterated that "la agricultura ya no da" ("agriculture doesn't pay off anymore," since yields, and thus profits, are negligible) several times. Although there has been a good deal of erosion, this seems to be another case of the truth effects Begoña Aretxaga (2000) wrote of. If you repeat it often enough, it becomes true.

Some Mapuche activists saw this program as a means to generate consent for the timber industry among the Mapuche, a point that matches Seguel's analysis. Horacio Quilapan, a member of CITEM (Coordinación de Identidades Territoriales Mapuche, Mapuche Territorial Identities Coordinating Organization), argued that the manner in which the industry has expanded in his comuna in Cautín—by providing small farmers with seedlings and support—was very "undercover and ominous" compared to many comunas in Malleco, where the presence of timber companies was more obvious. I asked if Mapuche participants were happy with the program, because that was the impression the municipality gave. He said they were; they get free plants, consultants, fences, preliminary compensation, and management plans. But, he said, people participated to get money quick, without thinking about the consequences. Perhaps, he mused, ten years down the line, they would see problems with water shortages and land degradation, and then some would react. Another CITEM member, Gabriel Ancamil, added: "Obviously, they are going to take what they are told is good. It is not that they come up with the idea that it's good, you understand." Mapuche communities are subject to a lot of misinformation at the hands of people who come to them with "projects," he suggested, adding that if people do not know if something is good or bad, they look at it in economic terms: "In ten years, you are going to harvest, and CONAF is going to give you the wire, the fence, to close it in, and on top of that, they are going to compensate you, that's good, isn't it?"

Since the beginning of the conflicts, the timber companies themselves have developed Buena Vecindad (Good Neighbor) plans, meaning that they open up their plantations for Mapuche to gather native plants and offer special programs and resources to the communities. Mininco's plan states its main objectives as "insert[ing] the company into the life of the community in general" and helping neighboring communities overcome extreme poverty. Their actions are focused on rural employment, educational support, and development (Forestal Mininco 2010). In parts of Cautín the timber companies have begun to focus on increasing output not by buying new land but, similarly to the Forestation Program for Small and Medium Landowners, by subcontracting and providing resources for people, including the Mapuche, to plant on their own land.

Another area through which municipalities participated in neoliberal multiculturalism involved marketing Mapuche culture. Some of the Concertación's indigenous policies directly linked into neoliberal values, sponsoring programs through which elements of Mapuche culture could be exploited in the global marketplace. Often these policies were implemented through the municipalities, implicating them in the creation of neoliberal multicultural citizens. Among the comunas I focused on, this was especially true of those located in Cautín. In the Malleco comunas municipal governments were not similarly inclined. Andrés Lonkomilla, a forty-something Mapuche state worker in Malleco, felt authorities in his comuna tried to do as little as necessary to not have the Mapuche "knocking at their door." State workers in Cautín tended to see the Mapuche as a client base but also as a resource, whereas in Malleco, they were seen as a burden. This was likely related to historical factors (more colono settlements were established in Malleco; lonkos in Cautín have a long history of negotiating with the Chileans) as well as contemporary ones (the worst of the conflicts have taken place in Malleco, where the timber companies have a greater presence).

One of the Cautín municipalities had a microenterprise department that helped establish small organizations and sell products in Chile and abroad. The department worked with Mapuche and non-Mapuche people, but as Emilio Meza, a young Chilean who worked there, put it: "We are selling . . . artisan textiles not because a Chilean makes it, but because a Mapuche makes it. And we don't sell *artesanía* because it is a pretty rug, . . . we sell [it because it has] a cultural element. Because people elsewhere value this, it makes sense for [our comuna] to value it as well." He added: "I think some comunas that are really in indigenous conflict, . . . Lumaco, Ercilla, and a ton of others in the North, I think they have looked at the indigenous issue more as a problem than as an opportunity. I think in recent times, we've transformed it into an opportunity." Meza, whose job involves commercializing the products in Europe, said "culture" gave Mapuche products a competitive edge in the global marketplace. "Culture" is in fashion, he explained, and cultures denigrated or attacked in the past are highly marketable today.

But Meza had mixed feelings about emphasizing difference: "I think the issue of racial difference is not so critical, or it is not the problem. I think the problem is economic, socioeconomic. I think that is what puts a wrench in the issue of coexistence of people today. But specifically with our issue, in [our] work, for me, the issue of commercialization, it gives me an enormous facility because I have a way to differentiate myself from other similar products from whichever other place in the world, and this gives me something important in relation to . . . merchandising in European countries." Although I do not want to be overly critical of this strategy, considering that in Malleco the approach seemed to be to keep the Mapuche as subjugated as possible, Meza's comuna is a good example of how the state (through CONADI, Orígenes, and municipal governments) sponsored programs through which elements of Mapuche culture could be exploited in the global marketplace. In this sense, under neoliberal multiculturalism Mapuche culture became a brand to be sold, and Mapuche entrepreneurs the very salespeople.

The commodification of culture could be observed in "ethnotourism" projects—opportunities for tourists to visit "typical" Mapuche communities. These initiatives were usually run by members of the communities, with training and some support from CONADI or the municipalities. Oscar Arias, a left-leaning councilman in Cautín and the middle-aged son of a local elite family, spoke of his comuna's goals in this regard: "We want to develop tourism, ethnotourism, for which we have great potential that we don't see. Because I don't see it, but I know that for you [foreigners] it is something nice. . . . And we have to take advantage of it. . . . There are many people who live as they lived before, who have their *ruka*, their things. We want to take advantage of all that and also make a source of work for the people in the countryside." Arias displayed some ambivalence about ethnotourism; he felt it would take substantial work to convince "ourselves" (meaning, winkas in his comuna), even before convincing Mapuche communities to undertake such projects with municipal support. But he also found this alternative more favorable to quality of life than planting eucalyptus, which had already dried up a lot of the area's water sources. He felt it could become an important source of income for people in his comuna. Of potential tourists, he observed:

> They are going to say that in [our town], the Mapuche culture has a lot of roots. They know us for Mapuche culture. That is the important part, and that is what [others] don't understand much, that it is a benefit. It is a benefit that we have, and we have to exploit it, you could say. Exploit in what sense? In that that's the identity we have. If we want to be a touristic town, we'll be it for that [reason], not because we are going to make a beach or make a pool. Intercultur-

ality, as I say, is to respect ourselves and try to preserve it and above all, make an incentive so that the thing stays very intercultural, because we are the ones that arrived here. They were already here.

On one level, selling Mapuche culture through ethnotourism or craftwork seems like a thin definition of "interculturality." It certainly does not necessarily signal respect for Mapuche claims for autonomy or territory, and even some of its winka advocates (like Arias) were doubtful about the cultural value of such initiatives. It also relies heavily on market values as a justification for incorporating the Mapuche. Yet, as Sarah Radcliffe and Nina Laurie (2006) have argued, based on their work in the Andes, the appropriation of culture for development should not be read as exploitation alone, as it is also a product of shifting indigenous discourses, practices, and desires. This perspective does seem like an advance over that espoused by other local elites and state workers, especially in the Malleco comunas, who seemed to prefer to erase Mapuche culture rather than promote it. My point here is that municipalities were an important part of the implementation of neoliberal multiculturalism in Chile, provided for some of its variability of form, and influenced how "authorized Indians" would be constructed. At the same time, because Chile is so centralized, the possibilities for regional variation in policies were relatively constrained.

THE CONSEQUENCES OF NEOLIBERAL MULTICULTURAL SUBJECT FORMATION

In this section I explore the consequences of the Concertación's approach in terms of the subject formation framework suggested by Hale (2004, 2006). I did not observe in Chile the decentralization and (however limited) opportunities for local autonomy documented in other cases (e.g., Horton 2006; Postero 2007; Yashar 1999). However, I do consider that state programs might contribute to the creation of alternative, more liberatory notions of interculturality on the part of Mapuche and their advocates. My main focus, though, is on the ways that neoliberal multiculturalism has served to delimit the possibilities for legitimate interlocution between indigenous actors and the state.

It is important to note that the permitido and the insurrecto are prescriptive subject positions—they are what the state wants indigenous people to be, and the basis for how it will respond to indigenous people, not an accurate reflection of who indigenous people are. In this sense, these subject positions are designed to facilitate the state's efforts to avoid political dialogue with Mapuche actors on their terms. That is, the construction of this dualistic model allows the state to reject Mapuche assertions that they are political actors and deserve to be heard. Nevertheless, this is not a total rejection. The model allows the state to set the very narrow terms for what it means to be an authorized Indian in Chile. If the Mapuche insist too much on being something else, they will be labeled insurrectionary and face repression. It is not just those labeled "insurrecto" whose participation as valid political actors is curtailed. The "permitido" subject position is defined so narrowly that even those Mapuche who more or less occupy it are not allowed space for any authentic dialogue or interchange. (There is little if any opportunity to address any disagreement with state policy.) Moreover, the construction of the Mapuche as either authorized or terrorist is consistent with William Robinson's (2001) characterization of the role of peripheral neoliberal states in maintaining social order on behalf of capital; if subjects will not consent to what the state offers through (neoliberal multicultural) development policies, they face direct coercion.

In Chile as elsewhere, intercultural discourse and policy are central to setting the range of acceptable behavior for indios permitidos. Were there *any* openings within the Concertación's programs for exercising autonomy? Focusing respectively on healthcare and education, Yun-Joo Park (2006) and Patricio Ortiz (2007) have shown that intercultural programs were developed with two issues in mind: movement demands and neoliberal priorities. Mapuche demands at the return to democracy included the establishment of intercultural programs. Movement actors saw practical as well as political ends in interculturality: not only would these programs contribute to the survival and revitalization of Mapuche traditions, practices, and ways of knowing, but they could help legitimize the Mapuche as a people with collective and cultural rights and thus contribute to the broader struggle for autonomous institutions. But the creation of these programs was also a relatively inexpensive way for the Concertación to gesture at addressing the fact that Mapuche were at the bottom of the barrel, according to most inequality measures.

In developing these programs, the Concertación tended to focus on increasing access to healthcare or education, rather than on their intercultural substance (Park 2006). Park and Ortiz have shown that, as a result, these programs fell far short of Mapuche visions of what intercultural programs should look like. For instance, although they usually made machi and other Mapuche health experts available to patients, intercultural health programs did not require Western-style practitioners to consult with them. And bilingual intercultural education was limited to rural Mapuche schools, such that Chileans were not educated interculturally. Even in the Mapuche schools, Mapuche ways of knowing were not integrated throughout the curriculum.

In health as well as education, Mapuche actors were given few opportunities for consultation and control over decision making. In the end, by creating these programs, the Concertación drew attention away from the political aspects of demands for interculturality, constructing the Mapuche instead as a mere ethnic group whose culture it respects.

Still, Park (2006) did find some expressions of autonomy in intercultural health programs, as did Guillaume Boccara (2007) in Orígenes-sponsored intercultural training workshops for state workers. Park has emphasized that when intercultural health programs emerge from the efforts of Mapuche organizations, perhaps receiving state support after they are well established, they are more likely to represent indigenous visions of interculturality. Boccara has observed that facilitators of the Orígenes workshops, often Mapuche educators or holders of traditional knowledge, had substantial control over the information they presented. Because Chile remained so centralized, however, opportunities for the growth of expressions of autonomy or oppositional politics from out of intercultural programs was less common than, say, what Postero (2007) has reported in pre-Evo Bolivia. Indeed, the instances in which this sort of thing happened in Chile were those few in which, for whatever reason, decision making was more decentralized. For example, the facilitators Boccara discusses were subcontractors, not direct state employees.

Postero (2007, 153) observes that NGO workshops about the Popular Participation Law in Bolivia "were part of the process by which citizens were trained to speak a common language of administration, financing proposals, development, budgets, monitoring—the idioms of modern bureaucratic democracy." This, too, could be a function of Orígenes trainings and projects. At the same time, it could also be argued that Mapuche employees learned important skills through working in these programs, which could be useful down the line for autonomy-related projects. While I think cynicism about intercultural policies is well placed, it is not impossible that they could lead to or support more autonomous practices—perhaps not in the short term but in the long term, although this depends on what happens to these programs under future administrations. On balance, however, these policies appear mostly about generating consent for neoliberalism and pacifying some sectors of the movement—which are, in the end, closely intertwined goals.

What were the consequences of neoliberal multicultural subject formation for Mapuche communities? That my attention is focused here mostly on indigenous actors is not to suggest that the conflicts did not have personal costs for colonos and other local elites. A former dean of a local university, who introduced me to several colono respondents, reflected that he knows these colonos to be good, honest people. The more interviews I did, the more

I saw this as a core dilemma. People may be good and honest, at least from the perspective of their own social group, but they may simultaneously be implicated in a system of extreme social inequality, in which they benefit at the expense of others. Daniel Hauri, who had seen buildings and crops on his farm go up in flames, broke down in tears during our interview. "One feels very badly," he said, "because one adores his homeland, and everything, and even more the place where one lives, where one was born, where his roots are, being a country as beautiful as ours, that these barbarities happen." It is painful, he said, because his ancestors worked hard to make the farm what it is and would not expect him to give up. He wondered how rich people could own huge expanses of land, and he could not even have his small farm to provide for his family. Adalberto, a young landowner in Malleco with only thirty hectares, said he had been assaulted and told to leave his land. He noted that the situation was painful "because one is born and raised in that place, but what are we going to do?" Several atentado victims mentioned emotional and psychological traumas, including fear, defenselessness, nervousness, psychosis, and paranoia.

Nevertheless, because neoliberal multiculturalism is a policy response focused on indigenous people, I focus here on its consequences for Mapuche communities. Although the Concertación's indigenous, intercultural, and multicultural policies created some benefits for Mapuche communities, in terms of material goods and services if not enhanced participation or political rights, the punitive response to Mapuche claims has taken a huge toll. During police raids people have been subject to verbal abuse, shot with rubber bullets and birdshot, punched or hit with weapons, and dragged across the ground. Limbs of young and old have been broken, and women have lost pregnancies. Their houses have been turned upside down, their windows broken. Police often carry away people's hunting rifles and other tools, claiming they are weapons. These measures only increase the sense of impotence and rage within the affected Mapuche communities. For a long time in several communities in conflict, police set up roadblocks where they stopped, searched, and registered the identities of all individuals and vehicles—a clear violation, observed Gaspar Curamil, a young Mapuche intercultural health worker in Malleco, of the freedom and sovereignty guaranteed to individuals in the Chilean constitution.

One respondent described ongoing police presence in the communities as psychological warfare, and indeed a report prepared by two workers at the Mapuche Health Program documented the psychological wounds in children produced by police raids and violence in the Mapuche community of José Guiñon, members of which were accused of terrorism in the Poluco Pidenco trial (Sepúlveda Navarro and Millaqueo Millapán 2004). These included mood swings, sleeplessness, hypervigilance, flashbacks, difficulty with concentration, and depression. In 2007 a community in Ercilla issued a formal complaint against police who had been going to the local schoolhouse to interrogate young children about their parents' activities. People worry their children will forever fear the police. Ramiro Raipillan, a young man from the community in conflict with Hauri, remarked that police protection of winka fundos contributed to the sense of insecurity in Mapuche communities. The police guarding Hauri's fundo harassed community members, stopped them on the road, and filmed their movements. Ramiro's own house had been raided at least seven times by the time I interviewed him. There are accounts of torture at the hands of police during interrogation, involving beatings, electrocution, and asphyxiation (Ray 2007). These forms of violence are violations of human and citizenship rights. National and international observers have argued that they demonstrate a lack of equal protection and a failure to respect the International Convention of the Child, other human rights agreements, and Chile's own Constitution and Indigenous Law.

The state violence associated with the conflicts was at times reminiscent of the dictatorship. The level of police violence I witnessed at Mapuche demonstrations on college campuses and marches through Temuco was shocking. It frequently struck me that the students did not start behaving violently until after the police began to throw tear gas and soak them with water cannons. It seemed straight out of the dictatorship, as did other tactics. For example, during the Illicit Terrorist Association trial in 2002 the evidence used against the defendants included their possession of ETA (the Basque separatist group) pamphlets, cassettes from Victor Jara (a Chilean folk musician tortured and killed shortly after the coup in 1973), and photos of Che Guevara (Terwindt 2004a). Similar types of evidence were used to "prove" subversive activity during the dictatorship. Several incidents of theft and harassment of Mapuche organizations and advocates have also been reported. A number of computers belonging to advocacy organizations have been stolen, and in 2002 the car of Jaime Madariaga, a defense lawyer in the Trial of the Lonkos, was set on fire in the center of Temuco.[19] Such violations represent the punitive, disciplinary face of neoliberal multiculturalism.

Police protection of colonos and maltreatment of the Mapuche also made clear whose side of the conflicts the state supported; colono claims were implicitly legitimated, even though no guilty parties had been found in most cases. But in fact, fundo owners and local elites were critical of what they considered an inadequate state response, claiming that the conflicts had grave economic consequences for the region, consequences they associated with their own economic interests. Iván Isler, a colono who had experienced numerous atentados, declared: "I cannot keep silent. I cannot, because I do not want to be an accomplice to a government that is destroying the region, destroying it deliberately." Agrobusinessman Franco LaPorte maintained that while the big businesses already in the region had remained, other sources of capital had distanced themselves. Angel Durán, who worked for a timber company's "good neighbor" program, complained that the region was losing tourism because foreigners were afraid to come to the region.

I could find no evidence to support these contentions. University administrator and former rightist politician Armando Torres said real estate ads had begun to include the expression "good neighbors"—code for no Mapuche—because no one wanted to buy land bordering Mapuche communities anymore. Nevertheless, he acknowledged: "The wheel of economic growth is greater than the capacity of the conflict to detain it." Elites' complaints about the economic impacts of the conflicts are reminiscent of the "suicide belt" discourse of the mid-1900s, a discourse rooted more in racial animosity than economic reality. In the years of this study as before, the Mapuche were a convenient scapegoat for broader economic changes affecting the region, even as they too suffered the consequences of those changes.

The criminalization of the conflicts, the refusal to consider the legitimacy of Mapuche complaints, and the use of dirty war tactics not only escalated the conflicts but also hardened Mapuche attitudes toward the state and elites. When I asked Jorge Millan what the future held for his community, he said they would keep fighting. Then he paused, laughed softly, and added: "Get Marcial out of there." "Now, yes?" I asked. "Now, yes." Ramiro Raipillan, too, said that after all this conflict, the community does want Hauri to leave. "We didn't start it. It was he who started this issue of hatefulness. We weren't the ones who asked for police protection to protect ourselves from him." The pain that has resulted, he explained, means that now the only thing they want is for him to leave and allow the community to move on. The hostility toward Hauri as well as the perpetrators of state violence is noted in graffiti in the town nearby: "[Hauri] son of a bitch," "Comrade Evo," "Murderer Cop," and "Lemun lives." Raipillan felt Hauri began to hate his family when they began to speak out in defense of their community. He thought Hauri's resentment of them for standing up to him as an old patron was at the root of his accusations against them. This account serves as a metonym for the larger conflict; Mapuche asserting agency in the face of oppression leads to a push back on the part of the colono, who seeks to discipline the Mapuche and keep them in their place. Whether it is fair to place Hauri and other colono

families as the stand-in for the invasion of their lands is questionable, but that
the Raipillans have reason to feel animosity toward the Hauris is much less
so. Ramiro's account is indicative of the broader pattern created by neoliberal multiculturalism, beyond the relationships between particular colonos
or Chileans and Mapuches: those Mapuche who refused to consent were subject to discipline and state violence.

Beyond criminalization, many Mapuche argue that the conflicts simply
point out a deeper problem. Antonio Queipul, a former member of the CAM
who now is active in the movement in other capacities, explains:

> The conflicts, for us, operate as a kind of opportunity to make visible the
> contradiction between a people that doesn't have rights, that doesn't have the
> opportunity for self-rule or self-determination, and colonial states that, let's
> say, without respect . . . occupy your territory, occupy your resources, con-
> taminate you, run over you, deny you the basic [necessities]. The transnational
> companies are the modern armies of the states. . . . Better said, the big transna-
> tionals today *are* the great empires that colonized us in the old days. That is, if
> in the old days the state, the Spanish empire did it, today Repsol, which is also
> Spanish, does it, or Endesa does it. And if, in the old days, the Italians colonized
> Argentina, today Benetton, which is also from Italy, does. If, in the old days . . .
> on the Chilean side it was [José] Bunster with his wheat business that financed
> the military occupation of the Araucanía, today Angelini does it through the
> timber companies, or a Matte through the paper and pulp companies. So in the
> end, it is as if the conflicts permit us, before our people, to open a reality and
> realize that they are symptoms of an illness and also so they understand that if a
> particular conflict is solved, the illness continues.[20]

Queipul pointed out the extent to which the interests of the state and corporations are tied up together; neoliberal multiculturalism is designed to address some indigenous claims without threatening those interests. In contrast,
only the recognition of Mapuche rights to self-determination, according to
Queipul's position, stands a chance of reversing the continuing dispossession
in the Araucanía. But clearly that recognition does not fit within the neoliberal multicultural model. As Mapuche, even if you do not engage in violent
tactics, you are not an authorized Indian if you insist on making such claims.

Mapuche and their advocates associated the conflicts with violations of
Mapuche rights. While rightists echoed the official Concertación position in
contending that the CAM and other Mapuche activists do not recognize the
rule of law, Mapuche and their advocates forced the question of *whose* rule of
law is at stake, emphasizing the inequalities that result from epistemic privi-

lege. Some suggested that in failing to adhere to the old *parlamentos* between the Spanish and the Mapuche, the Chilean state violates international law. In doing so, they insisted that Mapuche ways of making law are equally legitimate as Chilean ones. Others pointed out that the fact that it is almost exclusively Mapuche who have had the antiterrorist law thrown at them constitutes a lack of equal protection. Human Rights Watch and the Observatorio de Derechos Indígenas (2004) pointed to a lack of due process. The UN Special Rapporteur for Indigenous Rights, as well as the International Federation for Human Rights (FIDH), expressed similar concerns. That so many transnational organizations expressed doubts about whether Mapuche rights were being upheld, as opposed to whether Mapuche were violating the rule of law, is telling. It reinforces the extent to which the state's priority was to control Mapuche activism in the interest of capital, at the expense of the rights of indigenous citizens (Cuadra 2010).

Mapuche and their advocates argued that by reframing the political character of Mapuche claims as criminal acts, the state and elites ignored the historical and political-economic roots of the conflicts. In my view, one of the most important consequences of how the Concertación chose to address the conflict—through a dual approach that rewarded the indio permitido and castigated the "terrorist"—is that it made clear that *no* Mapuche are considered valid political interlocutors. Authorized indigenous behavior is narrowly defined and leaves little room for participation in political decision making or negotiation. Any other behavior is subject to repression, even if it does not involve extreme forms of protest. Mapuche status as a people with political rights is thus denied. But as young Mapuche scholar Eugenio Huentelican noted, neither was the movement capable of developing a coherent and consistent response to the Concertación. There is a lack of unity within the movement. It has been slow to develop alliances with other social actors and arguably lacks a coherent political project for change, suggesting that the neoliberal multicultural response has been successful in demobilizing Mapuche activism.

Chilean and colono farmers in the Araucanía often told me that they live "surrounded by Mapuche." But from the opposite perspective, it is Mapuche communities that have been encroached upon over time, first by the Spanish, then the Chilean military, colono settlers, and now huge timber plantations and other megadevelopment projects supported by the state. Chileans and Mapuche in the conflict zones exhibit a mutual distrust and an animosity that has reached the breaking point. I am unable to take a clear position on what is true or untrue in Chilean and Mapuche accounts of specific conflicts, but the conflicts indicate just how much is at stake for state, indigenous, and local elite actors in the neoliberal multicultural context. The chapters that follow explore how the historical and the contemporary; the local, national, and global; and the political, economic, and cultural inform state and societal responses to Mapuche claims.

Thus is the content of neoliberal multiculturalism in Chile. The particular form it takes is a product of Chile's goals in the global economy as well as the conflicts and Mapuche mobilization. Although neoliberal multiculturalism represents a shift in discourse and policy toward the indigenous, few Mapuche leaders and communities express full satisfaction with the paradigm. This is so for a number of reasons, among which the Concertación's failure to achieve formal recognition of indigenous peoples in the Constitution, the privileged status given to economic interests above indigenous rights, and the criminalization of Mapuche demands for the return of ancestral territory rank most highly. Interestingly, Mapuche and their advocates and local elites and colono farmers alike called for more government intervention to resolve the conflicts, though Mapuche and their advocates tended to emphasize recognition of indigenous rights and negotiation as the solution, whereas local elites and colonos might call for negotiation but generally supported criminalization.

Constructions of Mapuche as "authorized" and "terrorist" seem contradictory but ultimately sustain one another. That is, the punitive policies are part and parcel of neoliberal multiculturalism. Authorities emphasized the role the Mapuche could play in enhancing diversity in Chilean society but downplayed claims for recognition of their collective and cultural rights to territory and self-determination, particularly insofar as these were perceived to violate development goals and the property rights of timber companies and local elites. The Concertación had to balance the interests of a wide range of social actors in developing this paradigm, but it did not act as a disinterested mediator. Indeed, the Concertación generally advocated for big capital and against Mapuche communities as well as, it must be said, small- and medium-scale Chilean farmers (even though specific farmers were favored over the Mapuche in the context of the conflicts). In this way neoliberal multiculturalism took specific form given the particularities of Chilean history and social relations.

Before moving on, it is worth emphasizing the Concertación's reticence to consider the legitimacy of Mapuche claims, which are in their essence not simply social claims easily resolved by handouts and development-oriented solutions but political ones linked to collective rights to territory and autonomy. José Aylwin (2002) has observed the irony of Chile's simultaneous commitment to economic globalization and rejection of the globalization of indigenous rights. He asks how Chile can talk about Mapuche violations of the rule of law, when it does not respect their most basic rights as a people. For the Chilean state a colonizing logic remains strong: the Mapuche cannot be allowed to be actors in their own right, with the right to a form of knowledge, a way of being. Rather, they continue to be a problem to be solved, a rogue element to be controlled, objects to be acted upon. In this sense, as a racial project, neoliberal multiculturalism represents a continuation of the history of colonial dispossession. The state violence that is part of the negative side of neoliberal multiculturalism is punishment for Mapuche who refuse to consent to this form of governmentality, and it is legitimated by the Eurocentric racism that is at the base of the modern/colonial system.

The situation was not much better within civil society. Increasingly, sectors of the Mapuche movement seemed to recognize that in order to have success in meeting their goals, they needed alliances with non-Mapuche people. Most also recognized that some Chileans supported their cause. All the same, there was a feeling, as intercultural educator Pepe Morales observed as he reflected on the hardships the Mapuche faced as a result of the intervention of the timber companies, "that Chile doesn't see what we suffer."

The extent of this suffering became particularly clear to me when one day I sat in on a meeting between Andrés, a human rights worker, and Aurora Kalfupange, a young woman who had participated in the fight against the construction of the Ralco dam. They were meeting to discuss how to ensure that the state lived up to commitments it had made before the Inter-American Human Rights Commission. At the end of the meeting, Aurora asked Andrés what he, as an expert in these things, thought. "What is going to happen with us in the future? What is going to happen with us, the Pewenche? Are we going to disappear, or will we continue *en pie de guerra* [on the warpath]?" This question, so pure and sad, carried the legacy of centuries of oppression, invasion, and dispossession. Weeks later, I was talking to some friends and acquaintances in Santiago. Delfina, a wealthy elderly woman who voted for the Concertación, said she had heard the Pewenche affected by Ralco were now running a tourism project and making lots of money, because foreigners like that kind of thing. She, like so many others I had spoken to, seemed to want to prove the Pewenche were better off after Ralco was constructed. I told everyone present the story of Aurora and her question: "What will become of us, the Pewenche?" They were clearly affected by the story, and the conversation paused briefly, before Delfina shrugged, insisting that the nation's problems with electricity were too serious to have done anything else but build the dams in the Alto Bío-Bío. How to have Mapuche claims heard, understood, and legitimized—not just by the state but by Chileans in civil society—is a formidable struggle.

CHAPTER 5

LOCAL ELITES CONFRONT MULTICULTURALISM

How did the Chilean public construct the Mapuche in the context of the conflicts? Large-scale surveys give contradictory impressions. While some surveys conducted in major cities (all outside the conflict zone) indicated endorsement of Mapuche claims (IDEP 2003), others showed support for use of stronger tactics against Mapuche activists (Libertad y Desarrollo in La Tercera 2002). One study examining attitudes in ancestral Mapuche territory showed many Chileans there harbored beliefs that the Mapuche were lazy, violent, drunk, uncivilized, and primitive (Merino et al. 2004). Rejection of the Mapuche was not monolithic, of course, but negative attitudes about Mapuche claims prevailed, indicating that the ideologies and discourses that sustain systemic racism were alive and well, particularly in the Chilean South.

I explore these discourses through the lens of local elites (and to a lesser extent, state workers). How did these groups respond when confronted not just with growing Mapuche activism and social conflict but with the emergence of new ideas about multicultural citizenship that filtered down through state policy, political discourse, and the media? Earlier in this book, I have documented Mapuche and local elites' contested memories of the region. I have shown how epistemic privilege—encoded in law, policy, and social understandings—supports elite views while constructing Mapuche ones as invalid. I have demonstrated that although neoliberal multiculturalism is a set of transnational discourses and practices, it takes specific form given the particularities of Chilean history and social relations. Contemporary local-level attitudes and relationships, shaped by historical ideas about race and ethnicity as well as new state discourses and practices, are crucial to understanding how neoliberal multiculturalism plays out. Local practices and social imaginaries are not always an easy match with state-driven discourses. In fact, many local elites resisted multiculturalism to preserve their own interests. This resistance represents an effort to assert themselves as self-constructing subjects in a changing political context and is informed by long-standing ideas about race and belonging. Yet, despite this dominant trend, resistance to multiculturalism was not universal. Alternative discourses existed among some state employees and, of course, the Mapuche; they signal the possibility of distinct visions for the shared future of the territory.[1]

My analysis focuses on the responses of local elites to the Concertación's indigenous policies. Policy is a useful filter through which to view the persistence of social hierarchies and discriminatory views. Indeed, the historical moment of the Concertación governments provided a distinctive opportunity to see points of conflict between new state and transnational discourses and local "common-sense" understandings of race and belonging. Respondents' reactions to multicultural and indigenous policies thus reveal more than their views regarding those policies; they expose ingrained positions regarding the Mapuche and their claims for collective rights. Examining reactions to policy therefore has the potential to show how deep-seated ideas about race and social hierarchy interact with a changing sociopolitical context.

My sample does not account for potential differences among Chileans of different social classes.[2] Moreover, while the local elites I interviewed tended to be relatively well off economically, in terms of social status, they were not a monolithic group; some were extremely wealthy, whereas others were medium-scale farmers struggling with changes wrought by Chile's insertion in the global economy. Not *all* elites expressed *all* of the views discussed here, and some expressed them with what seemed to be a virulent anti-Mapuche racial hatred, whereas others did so with a sense of benevolent paternalism.[3] I seek to explore not who thinks what and where—a nearly impossible task as elites from different comunas frequently mixed various aspects of these often-contradictory narratives. Rather, I seek to delineate the *dominant* narratives that circulated among local elites regarding indigenous policies and to explore what this suggests about their receptiveness to multiculturalism and Mapuche demands. To be dominant, these views do not need to be held by all; the point is that their very existence—particularly among the elite—complicated the state's objectives in constructing "acceptable" ways of being indigenous as well as Mapuche efforts to envision an alternative future for the region.

In discussing indigenous policy and the Mapuche, respondents drew from, but did not strictly follow, the terrorist and authorized archetypes I examined in the previous chapter. Instead, four groups of narratives (or in Ruth Frankenburg's [1993] terms, "discursive repertoires") anchored discussions of indigenous policy in the region. These narratives centered on terrorism, culture, poverty, and integration. By calling the Mapuche "terrorists," local elites matched, and even fueled, the punitive policies associated with neoliberal multiculturalism. In contrast, the remaining narratives suggest a dominant (though not universal) rejection of multicultural values and demonstrate that purportedly vestigial views about racial hierarchies in the region are thriving in the context of the conflicts. Scholars including Mariella Bacigalupo (2007), Florencia Mallon (1996), Jean Jackson and Kay Warren (2005), and Robert Andolina, Sarah Radcliffe, and Nina Laurie (2005) have observed that questioning indigenous peoples' authenticity is a central means by which the state and elites counter and regulate indigenous claims. In the culture narratives, elites questioned the authenticity of those who purport to be Mapuche and suggested they did not deserve land and other privileges because they were corrupt and lacked a work ethic. In the poverty narratives, local elites reduced Mapuche cultural and collective claims to poverty, asserting that culture was a choice and indigenous policies were unfair to other poor Chileans. In the integration narratives, they sustained that for the Mapuche to survive, they must leave their culture and land claims behind and integrate into the Chilean nation. Although these narratives sometimes contradicted one another, they were not mutually exclusive in the discourse of those who used them. Ultimately, the narratives reinforced one another, justifying the dismissal of cultural and collective rights claims. The contradictions in how respondents talked about the Mapuche indicate the complex interplay of multicultural discourses filtering down from above, their own "selective remembrances" (Stern 2004) of times past and their fears and desires for the future. Taken together, these narratives suggest the obstinacy of local, sociohistorical understandings despite official efforts to promote multiculturalism.

Racism is built into social structure and reflected in the discourses, beliefs, and practices of individuals and communities (Bonilla-Silva 2001; Feagin 2006). In Chile the creation of new neoliberal and multicultural policies represented a shift in how racial understandings, always laden with power relations, were built into the state. Examining beliefs and attitudes in the Araucanía is essential to understand how this shift might reshape, harden, and even build on elites' understandings of the Mapuche. Looking at these narratives also shows racism is produced not just in a top-down manner but through everyday beliefs and interactions. Local histories and lived experience influence how people interpret national and transnational discourses and how they play out on the ground (Speed 2008). As Eduardo Bonilla-Silva (2001, 118) has pointed out, shifts in racialized social systems are always incomplete, as new "mechanisms and practices" of racism take time to become institutionalized and previous racial systems continue to impact upon people's lives.

Local elites' narratives are perhaps typical of settler societies and may seem archaic at times. Their continued use indicates the extent to which local elites felt established patterns of interaction and privilege were threatened in this changing context. I argue, however, that these narratives should not be understood as simply vestigial. Rather, elite narratives partially challenge and are partially functional to state neoliberal multicultural objectives. On the one hand, through the neoliberal multicultural project the state seeks to erase the most visible racism. Resistance from local elites, who reject even superficial, symbolic forms of recognition, threatens to derail that project. On the other hand, vocal citizens calling for the state to criminalize the Mapuche struggle and not recognize indigenous rights in a more meaningful, material way provided a justification to state and industry actors who viewed collective Mapuche claims as a threat to the neoliberal project. While elite resistance to symbolic recognition was a problem, as a new racial project, neoliberal multiculturalism does not reject and in fact enables some forms of local racism to thrive.

By acting in their own perceived self-interest, local elites reinforced the constructions of indigenous subjects disseminated at the national level in some ways but refused to consent to them in others. Their racial attitudes and practices were at times functional to the state's project, and at other times disruptive to it; in either case they contributed to the shape of neoliberal multiculturalism in Chile. To highlight the contested character of these narratives, I also incorporate some of the responses and visions of state workers as well as those of the Mapuche.

TERRORISM NARRATIVES

From colonos who rolled their eyes when I asked what the Mapuche had contributed to the Chilean nation, to an English missionary living in Chile since 1961 who made a biblical reference to "malicious hordes claiming territory" and argued that most *machi* were "doing the work of the devil," it was numbingly common to hear the Mapuche described in shockingly negative terms. But the advent of the conflicts revived an additional descriptor to apply to the Mapuche: terrorist. Owners of lands in conflict frequently used the word "terrorist" in describing their relations with the Mapuche. Their use of the term tied their experiences to contemporary global security discourses and hearkened back to the dictatorship, when the term was used to describe leftists.

Iván Isler, a colono and owner of land in conflict, reflected: "What is terrorism? It is nothing more than producing terror, threatening the people." He maintained that the CAM (the Coordinadora de Comunidades Mapuche en Conflicto Arauko-Malleko) was a group of "radicalized Mapuche Marxists" seeking to create an autonomous country. To achieve that goal, he told me, they were "harassing certain sectors" into abandoning their land and simultaneously decreasing its value so no one else would purchase it.[4] Máximo Ordóñez, a national-level politician seeking to create a resort on land in conflict, argued that the perpetrators did not necessarily seek to intimidate him on an individual level but were looking for publicity: "Terrorism is basically communicational. It seeks impact. It seeks diffusion."[5] It is worth remembering that in most cases, the incidents construed as "terrorism" involved violence against property. Contrary to international standards, Chile's antiterrorist law supports this association.

In an interesting twist, some landowners used the concept of human rights to defend their position. In calling for the government to take a stronger stand against the Mapuche, Ordóñez observed: "Terrorism is against human rights by essence, the Chilean Constitution says so." Colono Daniel Hauri was involved in a long-term conflict with a nearby community and had police protection on his land. Much despised for his heavy-handed ways, he was rumored to have held Mapuche at gunpoint on behalf of the military at the time of the coup. Over a few years prior to this interview, several buildings and crops on his land had been destroyed by fire. Hauri used a human rights frame to discuss his situation: "If they have need, give them what they want, but give them what is theirs, what it corresponds to the state to give, but don't do a hidden expropriation, coming to terrorize us, to take away our things. . . . Anything can be done, but with respect, and respecting the human rights, that come out so much these days, human rights, human rights, and we haven't had even half a human right, and that's what hurts most." The use of the human rights frame represents the co-optation of a concept usually associated with the Chilean Left. It is particularly incongruous because many local landowners were associated with paramilitary groups that contributed to toppling the Allende government and the subsequent human rights abuses. Hauri's reference to expropriation, which hearkens back to agrarian reform, is also striking. Like many others, Hauri opposed agrarian reform and cited it as the point at which these troubles started. While I do not want to minimize his suffering, his lack of reflexivity about his possession of land that was expropriated from the Mapuche and given to his ancestors is a sadly ironic selective remembrance.

Local elites and landowners considered it the responsibility of the government to resolve the conflicts and complained vehemently that the Concertación downplayed the conflicts. Fundo owners continuously mentioned feeling abandoned by the government. Ordóñez went furthest, suggesting that the government not taking responsibility for the conflicts was like telling the families of those who died on September 11, 2001, in the United States that they had to fight Al Qaeda themselves. Hauri and his family spoke of "unjust justice," a justice system that did nothing to support them. They felt the government was siding with the Mapuche, an assertion that, while it might have made sense to them, seemed incredible given the antiterrorism trials that were taking place at the time.

Fundo owners' claims that the government was not doing enough or was on the side of the Mapuche can be read as an effort to taunt the government into action. In fact, through their contacts at the national level, local elites in the conflict zones fueled the use of the antiterrorism law. It was Juan Agustín Figueroa, lawyer and minister of agriculture under Aylwin, who brought the first terrorism case before the courts for a fire set to a house and sixty hectares on his eighteen-hundred-hectare property. Figueroa was also named by Lagos as a member of the Constitutional Tribunal and was known to be close to many members of the Supreme Court (Narváez and Alonso 2006). His influence over the use of the antiterrorism law cannot be overestimated. Landowners were also recruited by Senator Alberto Espina to contribute to a Senate report which sustained not only that the Mapuche were a threat to public order and security but that the state was not doing enough to protect its citizens. National and regional agricultural associations publicly called for state action. Altogether, local elites and landowners in the Araucanía and their allies at the national level pressured the Concertación to take a harder line and criminalize the Mapuche struggle. Eventually they were successful;

in all terrorism trials that took place under Lagos, the state participated as a complainant on behalf of citizens. Elite landowners' use of the terrorist construction thus served to mobilize opposition to the Mapuche not just among their peers but among state authorities as well.

Despite their claims that the government was not doing enough, fundo owners almost universally supported the application of the antiterrorist law. Landowner Esteban Marcial had national connections and was involved in the early application of the law. He recalled that it was difficult to convince the government to agree to it. His position that the application of the law was necessary and legitimate reflected the value he placed on liberty and private property: "I don't accept being a second-class Chilean. I elect the place where I want to live, and I defend myself so that my liberty to elect the place where I want to live is respected. Now, I recur to the means of law that the state proportions to me. I don't go with armed patrols or bulldogs or a machine gun, but rather recur to justice when it corresponds."[6] Ulises Ibáñez, lawyer for a major timber company, also defended the use of the antiterrorist law. Ibáñez said it was the government that first asked for the application of the law in the Poluco Pidenco case because they had to fend for the interests of the collectivity—the collective right of the Chilean people to be safe. Such statements strike Mapuche and their advocates as ironic; no one recognizes the collective rights of the Mapuche, but the state defends the Chilean people's collective rights against them. It is hard not to see the application of the antiterrorism law as race-based, and the sense of fear and terror among the fundo owners as a racial fear of Mapuche uprising, similar to the fear that motivated the media and politicians to call for the subordination of the Mapuche in the second half of the nineteenth century.

Indeed, the terrorist construction intersects with historical factors. Not only was the antiterrorism law designed to control leftists under Pinochet, but in addition, fundo owners have on several occasions announced to the media their plans to organize self-defense brigades—essentially paramilitary organizations—to defend their property. The most commonly identified group is the Comando Trizano, named after Captain Hernán Trizano, who was charged with defending colono settlers at the end of the nineteenth century and known for his brutal behavior toward the Mapuche. The decision to use Trizano's name can be read as a symbolic reenactment of the original colonial assault. Altogether, elites' construction of the Mapuche as terrorists provided justification for the state's application of the antiterrorism law. While I have argued that local elites both consented to and encouraged the negative side of neoliberal multiculturalism (i.e., the consequences assigned to the *insurrecto*), it should be noted that this consent was less about neoliberal multiculturalism than it was about repressing Indians who had stepped out of line according to local norms that until recently were fully sanctioned at the national level. The following sections, in contrast, examine local elites' resistance to affirmative multicultural values.

CULTURE NARRATIVES

In defining "culture," social scientists often turn to Raymond Williams (1981, 13), who has called culture "the signifying system through which . . . a social order is communicated, reproduced, experienced, and explored." "Culture" involves collective meaning-making as well as the material practices that communicate and ground those meanings (Jordan and Weedon 1995). In the narratives that follow, local elites have challenged Mapuche meaning-making, particularly insofar as it identifies land as a central element of cultural survival. But they also talk about culture in a more colloquial way, insisting the Mapuche "don't have culture." By this they mean the Mapuche are less civilized than Chileans. Equating "culture" to Western norms and practices, elites suggest the Mapuche are corrupt and lack a work ethic and therefore do not deserve to have their demands addressed. Ideas about land, work, and culture are tightly enmeshed in these narratives, which together demonstrate that culture itself is a site of contention in southern Chile.

Delegitimizing the Association between Land and Culture

Land has long been a central demand of the Mapuche movement. Mapuche emphasize its importance as a material and symbolic resource. Land loss is linked to the extreme poverty faced by many communities. Land is seen as central to cultural continuity, because of the spiritual and cultural significance of particular territories to communities and because ongoing dispossession has resulted in high outmigration, which is associated with the loss of Mapuche identity and collective practices. But Mapuche especially emphasized that the land belonged to them historically; they were dispossessed of it following their military defeat and later as a result of shady practices on the part of *winka* landowners. Some Mapuche framed their demands for land in terms of the collective right to territory, reflecting a desire to reestablish the Mapuche nation. The Concertación's land policy was a response to these claims. It was also the most criticized aspect of the Indigenous Law. Many Mapuche considered the policy insufficient. Local elites and some state workers, in contrast, rejected the idea of returning land to the Mapuche or subsidizing its purchase at all. Disputes over land policy get at the crux of debates over indigenous authenticity, dependency, and rights in the context of globalization.

The elites I spoke with sought to disassociate land and culture, claiming it was the Mapuche obsession with land that led to high levels of poverty in their communities. These narratives brought home the conflict between individual and collective conceptions of rights. Indigenous demands encompass claims for individual civil, political, and social rights as well as rights that are collective in character and differentiate the indigenous from other citizens, such as the right to language, cultural practices, collective representation, territory, and self-determination. Many elites considered collective aspects of Mapuche claims a threat to their own interests. Recognizing the Mapuche right to territory, for example, might have a direct impact on elite landownership and economic power. Some elites were opposed to collective rights on principle; a commitment to neoliberal values led them to privilege personal liberties, and private property in particular, above all other claims. As a result, they worked hard to delegitimize the claim that the Mapuche as a people had a right to the land. This involved questioning the cultural (and thus collective) basis for Mapuche claims.

Some local elites as well as their rightist counterparts at the national level opposed the land policy with economic arguments. They criticized the Concertación for "tying the Mapuche to the land" and promoted the idea that "it is possible to be Mapuche without land." Reflecting a neoliberal developmentalist position, they believed distributing land subsidies in the context of a globalized capitalist economy was inappropriate. For example, Carla Becker, who worked for a rightist think tank in Santiago but was raised in the region, suggested that by providing land subsidies, the state was repeating the historical wrong of deceiving and disrespecting the Mapuche. Her rationale was that having more land would not improve their economic situation because today agriculture can only succeed on a large scale. Becker's logic reduced Mapuche land claims to their material aspect, ignoring their ancestral character. In addition, she seemed to accept as unproblematic the concentration of land (and wealth) that results from the global economic model she advocated. In a related argument, Manuel Borja, who headed a regional agriculturalist association, suggested that rather than land, what the Mapuche needed was "direct assistance," meaning socioeconomic subsidies. This was a common position among local elites, though it often seemed rooted less in concern for Mapuche well-being than in their own self-interest. For Becker and others, opposition to the land policy was rooted in a belief system that privileged neoliberal values (Chile's competitiveness in the global market, private property). In contrast, while Borja opposed returning Mapuche lands, he argued in favor of economic policies that would lessen the impacts of global trade on the region's small- and medium-scale farmers. In both cases, land clearly had material worth for elites, which is why they sought to keep it out of Mapuche hands, even as they claimed to have their best interests at heart. These narratives demonstrated continuity with mid-twentieth-century apprehensions that Mapuche communities were a "suicide belt" impeding development in the region.

Despite these economic arguments, elites more often based their criticisms of land policy on culture, or what it meant to be Mapuche. Conveniently, these cultural critiques defended elites' economic interests. For example, Armando Torres, a university administrator and former politician, denied that land was a central part of Mapuche identity, repeating the common argument that they were hunters before the Pacificación, not farmers. Angel Durán, who worked for a timber company's "good neighbor" program, argued it was wrong to give the Mapuche land unless "they are really, typically Mapuche," in which case it was appropriate to create "development areas" but "only if they want to live as they should." Others, like Máximo Ordóñez, maintained that the land policy rewarded the "wrong" Mapuche: "the orchestrators of this conflict."[7]

All of these arguments suggest that Mapuche who actively claim land are somehow not authentic: either they are not really farmers, not Mapuche who live in the old way, or not good Indians. In questioning the authenticity of the Mapuche, these respondents are working with implicit dichotomies. As Jean Jackson and Kay Warren (2005) have observed, indigenous peoples' use of anything modern, Western, or new leads to accusations of inauthenticity. The politicization of culture by indigenous movements, they suggest, opens them up to accusations of falseness or lack of adherence to tradition. For these elites it seems an authentic (and "good") Indian was a passive one and "real" Mapuche culture involved living as elites imagined they did in the past.[8] Such views ignore that culture is ongoing, always changing and being created (Mallon 1996; Wade 1997). They assert a monolithic and static view of culture in order to deny contemporary Mapuche claims.

Elites argued that Concertación policy conflated culture with land and was therefore wrongheaded. Torres couched this view in a broader critique of Mapuche ways of life: "The big drama is when they want to be Mapuche in the old way, living on the land, having some oxen, planting little. But at the same time, they want to enjoy the benefits . . . of global society." The solution, he felt, was to convince more Mapuche that it was possible to "maintain aspects of identity doing something distinct from working the land." He insisted that it was leftist academics and politicians who associated the Mapuche with land, not necessarily the Mapuche themselves. Doing so, Torres claimed, was "to condemn the Mapuche to poverty, because the land doesn't provide." He disagreed with Durán's opinion that people who lived in "the old way" deserved land. Yet Torres too insinuated the inauthenticity of those who seek to live in "the old way" and simultaneously desire to be modern. He considered it essential to break the association of Mapuche culture with land, suggesting that this association—rather than systemic, historical inequalities and dispossession—led to Mapuche poverty. In asserting the possibility of maintaining Mapuche identity without having land, Torres argued against essentializing Mapuche culture. But at the same time, he summarily delegitimized all land claims and reduced the multitude of factors that led to a situation in which more than half of all Mapuche resided in urban areas by the early 2000s to the notion that "the land doesn't provide." Some Mapuche also critiqued the focus on land, but for different reasons: they maintained that political demands like autonomous territory and self-government were more likely to advance the collective cause than focusing on land alone.

Other local elites believed the Concertación was giving in to unrealistic demands that disregarded the passage of time and felt this created an unhealthy dependency on the state. Agrobusinessman Guillermo Hanssen found demands for ancestral territory "infantile" and compared them to him going to northern Europe and demanding the land his ancestors possessed in the Middle Ages. In his view, to claim ancestral territory is to refuse "to recognize the development of humanity." Gastón Muñoz, the self-styled historian from Malleco, said these demands were even more untenable because the Mapuche "continue overpopulating," so giving the Mapuche land today is not like returning it to the people from whom it was taken (which he estimated to have totaled ten in his comuna). Muñoz agreed that the policy created dependency, and the Concertación's attempts to change "the misery they have surely lived" were inappropriate.

He explained: "They have wanted to live that way. Because everyone is the constructor of their own destiny, no? So they have lived, obviously, in a *ruka*, without water, without this, without this other thing, but it is because they have wanted to live that way all their lives. So the state, in my view, is committing an error by giving them land." Part of this error is not giving them machinery to work the land, he conceded. However, in a common narrative about the poor throughout the world, Muñoz concluded that the state is too "assistentialist." (*Asistencialismo* refers to a social system dominated by reliance on state subsidies and programs.) The Mapuche, he said, are "the same as the child who asks for everything from the father." Here we see one way in which Mapuche poverty and culture become entangled in the dominant narratives: Mapuche should not receive land because it fosters dependency, and in any case, Mapuche poverty is a product of personal choice (or perhaps, of collective, cultural choice). Rather than making demands on the Chilean state or society, Mapuche simply need to grow up and assume responsibility for their condition. Comments like these reflect positivist notions of progress as well as an ethos of individual responsibility. Part of elites' opposition to land policy was a critique of the Concertación based on ideological differences. Yet their rhetoric also revealed their opposition to Mapuche claims, in terms of either the authenticity of those making them or what they perceived to be a false association between culture and land.

Some municipal employees also criticized the land policy, but they were more likely to focus on the type of land the government purchased on behalf of the Mapuche. For example, Miguel Angel Carrizo, head of rural development in a Malleco comuna, objected to purchasing land in places that lacked water because of the limited possibilities for agricultural production. Ximena Ortíz, who worked for INDAP in Malleco, placed some of the blame for these purchases on the communities themselves, because they have a say in the lands they buy. Speaking of the community I visited with her and fellow-INDAP employee Gonzalo Arellano (discussed in chapter 1), she said: "I don't know [about] their decisions sometimes. The attachment they have with the land is so great that they bought land that is practically [only good] for timber usage." Sometimes communities buy such land because it borders on land they already own, or because it has historical or spiritual significance for them. Moreover, buying elsewhere requires picking up and moving, often far from home, in a process that may result in the division of the community, as some families stay in the original location (see Mallon 2005).

Mapuche state workers generally had a more complex understanding of communities' relationship to the land. Gaspar Curamil, a young intercultural health facilitator in Malleco, drew a distinction between purchasing land for use and doing so to reconstruct Mapuche territory. Speaking specifically about Temucuicui's purchase of the Fundo Alaska, he said:

> There are many winkas who say, "Why did the Mapuche buy hills? What are the hills going to do for them?" . . . [From] a productive development logic [one] could think the same thing, if, of course, they can't produce wheat, they can't produce crops. Animals, maybe. But why do they want the hills? . . . Think, here I am talking about a different worldview. I, the other day, talked with an old person from the community, and I also visited that sector and saw with my own eyes how everything that is natural is emerging anew, the trees, land, and water alike, everything is sprouting anew. So . . . here there is clearly a cultural intentionality. Here the people didn't struggle for a productive [in the economic sense] reason. Here the people struggle to rescue their space and territory. So the people fought for a completely cultural, territorial, reason.

Curamil's words indicate the symbolic importance of reclaiming the land. Most local elites rejected this logic. Instead, they opposed land policy mostly on the basis of culture, asserting that the Mapuche *by culture* did not know how to work the land, doubting the authenticity of those making land claims, and altogether attempting to dismantle the association between land and culture. This narrative demonstrates not only their rejection of the land policy but also their skepticism about Mapuche claims.

Sometimes local elites went beyond simply challenging the association between Mapuche culture and land, instead contending that they had no culture to speak of at all. When I asked what he thought of the intercultural policies sponsored by the government, elderly Malleco landowner and businessman Simon Baum answered: "What culture? I wonder what culture?! They talk about culture. Culture for me implies certain basic understandings. Of what? Well, to start, the oldest things: a religious belief. . . . [The Mapuche] practically didn't have religious beliefs. Now what [else] could they [use to defend] themselves?! Culture? Language? Now [these] Mapuche medicines are appearing. These are tricks to keep them going." In contrast to the government, which integrated aspects of Mapuche culture into intercultural health and education programs and even sponsored annual Mapuche New Year celebrations, local elites like Baum asserted that the Mapuche were inventing culture in order to claim a right to land and special benefits. They were trying to recover language or inventing words, celebrating ceremonies they had not before, and all of this was seen as manipulative by local elites. Whereas Baum asserted that the Mapuche never really had a culture to speak of, others said the Mapuche had *lost* their culture, not because of the history of dispossession and discrimination, but because they were not interested in maintaining traditions or teaching their children their language. All of this mattered to them because if the Mapuche do not have a culture, if they are the same as other Chileans, then how could they deserve rights as a people?

Deservedness, Corruption, and Work

In a second set of narratives, interrelated with those explored above, local elites and several state workers asserted that the Mapuche had corrupt leaders and no work ethic, both of which cast doubt on their deservedness of land and other resources. As with the critiques of land policy, these narratives entail a negative appraisal of Mapuche culture. In the first case, the authenticity of Mapuche leaders is called into question. In the second, the perceived absence of a work ethic represents a cultural shortcoming that makes Mapuche undeserving of state support.

Ximena Ortíz thought it was "totally valid" for the Mapuche to claim their rights, but she criticized some leaders for using their communities to get benefits and then keeping them all for themselves. The notion that some people "live off being leaders" is very common. Angel Durán commented: "They [Mapuche leaders] live very well. They take advantage of the situation. They change clothes, today they go around in the latest model pickup truck, they go by car, they have *estancias* [estates] outside of Chile, they buy land in Valdivia." Bruna Pentz, a middle-aged woman from Cautín whose family had owned a prominent business in the region, related a rumor that Aucan Huilcaman, leader of the Consejo de Todas las Tierras, went to Europe, received two million dollars in donations, brought one million back to Chile, and put the other in a Swiss bank account. Others argued that leaders are not authentically Mapuche because they got fancy ideas in exile during the dictatorship, or because they travel abroad and network with other indigenous peoples. Such assertions, commonly made about indigenous leaders throughout Latin America, imply that Mapuche leaders and their followers lack an ethical culture and thus are unworthy of government support.

But the concept of work was the major filter through which elites and state workers talked about Mapuche deservedness. Carol Nagengast (1994, 123) has observed: "The discourse of work has historically been an effective instrument of state control." She makes explicit the relationship between work and culture under capitalism: "The unproblematized equation in the capitalist world of work with society and culture entails a compulsion to represent political, cultural, or ethnically subordinate dissidents as the negation of the proper working self. So represented, we cannot help but take their Otherness personally." Some respondents blamed the purported Mapuche lack of work ethic on individual character. In this sense, work ethic was an important element in the distinction between "good" and "bad" Mapuche. More often, though, "work" was used to express hesitations about Mapuche culture, to justify their impoverished condition, to suggest they are undeserving of government assistance, and ultimately to delegitimize their demands for land and other reparations. Jorge Luchsinger explained why, in his view, returning land to the Mapuche is a worthless endeavor: "The Indian has never worked. The Mapuche is predatory, he lives from what nature supplies, he doesn't have intellectual capacity, he doesn't have will, he doesn't have economic means, he doesn't have income. He doesn't have anything" (in Corvalán 2005, 17). For Luchsinger, if they do not work, they do not deserve the land they are reclaiming.

"Lazy" was one of the most frequent descriptors to come up in my interviews with non-Mapuches. When I told an English missionary who had lived in Cautín for several decades that I thought the situation in Malleco was unjust, given the encroachment of the timber companies and the lack of water in many communities, she only replied: "Yes, but you also have to change their laziness." Such assertions were often accompanied by anecdotes to prove the point. After a long tirade, in which she described various Mapuche faults, Nilda, the wife of a man who was mayor of a Malleco comuna during the dictatorship, added: "And the other thing is, they are lazy." She told about a time she and other women involved in the Centros de Madres went to a Mapuche community, now involved in a major land dispute with a colono landowner, to teach the women to knit.[9] All the men were standing around watching. She asked, "And the men, don't they have something else to do?" Some of the men left, but most stayed, so she added: 'If all of these men hang around, we're going to give them knitting needles! Go do something, don't you have a fence to fix, planting to do? At least cut some of these weeds that are all over the place!'[10] Most of the men left, but one stayed behind to "make sure we weren't inciting rebellion among the women." As Francesca Polletta (2006) might put it, personal stories like this one served to "harden" differences between Mapuche and colonos. Through repetition they took on a mythic character over time, becoming, for the individuals who told them, the ultimate proof of Mapuche unwillingness to work to improve their position. As in Nilda's anecdote, gender was a frequent component of such stories: non-Mapuche respondents drew a distinction between lazy and abusive Mapuche men, and Mapuche women, who were long-suffering and tireless at toil.

In a link to the argument that government programs generated dependency, others suggested that these programs also produced laziness. When I visited the Hauri family, we drove from one of their fundos to another, a short distance away. On the way, Daniel and his grown daughter, Renata, told me I would notice whose land was whose because Mapuche land was messy and untended. As we passed some Mapuche men building a fence at the side of the road, Daniel and his daughter joked that the men dig once and rest for fifteen minutes. Later, one family member asserted that government benefits caused this laziness: "If they lack something, they go ask for it at the municipality, and they give it to them. . . . So, it is like they maybe become accustomed to donations, to always be given [things]. . . . And they are becoming, perhaps, a people that doesn't work, maybe lazy, and losing their identity in that sense." Culture is not absent from these observations. For example, Miguel Angel Carrizo blamed an "assistentialist culture" for Mapuche laziness rather than an "assistentialist state." He said the Mapuche want things to be given to them, and demand a lot, but if they have to work to get it, they resist.

Mapuche also frequently critiqued the state for being assistentialist, but their point was different. Longtime leader Victorino Manque claimed the state did not support projects that exercised or worked toward autonomy, adding: "This assistentialist system, of receiving crumbs, is the most harmful and perverse for the Mapuche. That is not development, in any way. It is just to continue with colonialism." Although Manque's critique may seem similar to that of elites, it comes from a substantially different political worldview, one that challenges the colonialist system that benefits elites at the expense of the Mapuche. From this perspective, dependency is a *goal* of indigenous policies. Mapuche teacher Pepe Morales likewise criticized assistentialist Concertación policies for failing to address "the root issues" of dispossession and self-determination. He argued that indigenous policy reflected the general trend of policy in Chile, inherited from the dictatorship and "very functional for transnational corporations." These views suggest cognizance of the objectives of the neoliberal multicultural project.

The notion that Mapuche do not have a work ethic was consistently linked to their lack of deservedness. Perhaps the most repeated assertion in my interviews was that the Mapuche *dejan la tierra botada* (leave the land messy and abandoned), which was taken as proof that they were lazy and land policy was wasteful. Guillermo Hanssen observed that his fundo was sold to a Mapuche community in 2003 and soon "will have been left to waste [*botado*] for four years, with no activity. Zero." Although it was sometimes the case that Mapuche did leave land uncultivated, local elites rarely delved into why this was the case. Sometimes, even after receiving land through CONADI (the Corporación Nacional de Desarollo Indígena, the National Indigenous Development Agency), Mapuche lacked the capital to invest in seeds and equipment necessary to plant crops. Many also were obliged to seek out day labor or other sources of income. By attributing these problems to laziness endemic in Mapuche culture, elites could wash their hands of responsibility for the situation and simultaneously declare Concertación policy ineffective.

A related assertion was that the Mapuche did not work well together. Many Chileans seemed to believe that to be indigenous is to work communally. Because the Mapuche did not necessarily do so, Chilean respondents felt giving them state resources was a waste; the Mapuche would just fight over resources and projects would come to no productive end. The stereotype about communal work served the argument that Mapuche communities were not really traditional communities, once again calling the authenticity of contemporary Mapuche into question. Here again, "culture" entered into arguments against indigenous policy. Not only did something negative in Mapuche culture (or perhaps nature, as the two were often conflated) make them lazy, but Mapuche who receive benefits must not be authentically indigenous because they do not work together well. This notion was used against the Mapuche despite the extreme individualization in Chilean society, the assignation of state resources on an individual basis, and the lack of historical evidence to suggest that the Mapuche ever worked land communally.

As with other narratives, some respondents viewed the issue of work differently. A few Mapuche and their advocates tried to reframe this narrative by suggesting the Mapuche were not lazy, but rather only used what they needed and did not seek to acquire more and more like winkas did. Although it is possible to read it as an attempt to assert alternative values in contrast to the accumulation prevalent in dominant society, this narrative is somewhat problematic. It essentializes the Mapuche as uninterested in consumption and concedes that they do not work as much as they could. Moreover, it fails to address the role of dispossession, systematic inequality, and development policies in creating a situation in which Mapuche work extremely hard to achieve basic subsistence, which just looks like poverty to outside observers, who then turn around and blame that poverty on lack of work ethic. Indeed, other Mapuche altogether disputed the notion that their people lacked a work ethic, suggesting that if they did not work, it was because they lacked the conditions to do so. Ramiro Raipillan, from the community in conflict with Hauri, was frustrated with the limited options available for the land the community had reclaimed. Given the conditions of the land, he said, the only options were raising livestock (which they could not afford) or timber cultivation (which they rejected because of the negative effects of the industry in the region). They were aware that many winkas thought they were lazy and wasting the land, but they decided the best strategy for the time being was to try to improve the water sources to help native species return.

Andrés Lonkomilla, who is Mapuche and worked for a municipal agricultural program funded by INDAP in Malleco, strongly felt the Mapuche worked hard. Like Raipillan, he insisted on looking at the broader power structure, suggesting that even if they had land, many communities were so lacking in economic resources that there was not much they could do to work it. The greatest needs of the families he worked with, he said, were "to figure out how to get through the month . . . they seek out ways in which to survive." Speaking specifically of two communities involved in some of the most extreme conflicts, Lonkomilla said: "We were working there. . . . Later, two or three years ago, we left the sector. And we couldn't do much more for them anyway, because—it is complicated—because they needed something bigger, I don't know, [bigger] than us." When I asked if leaving the sector had anything to do with the conflicts, Lonkomilla responded that, to the contrary, the issue was that INDAP had funded the program to the extent that they met particular objectives. In these communities advances were few. The communities could not access credit, did not have water (a situation made more acute by nearby timber plantations), and could not afford to dig deep wells, even with a government subsidy covering part of the cost. People there survived by selling firewood, which they often took from gorges where there were still some native trees, but chopping down the trees contributed to the desiccation of the gorges.

Lonkomilla described a typical situation of poverty becoming a deeper and deeper hole, made more severe by the impacts of neoliberal policy. Of about sixty families participating in the project, at most ten were able to engage in productive work: "The rest didn't have the conditions for the work. That is, soil, water, I don't know, there were minimal things they didn't have. So if they didn't have enough to eat, even less were they going to be able to work agriculture. They wanted a project, but they wanted the money from the project to buy food, not to plant something that a couple of months later would give them something. They had necessities right now." What INDAP wanted were "commercial results. . . . They want the people to do productive things and to sell, to get into the market." Lonkomilla's team realized this was going to be impossible. The best they could hope for was to create a situation in which the communities could feed themselves. He noted an added contradiction: while INDAP wanted communities to access the market, the municipality just wanted people to not come around asking for help. Lonkomilla's account disputes the notion that Mapuche are lazy and also makes clear that poverty is of central concern for many communities. At the same time, these particular communities were associated with the Coordinadora Arauko-Malleko (CAM), suggesting that poverty-related concerns are not easily disentangled from claims for territory and other collective rights.

Despite the existence of some alternative discourses, the dominant narratives about land, deservedness, and work are a critique of Mapuche culture, an assertion that on some level it is because of their cultural inferiority that the Mapuche are poor. They do not deserve special policies, and conversely such policies are a waste of state resources. By critiquing Mapuche culture, local elites in a sense recognized the Mapuche as a collectivity. Ultimately, though, their criticisms signaled resistance to multiculturalism as well as claims for collective rights.

THE POVERTY NARRATIVES

In a contrasting group of narratives, local elites contended not that the Mapuche were culturally inferior but simply poorer. By emphasizing ethnicity rather than poverty, they suggested, indigenous policies concentrate on the wrong issue. Because the real issue is poverty, local elites argued, special policies for the Mapuche were unfair to other poor citizens. What the Mapuche really needed, they suggested, were equal opportunities and freedom of choice. The same individuals who viewed Mapuche culture as inferior also frequently said poverty was the important issue, not culture. Despite this contradiction, the poverty narratives contained a cultural critique: insisting on poverty as the explanation implicitly called into question the legitimacy of Mapuche claims based on cultural difference.

It Is Only Poverty

While most Mapuche respondents and some state workers associated economic need in the communities with the history of colonialism and racism against the Mapuche people, many elites sustained that there was little cultural difference between Mapuche and non-Mapuche. Any difference that existed was socioeconomic in character, they felt, and culturally specific programs were therefore unnecessary. This narrative is connected to, and facilitates, the sameness narrative discussed in chapter 2, in which elites contended that before the emergence of contemporary Mapuche demands for cultural and collective rights, Mapuche and Chileans lived together peacefully and were the same. It exists on the left and the right, although on the right it was more often used as fodder for doing away with indigenous policies altogether, whereas on the left, it was justification for not addressing issues of recognition. During the Lagos government, for example, Interior Minister José Miguel Insulza declared that Mapuche land issues were a class problem with roots in the dictatorship (Bell 2001). It makes some sense that elites and politicians on the left would say this, as social class has long been a banner issue for them. Politicians who came of age in the 1960s and 1970s are likely to have been influenced by a Marxist perspective that saw class revolution as the solution to all social inequalities. The belief that Mapuche demands are rooted in poverty was reflected in much of the Concertación's indigenous policy (Richards 2004).

But it was stranger to hear this argument coming from rightist political and economic elites, who never before seemed to express much concern about economic inequality. To some extent, both groups ignored the complex intersections among economic poverty, racial and ethnic discrimination, and the historical disregard for indigenous rights. Nevertheless, if we take them on their word, it is puzzling that elites disliked the Concertación's policies, which were focused overwhelmingly on poverty alleviation. Ultimately, it seems they simply did not like these policies because they were for the Mapu-

che. Any policies that might challenge dominant racial hierarchies by privileging the Mapuche were highly suspect to local elites. This was especially
true when they involved a resource as symbolically and materially important
as land, but respondents also complained about intercultural programs as well
as indigenous scholarships and development funds.

As quick as rightist elites were to attribute the conditions behind Mapuche claims to poverty, in most cases they were still reluctant to advocate
significant redistribution. For example, although he believed Mapuche communities needed "direct assistance," agriculture association leader Manuel
Borja seemed to suggest that leaving the land behind was a better solution,
asserting that when Mapuche moved to the cities, they lived relatively well.
But according to the 2006 CASEN (Encuesta de Caracterización Socioeconómica Nacional, the National Socioeconomic Characterization Survey,
conducted by MIDEPLAN [Ministerio de Planificación, the Ministry of
Planning]), 18.4 percent of the urban indigenous were poor or indigent, versus 13.6 percent of nonindigenous. In rural areas the figures were 20.2 percent
for indigenous and 10.8 percent for nonindigenous.[11] Thus indigenous urban
dwellers are only slightly less likely to be poor than their rural counterparts
and are significantly poorer than nonindigenous urban residents. Borja's assertion draws attention away from the causes of poverty that lead to Mapuche
migration, including colonial dispossession and ongoing capitalist intervention in their ancestral territory. By blaming the "Mapuche problem" on poverty without reckoning with these complexities, elites elided the ways they
benefited from Mapuche subordination.

Martin Rahm, the lawyer and regional politician whose family lost several hundred forested hectares to arson, compared indigenous identification
cards provided by CONADI to pass cards in apartheid-era South Africa.
Drawing attention to race or ethnicity, he said, led to problems:

> I was always in disagreement with the Indigenous Law because I believe people
> shouldn't be catalogued or divided by ethnic group. I believe that precisely
> Chile had the luck of not having racial or ethnic problems. There weren't racial
> or ethnic problems, just as there weren't, fortunately, religious ones, which are
> destructive [for] nations. Because we've seen in Europe how they've destroyed
> Yugoslavia, how it was destroyed by ethnic problems. Prosperous countries, old
> countries, not countries in formation. And here we have introduced a strange
> element brought from the outside, I insist, in which we are cataloguing people
> by ethnic group.

Although Rahm was somewhat inclined to invest state resources in helping
the poor ("without considering their gender or racial condition"), he rhe-

torically conflated multiculturalism with segregation and political upheaval. Similar to elites' discussion of the causes of the conflicts, Rahm saw multiculturalism as an outside force and was suspicious of it.

It is interesting that in Chile, where class conflict featured so prominently in the mid- to late twentieth century, conservative elites now turn to the concept of poverty to explain away indigenous demands. It seems as if talking about poverty (and hence social class) is somehow less threatening than addressing race, ethnicity, and nation. Neoliberalism and the legacy of the dictatorship may have something to do with this. Not only did the elite live through a major class-based transformation in their society and come out relatively unscathed, but the neoliberal model has effectively limited the possibilities for change—Chilean rightists can support some policies for the poor, because the sectors of the Left with access to political power, who also bought into the neoliberal model, are no longer likely to propose a fundamental restructuring of society that might threaten elite interests. Under neoliberalism, addressing poverty does not mean redistribution; it means establishing some ameliorative policies, providing "opportunity" and making a few "projects" available. Mapuche claims, on the other hand, *are* considered a threat to elite interests. So like the Concertación, rightist elites reduced Mapuche demands to class, but unlike the Concertación, they felt even a lukewarm appreciation for diversity had little place in policy. Elites might have insisted that poverty was the problem in part simply because they did not want to admit the legitimacy of Mapuche claims for collective and cultural rights.

Some respondents supported their focus on poverty with the argument that seeing difference itself amounts to discrimination. This perspective is similar to the "color-blind racism" discussed by Eduardo Bonilla-Silva (2001). As Miguel Angel Carrizo put it: "Just saying they are different is discrimination." The resistance to acknowledging difference sometimes bordered on the pathological. César, a middle-aged Mapuche leader, told me what he remembered from the military coup, which occurred when he was about seven years old. His teacher, he recalled, announced to the class: "From now on, there will be neither rich nor poor, we are all the same." This story suggests that as with the Mapuche claiming rights on the basis of difference, opponents of Allende may have felt the Unidad Popular's naming of social inequality was the problem, rather than inequality itself. Perhaps this reluctance to recognize (or more accurately, to do something about) class difference in the past has shaped reluctance to recognize the Mapuche. Again, I am struck by the role of the power to define—to be a knower, to be the creator of knowledge. If the subjects of the social world say everyone is the same, and it becomes ingrained in common sense, then so be it.

I do not suggest that non-Mapuche assertions of simultaneous sameness and difference were just about deception. After all, even as the Mapuche demanded rights related to cultural difference, they also demanded human rights (to a fair trial, to be treated with dignity, for example) that imply commonality with non-Mapuches. For both groups assertions of sameness and difference worked dialectically. But whereas the Mapuche used the dialectic to claim rights not just as citizens but based on their status as a people (claiming equality but specificity), colonos and other local elites used the concepts of sameness and difference to maintain social inequality and marginalization (claiming sameness to deny rights) and perpetuate their own relative local power (using cultural difference to disparage).

Multiculturalism as a discourse stakes a claim on culture; the state's adoption of policies that recognize cultural difference, however inadequately, stands in contrast to local elites' insistence that the "Mapuche problem" is one of poverty. We might think seeing Mapuche issues as poverty-related would lead local elites to support Concertación policies, which were focused on poverty-resolution with relatively minor attention to interculturality and diversity. Yet that was not generally the case, perhaps partly because most local elites sympathized with the political right, but more important, because they saw Mapuche culture as negative and recognition of collective and cultural claims as a threat to their own interests.

Fairness

Many non-Mapuche understood indigenous policy not as recompense for historical wrongs but as benefits the Mapuche received simply because they were Mapuche. They thus challenged indigenous policy on the basis that it was not fair to poor Chileans. Much of the rural population, both Mapuche and non-Mapuche, was poor, they emphasized, and providing the Mapuche with special programs and resources amounted to discrimination against the non-Mapuche. This was one of the most common themes brought up by non-Mapuche respondents, including campesinos, state employees, local elites, and elites with national connections.

Respondents asserted that special programs for the Mapuche were responsible for generating hatred against the Mapuche and conflicts with their neighbors. For example, when I asked Iván Isler if he thought discrimination against the Mapuche existed, he alleged that "Aylwin created discrimination with the Law," which gave the Mapuche special access to resources, and as a result, there was "much more hate" than before. Hernán Rohrer likewise argued that the new policies were creating hatred of the Mapuche, which did not exist before, "when everyone was the same." State workers frequently mentioned that indigenous policy discriminated against Chileans, arguing that poor Chileans did not have the same access to subsidies. Elvira Sandoval, who directed community development in a Malleco comuna, added: "There are people who say, 'Now we have to change our last name to get benefits.' What does this reflect? Today, if you're indigenous, you have it all."

Although it is true that the nonindigenous poor do not receive the same benefits as the Mapuche, rather than advocating that all poor receive these services, many elites seemed to be saying the solution was to do away with the policies altogether. This narrative was not couched in terms of better redistribution of wealth; it was couched in terms of unfairness. Even a high authority in the Catholic Church went so far as to suggest the rural Mapuche were "in a better situation than non-Mapuche campesinos." Nevertheless, a look at the CASEN statistics demonstrates that although the gap between indigenous and nonindigenous has narrowed, the indigenous as a group are still worse off. Indeed, the gap in poverty rates, in combination with the conflicts, is what led the state to create subsidies and programs for the Mapuche in the first place. In 1996, nationwide, 35.1 percent of the indigenous were poor or indigent, compared to 22.7 percent of the nonindigenous. In 2006 the figures were 19 percent and 13.3 percent, respectively.[12] While the rate of poverty, as well as the gap, shrank over the years the Concertación held the presidency, it did not disappear. In the Araucanía poverty rates for everyone were much higher over the entire period: 40.7 percent for the indigenous and 33.8 percent for the nonindigenous in 1996, and 24.7 percent and 18.2 percent, respectively, in 2006. Although poverty rates in the region also lessened over time, the gap between the indigenous and nonindigenous barely shrank at all. In fact, it seems the Concertación was more effective in reducing the gap between the indigenous and nonindigenous poor elsewhere in the country, although the 1996 gap in the Araucanía was smaller than for the nation overall.

The persistence of disproportionately high poverty for the Mapuche suggests it makes sense for them to continue to receive special subsidies. However, if we shift our focus from population groups (Mapuche versus non-Mapuche), and consider the effects of poverty on *any* individual or family, it is ethically untenable to argue that anyone who is poor should not receive similar levels of state assistance. Nevertheless, this would go against the neoliberal notion that "opportunity" and "access to the market" are what is most needed to help people rise out of poverty. (This is not to say non-Mapuche poor did not receive state support; the Concertación reduced poverty in part by expanding social programs—including many that focused on opportunity and market access—for all poor citizens.) But to some extent, multiculturalism contradicts the neoliberal ethos in order to buy the indigenous into the neoliberal project. Rather than making a generalized demand to end socioeconomic inequality, local elites who embraced the neoliberal ethos simply sought to eliminate programs benefiting the indigenous. It is striking that local elites, who have so much more than Mapuche and non-Mapuche campesinos, and opposed agrarian reform that would have benefited both, are willing to stick up for the non-Mapuche poor in order to deny indigenous rights. This again demonstrates how race complicates the class dynamic that has historically dominated Chilean politics.

Some questioned Mapuche authenticity as they criticized the benefits, demonstrating one sense in which the sameness, fairness, and poverty narratives are also a rejection of Mapuche cultural and collective claims. For example, Miguel Angel Carrizo believed the Mapuche choose their identity at their convenience; when they want benefits, they say they are Mapuche, but for other things they say they are Chilean like anyone else. Despite the fact that the military defeat of the Mapuche essentially forced them to be both Mapuche and Chilean, when it comes to services, Carrizo felt, they should choose one or the other. Others went further, contending that many recipients of indigenous benefits did not identify as Mapuche before the benefits existed or only lived in communities so they could get subsidies and were thus "acting out" their indigenousness. These individuals seemed to believe the Mapuche should live up to their standards of indigenousness if they want to receive government assistance. As with the question of who deserved access to the land, questions of fairness sometimes came down to casting doubt on whether beneficiaries were authentically Mapuche.

At the same time, resentment (or perhaps more accurately, frustration) did exist among some non-Mapuche poor. When I asked members of a multiethnic organization of women weavers about discrimination, the Chilean women dominated the conversation with talk of discrimination against non-Mapuches. They focused in particular on the indigenous scholarships, pointing out that nonindigenous kids had to maintain a higher average in order to receive subsidies. Most of these women lived in Mapuche communities and thought it unfair that "a last name" determined whether or not they received a benefit. One said: "I look at all people equally, be they gringo, Mapuche, Aymara, whatever race they may be. That is, I look at them as a person, I don't look at race. Why? We put race [up] as a wall." Although she perhaps did not agree with this color-blind rhetoric, at least one of the Mapuche women present felt the Chilean kids should receive the same scholarship opportunities. These women's comments reinforce the fact that many nonindigenous families, too, have unmet socioeconomic needs.

In most cases the exclusion of non-Mapuche who reside in the communities is a legal issue regarding who "counts" as Mapuche. However, I witnessed an Orígenes meeting in Malleco during which members of a community debated whether the one or two non-Mapuche who lived in the community would be allowed to participate in the Orígenes project. Although according to CONADI, these individuals did not "count" as part of the community, the Orígenes adviser told them that if they wanted to include these people as beneficiaries of the project, they could redo the paperwork. One older Mapuche man spoke out in favor of allowing their participation, saying: "With all the discrimination against us, if she [one of the non-Mapuche, who was present at the meeting] assumes the work and the struggle of the Mapuche, how are we going to leave her out?" As a discriminated group, the Mapuche should not go around discriminating against others, he insisted. But the Orígenes promoter remarked that one more family in the project meant less money per family overall.[13] In the end, after much debate, the community voted to leave the non-Mapuche out. Thus, even though the Mapuche, as a whole, are more disadvantaged than non-Mapuche campesinos, the existence of these new resources does make possible the exclusion of non-Mapuche in ways that could be conceived as unfair and definitely as unfortunate.

Still, there was variance among non-Mapuches with regard to perceptions of fairness. This was particularly true of state workers. Nancy Iglesias, who was born and raised in Malleco and worked for the regional government, felt indigenous subsidies were "historical compensation" and should exist for a limited time. Francisca Salas, director of community development in a Cautín comuna, bristled at the notion that the subsidies were discriminatory: "Personally, I would say the government is doing nothing more than a historical retribution for the damage caused." She listed the many subsidies available to non-Mapuche and maintained that land and educational subsidies for the Mapuche should be strengthened. Her views reflected those of many Mapuche, who considered the policies a necessary, if insufficient, response to Chile's historical debt with the Mapuche people. Most local elites of course scoffed at the idea of a historical debt. Mapuche demands for policies that recognized them as a people with all the rights that entails often fell on deaf ears in the state, and even the state's conciliatory policies met with race-based rejection among local elites.

In a clear assertion of sameness, respondents questioned the fairness of indigenous policy by suggesting the *Mapuche* were being discriminated against by indigenous policy, because it set them apart from other citizens. Máximo Ordóñez opposed indigenous law and policies "because I don't believe in any racial discrimination." He compared the Mapuche's situation to that of Black people in Harlem, whose "fragility is not a product of the color of their skin

[but] of where they lived, what their family conditions were." The references Ordóñez and others made to race relations in the United States and elsewhere suggest that not only local history but global discourses shaped their views on the conflicts and indigenous policy. He added: "When I transform race into a condition, I am making a segregation that later is very, very difficult to remove." Martin Rahm expressed similar sentiments: "The Indigenous Law starts with a concept that in my understanding is completely erroneous, that it is necessary to protect them, that they are like the disabled. I, to the indigenous, I tell them, 'You should be the first ones against the Indigenous Law, because they consider you like minors, as if you were stupid.' I tell them, 'And you aren't stupid, or are you?' I tell them, 'No, you know what you need, or don't you?'" Ordóñez suggested that the U.S. and Canadian policy of making "important [monetary] transfers to descendants of the indigenous" is being questioned today, because it has contributed to growing alcoholism. Taking this sort of color-blind perspective, whereby the problem becomes the policies that draw attention to difference, allowed these men to avoid giving serious consideration to the legacy of the Pacificación or ongoing dispossession and systematic inequalities that arguably can only be corrected through special policies. In this way they were able to ignore how unequal and racialized power relations have shaped the history of the region, contributing to symbolic violence.

Liberty, Equal Opportunities, and Choice

In another extension of the poverty narrative, local elites maintained that indigenous policy violated the rights of indigenous citizens to liberty, equal opportunities, and choice. This argument constructs the Mapuche as holders of individual—and not collective—rights. Indigenous policy denied indigenous individuals the right to private property, elites argued. All the Mapuche really needed was equal opportunities, so they could choose which aspects of their culture to maintain and which to leave behind. This narrative does not directly critique Mapuche culture, and indeed elites claimed to be defending Mapuche interests. Nevertheless, it obfuscated the collective and cultural aspects of Mapuche claims. In their insistence that cultural difference should be irrelevant to the lives of contemporary Mapuche, this narrative is in fact a critique of those claims.

Elites used the concept of liberty to assert the individual right to private property. For example, Carla Becker, the Araucanía native who worked for a conservative think tank, insisted Chile must give Mapuche individuals the liberty to sell land to whomever they choose. She contended that the state, not the Mapuche, had decided Mapuche culture was linked to the land. By denying them this freedom, the state had created a living museum. Each individual Mapuche must have the right to choose his or her destiny, she said, and if they choose not to tie their culture to the land or if they choose to integrate, that is their right. People cannot be obligated to maintain their culture, she insisted. This argument, based on an individual rights perspective and clearly the principle of choice, is pervasive among conservative elites. But for people like Becker, the principle of choice does not extend to collective aspects of Mapuche claims; the Mapuche do not have the right to *choose* autonomy because liberties inhere in the individual. By avowing that practicing one's culture is a choice, elites could construct collective and cultural rights as extraneous or even pernicious to policy making.

"Liberty" and "choice" have an easy affinity with another neoliberal value: equal opportunities. For university president and former politician Armando Torres, "to be or not be Mapuche" might have something to do with the language one speaks, but it is ultimately "a sentimental issue" linked to "the great issue of freedom of choice." While he advocated subsidies for the elderly because "you can't take a sixty-year-old person and tell them to do something else," he felt it was essential to increase education levels among the Mapuche "to get them out of poverty." Education, for Torres, involved "train[ing] them to compete in equality of opportunities." He assumed indigenous individuals with equal opportunities would leave their poverty (and their "Mapucheness") behind, choosing to be the same as other Chileans. For local elites who espoused this position, the ultimate goal of providing equal opportunities seems to be for the Mapuche to become more Chilean.

The concept of equal opportunities is pervasive in Chile, so much so that it often appears to have supplanted the principle of equality itself. Its predominance seems to have started with the concept of equal opportunities between women and men, promoted by the National Women's Service, and soon was extended to the poor as well as the indigenous. In my view the concept of equal opportunities is eminently neoliberal. It holds that all people need to make it is opportunity and hard work, rather than recognizing how institutionalized discrimination pervades the structure of opportunity as well as the payoff different individuals get from their investment of hard work. The pervasiveness of the equal opportunities discourse—in government programs as well as in elite narratives rejecting indigenous policy—is an excellent example of what Verónica Schild (1998) has called "selective appropriation," whereby the state incorporates some aspect of movement discourse (in this case, women's movement discourse) without addressing more substantive concerns. Not only does this discourse disguise institutionalized inequalities, but it is particularly nefarious when applied to indigenous policy, because it obscures the collective aspect of indigenous claims and effectively undoes the notion of a historical debt.

Equal opportunities came into the conversation at the level of municipal government, but in somewhat different ways. Some saw the shrinking poverty rate as proof of greater equality of opportunity. Others, like Gaspar Curamil, the intercultural health facilitator from Malleco, used the concept to implicate the state in the discrimination that continued to predominate in healthcare and other sectors. Curamil spoke of a study he conducted in Mapuche communities during the Lagos government, "which talked about equality for all, equality of opportunity in all environments." The study found extensive health problems and inadequate access to care. When he spoke with the machi, they explained that pine and eucalyptus plantations had crowded out their medicinal plants, which signifies, Curamil said, that they do not have equal access to practice their own type of medicine. He observed that a report on the violation of children's rights indicated the absence of equal opportunities when it came to security and protection from state violence (Sepúlveda Navarro and Millaqueo Millapán 2004). Curamil's observations signaled that systematic institutionalized discrimination meant the existence of special programs does not guarantee equal opportunities. Without attentiveness to such issues, equal opportunities discourse reinforces the structural roots of poverty and racism. Moreover, for many Mapuche the concept of equal opportunities is problematic to the extent that "equal" assumes "same," which makes it difficult to claim cultural and collective rights.

By representing the Mapuche as the same as other Chileans, local elites could construct any attempt at differentiated rights for the indigenous as unfair to Chileans. Their calls for equal opportunity and freedom of choice should be read in this context—Mapuche should be given the freedom to choose to be just like other Chileans. In construing state policies as unfair and insisting the "Mapuche problem" is "only poverty," local elites demonstrated their refusal to consent to state-driven multiculturalism and simultaneously refused to recognize the political validity of the Mapuche collective subject.

THE INTEGRATION NARRATIVES

So what policies *would* be appropriate? Although many elites were careful to note most Mapuche were "good," those who set fundos aflame and occupied land were few in number, and the impetus for such actions initiated with outsiders, they suggested the Mapuche needed to change if they were to survive. The solution, they felt, was integration, by which they often seemed to mean assimilation. Their visions entailed either a folkloric treatment of Mapuche identity or increased access to education.

Folklorization involves the view, often incorporated into policy as well as popular representations, that the cultural elements the indigenous should retain are those that bring up romantic images of a traditional past (Chamosa 2008). Folklorization recognizes the Mapuche to a point, but only insofar as that recognition does not represent a threat to its proponents' understanding of the Chilean nation. As Beatriz Quelin, a forty-something Mapuche woman who conducted intercultural workshops for Orígenes, noted, many people were willing to identify *mate*, *sopaipillas*, and the *nguillatun* as elements of Mapuche culture, but they were not willing to see the Mapuche as subjects of rights that might be different from those of Chileans.[14] This type of folklorization was clear at a We Tripantu (Mapuche new year) celebration in Cautín, when Priscila Álamos, the municipal director of education, did a double take upon seeing someone she knew dressed in Mapuche clothing. Álamos exclaimed, "Ahh, I didn't recognize her! She looks like a *Mapucha de verdad*"—a "real Mapuche," insinuating that the woman was just playing dress up and not in fact "real."[15]

In discussing recognition, Lourdes Caifal, a Mapuche woman who worked in intercultural education in Cautín, acknowledged that there have been changes over time: people are less likely to use the term "indio" and may know something about Mapuche celebrations and medical traditions. Despite that, she said, few develop a deeper understanding of Mapuche worldview, and many still believe Mapuche religious practices are witchcraft. Caifal asserted the importance of education, and moral and ethical formation, in changing this. She seemed to suggest it is possible to recognize the Mapuche in a folkloric sense while still contributing to a culture of nonrecognition and discrimination.

Sometimes folklorization lent itself to the good/bad Indian trope. For example, on a truck ride back to a Malleco municipality from a nearby Mapuche community, Teresita Castaños, a young woman who worked for a government assistance program called Programa Puente, said she did not like this community, which in years prior had a major conflict with a timber company. (The company is in possession of two hundred hectares that belong to the community in accordance with its *título de merced*.) She explained that the people have too many complaints and say she does not do anything. Gracia, a Mapuche woman from the community, who was riding with us and who Castaños liked because she was willing to talk to her about traditions, said Mapuche there are accustomed "to being given things." Castaños agreed, adding that she liked another community she worked in better because they were "warm" and let you take their pictures. The assertion that the Mapuche are accustomed to state assistance reinforces the notion that they are not willing to work to solve their problems, and minimizes the legitimacy of their rights claims. That it was Gracia who made the assertion here may reflect internalized racism. It also may simply be her opinion—she admitted to past conflict with others in her community, even though she shared many of their views. Alternatively, it may be that Gracia was telling the state representative what she thought she wanted to hear, a common survival tactic among Mapuche who feared continued repression of their communities.

Beyond folklorization, for many local elites education is the key to integration. The logic seemed to go like this: educate the Mapuche and the conflicts will be resolved, because they will take good jobs in the city and stop wanting land. Marcos Rohrer, who was a regional authority during Frei Montalva's government in the 1960s, experienced an *atentado* on his property in the early 2000s. He suggested it was fine to teach the Mapuche about their history; they should be proud of the fact they resisted. They are honorable people but should leave ancestral rights as something of the past. When asked in a magazine interview what policy changes were necessary, Juan Agustín Figueroa suggested "to recycle an important part of the Mapuche population and incorporate it into the active and productive life of the country" (Moraga Vásquez 2003). He proposed to do so principally through education. Like Armando Torres earlier, Figueroa said "the persons who aren't recyclable" should receive subsistence subsidies; he implied that these individuals—presumably the elderly—will eventually die off. Figueroa's choice of language reflects the extent to which the Mapuche were viewed as objects, less-than-human, a problem to be solved. At worst, they were disposable; at the very least, in need of transformation.

That elites would advocate investing in education and subsistence subsidies for the Mapuche seems to contradict their position that indigenous policies were both unnecessary and unfair to the nonindigenous. It seems to me, however, that these claims were interlinked. These elites preferred to believe indigenous policies recognizing cultural difference were unnecessary. They found such policies distasteful because they challenged their desire to believe "we are all the same" as well as their privileged socioeconomic position in the region. And yet persistent land claims, demands for rights to territory and autonomy, the intensification of the conflicts, and in some cases threats to their own property suggested the "Mapuche problem" was not going away. The most palatable response, in addition to the punitive policies they supported, was to establish indigenous policies that would eventually make the "problem" disappear—pacify the "unrecyclable" ones until they die off and educate the rest into submission.

Elites extracted recognition of cultural rights from the policies they rec-

ommended. For example, although they advocated education, many were
iffy about interculturality. Torres stated:

> I believe it is necessary to increase levels of education considerably, and perhaps
> within that educational policy, generate elements for the maintenance of cul-
> ture, but the only way to get them out of poverty is to train them to compete
> in equality of opportunities. You can't think that in Chile, the State of Chile is
> going to permanently subsidize an ethnic group. That is not possible, because
> otherwise they are going to end up the same as the indigenous reservations
> in North America that are waiting for the money or the casino to arrive, the
> alcohol, la la la la—that model is not possible.

Like Ordóñez, Torres pointed to perceived flaws in compensatory policies
elsewhere as justification for not implementing changes in Chile. He also returned to the concept of equal opportunities in order to downplay the importance of culture in designing educational policies. Although intercultural
policies are imperfect to the extent that they focus on diversity instead of
systemic inequalities, Torres would prefer removing from consideration altogether the role of racial-ethnic inequality in shaping people's life chances.

Torres felt the policies he advocated (education and nutrition programs)
were risky from the indigenous perspective because they could make maintaining identity more difficult. Poverty conserves identity, he said, but wealth
leaves it behind. In a sense his argument was different from those who claimed
Mapuche problems were just about social class. Torres recognized that identity matters, although he did not give much credence to the relevance of its
survival. Rather, he made a culture-of-poverty argument: being poor led the
Mapuche to retain their identity, or at least the aspects that prevented them
from getting ahead and fully integrating into Chilean society. If they just let
go of their identity, they could get themselves out of poverty. Torres's logic
was circular. Earlier he emphasized that getting the Mapuche out of poverty
would lead them to choose to set aside most aspects of their culture; here he
seems to be saying that getting out of poverty requires that Mapuche set aside
their culture. Either way, indigenous culture is not compatible with leaving
poverty and integrating into the Chilean whole.

Torres did not completely abandon the idea of retaining some aspects of
Mapuche identity; he said the challenge was to generate a symbiosis between
culture and development. Demonstrating the link between elites' folkloriz-
ing rhetoric and calls for education, he thought only relatively trivial aspects
of Mapuche culture should be maintained. Most Mapuche characteristics disappear upon becoming integrated, Torres suggested and seemed to think this
was positive. This notion of integration is really about assimilation, not the

coexistence of different cultures. For him, poverty was the consequence not of systemic racism and the legacy of colonialism but of aspects of Mapuche culture, particularly their attachment to land. Thus the goal was not just to reduce poverty but to eliminate these aspects of Mapuche identity. In their obsession over culture = land = poverty and advocacy of education as the solution to this dilemma because it would lead people to leave the land, these elites failed to consider the many educated Mapuche who are among those making claims for autonomy and territory (or, to the extent that they considered them, saw them as outsiders). They ignored the most important point: it should be possible to end indigenous poverty while allowing the cultural and political survival of the people, rather than forcing indigenous individuals to choose between being poor and Mapuche and maybe better off and Chilean.

Many Mapuche were ambivalent about formal education. On one hand, they valued it as a means to have a better life. On the other hand, as José Antiman, a member of CITEM (the Coordinación de Identidades Territoriales Mapuche, the Mapuche Territorial Identities Coordinating Organization), observed: "The schools were the principal actors in making us disappear," by denying language and cultural expression. Mapuche who sought higher education often struggled with the notion that becoming educated would cause them to lose their identity and make them more likely to seek employment outside their communities. Mapuche who worked for the state expressed ambivalence in this regard as well. For example, Andrés Lonkomilla agreed that education was important to change things in poor, conflict-ridden communities but said it was not likely to make it possible for them to make a sustainable living on their land. Rather, with education people would likely leave the countryside. These implications meant that getting a Chilean education left many Mapuche with mixed feelings.

And what happens when Mapuche become educated and continue to make demands? In fact, the participation of educated Mapuche in the movement has been central to its perseverance. Nevertheless, non-Mapuche often criticized educated Mapuche on the basis that they were not "real" Indians, bringing us back to the issue of authenticity. Such was the case of one Chilean bureaucrat at the Ministry of Agriculture's regional office when Malen, a college-educated Mapuche woman, visited her with several members of a rural Mapuche women's association, of which Malen was president. In Malen's recounting, the bureaucrat responded to the women's request that the ministry support their association by saying: "There are women here who say they are representatives, but there are some here who are not rural and who are professionals." In the bureaucrat's view a college-educated woman who speaks assertively and makes demands could not possibly be a "real" Mapuche woman, whom she expected, claimed Malen, to be rural, uneducated, submissive, and easy to manipulate. Although it *can* lead to integration, education can also be a space for liberation, and formally educated Mapuche play important roles in the movement.

Some Chilean respondents questioned whether it was worth trying to integrate the Mapuche at all. They felt the Mapuche were "closed" and did not want to share and live interculturally with Chileans. Several state and municipal employees in Malleco claimed the Mapuche refused to talk about their traditions to non-Mapuche and spoke Mapudungun among themselves at meetings so winkas could not understand. Curiously, several of the same individuals also claimed the Mapuche had already lost their traditions and language. Both of these positions were used to argue that it was not worth integrating the Mapuche—the first in the sense that they were not open to sharing with winkas (not considered were the possibilities that they were simply more comfortable speaking in Mapudungun or that winkas could make an effort to learn Mapudungun), and the second in the sense that the Mapuche were not authentic anymore anyway. Elvira Sandoval argued: "[The Mapuche] self-discriminate. They have to accept that we [as all Chileans] are a people, independent of the ethnicity we might have. Nor do I agree with the indigenous law that leaves them separated from others. The law boxes them in." I asked her to explain what this had to do with "self-discrimination." Sandoval responded with a question: "Why can't they insert themselves with the rest? Instead of a strength, it is a weakness for them." Her comments reflect anxiety that Mapuche claims challenge the substance of the Chilean nation. But she throws a common argument about discrimination back at the Mapuche: while many argue that it is through discrimination that the Chilean state and populace demonstrate they do not want the Mapuche to "insert themselves with the rest," here Sandoval asserts it is the Mapuche *themselves* who do not want to be "inserted." Of course, this is partially true; Mapuche claims are not only about integration; they are about recognition of rights that go beyond the extant citizenship agreement.

IMPLICATIONS FOR IMAGING A MULTICULTURAL NATION

When non-Mapuche landowners and elites interpret Mapuche claims as the product of laziness, revisionist inventions, or leftist conspiracies, they are expressing their resistance to what they perceive as a challenge to their place in the social order. Like the national and transnational discourses that shape political decision making, local elites' narratives are deeply rooted in coloniality, systemic racism, and a corresponding history of economic and political depredation. That history differs in important ways from today's global economy, but the contemporary narratives about race and ethnicity shaped by that history facilitate the economic conditions faced now by Mapuche communities. Elites' narratives allow them to attribute the conditions in Mapuche communities to flaws in their culture. By doing so, they in some sense recognize the Mapuche as a collectivity, but at the same time, avoid reckoning with the structural inequalities that have benefited them at the Mapuche's expense.

Local elites' views are crucial to understanding the continuing subordination of the Mapuche in Chile. Through their connections with regional and national politicians, local elites contributed to shaping the punitive aspects of indigenous policy in Chile. The history of denying and minimizing the Mapuche allowed this to happen without greater outcry. Whereas they directly supported the terrorist construction, local elites' culture, poverty, and integration narratives together represent their rejection of multicultural values and denial of Mapuche rights. When they perceived Mapuche demands as negative or threatening, they asserted there was something wrong with Mapuche *culture* that made them undeserving of state policies designed to address them. They simultaneously contended the Mapuche did not deserve special policies and programs because they were the same as other Chileans and the root problem was not discrimination or dispossession but *poverty*.

Even though these narratives are contradictory, they also reinforce each other. For example, one might ask, if the Mapuche are the same as everyone else, then why is there so much poverty among them? Whereas local elites might seek individual-level explanations for poverty, or might even advocate some limited form of poverty alleviation, they recurred to cultural inferiority to explain the generalized poverty in Mapuche communities. They did so because they were threatened by Mapuche demands as well as state policies that held up aspects of Mapuche culture as valid and worth retaining. The lack of coherence in elite narratives is unimportant. What is important is that culture and poverty narratives both allowed local elites to avoid dealing with historical and structural inequalities at the intersection of race, class, and nation. The integration narrative may seem somewhat more benign, but it ultimately fits into the same rubric; all three narratives are about refusing to recognize the Mapuche as subjects of collective and cultural rights.

Multicultural programs and policies represented a break with past erasure of indigenous peoples in Chile. Local elites reacted against this change, refusing to consent to official multiculturalism on the ground. Their multiple references to the failures of multiculturalism in the United States and elsewhere indicate that, although this refusal was influenced by homegrown fears and apprehensions, it was also to some extent deliberated and informed by transnational discourses. To engender the subjectivities necessary for the success of the neoliberal project, state-driven multiculturalism requires both punitive policies that sanction the terrorist and multicultural ones that reward the *indio permitido* (Hale 2004). Through their refusal to consent to even symbolic recognition, local elites cast doubt on the potential success of the neoliberal multicultural project. But as citizens calling for forceful measures against Mapuche activists, they provided a justification for the criminalization of the conflicts and the limited scope of the neoliberal multicultural agenda more generally. In both ways these actors contributed to the particular contours of neoliberal multiculturalism under the Concertación in Chile. To the extent that the state and transnational capitalists investing in the region sought to rein in Mapuche claims, elite resistance was functional to their objectives.

Multiculturalism under the Concertación did little to challenge dominant racial hierarchies in the Chilean South, and indeed multicultural reforms were not generally aimed at transforming the subjectivities of local elites. This should hardly be surprising, given that the rationale behind neoliberal multiculturalism is less about changing racial hierarchies than it is about creating self-governing indigenous subjects who will not challenge the state's political-economic goals (thus leaving systemic racism in place, if somewhat altered in form). Multicultural policies that are not directed at the whole population seem disingenuous. The lack of focus on local elites made it difficult to generate consent for multiculturalism among them. Local elites resisted indigenous policies and multicultural discourses based on their own memories and understandings of social relationships in the region. They did so to maintain their position at the top of the local hierarchy, a position threatened by neoliberal globalization and changing discourses about race and ethnicity. The case of the Araucanía demonstrates that persistent cultural disagreements, with important material consequences, not only complicate top-down analyses of changing political contexts but also can limit possibilities for social change.[16] But while elite resistance to the state's diversity and development measures was problematic, rejection of more substantive Mapuche claims provided support to the neoliberal multicultural project. In this sense neoliberal multiculturalism relies on some forms of local racism to thrive. Nevertheless, the quotations in this chapter from some state employees and Mapuche activists suggest the existence of alternative discourses, ones that might allow for envisioning a distinct shared future for the region.

CHAPTER 6

AUTONOMY, INTERCULTURALITY, AND A MORE INCLUSIVE FUTURE

In the 1970s and 1980s many Mapuche were active in the sociopolitical struggle to reinstate democracy in Chile. Like their Chilean counterparts, they anticipated that life under democracy would be an improvement over the brutal Pinochet dictatorship. Chileans and Mapuche alike hoped that under democracy the grip of neoliberalism would loosen, their participation would be solicited, and their opinions heard. Nearly two decades after the dictatorship ended, however, many expressed dissatisfaction with the substance of democratic citizenship. But in addition to the social and economic disappointments they shared with other sectors of the Chilean population, many Mapuche communities continued to experience repression and state violence. The extent of disillusionment became clear when I visited a community in Malleco that had faced state repression in the context of a conflict with a timber company in possession of land originally belonging to the community. When I asked what the future held for them, a spokesperson responded that they hoped to struggle against Chile's "false democracy." After seventeen years of dictatorship, the current context was not much different, he said—an assertion echoed by several respondents with a mix of resignation, anger, and profound sadness. "We have to reclaim our rights, or continue being dominated," the spokesperson continued. "We are not terrorists. . . . They say people come from the outside, but if I am hungry, I ask for bread. In [our community] we have needs and for that reason, we raise our voice."

Of course, the Chilean state had long failed to address Mapuche demands and ancestral claims. For many it was particularly disappointing that this remained true under the Concertación governments, which prided themselves on restoring human rights to the nation. They complained that the Concertación did not take *their* human rights, particularly collective and cultural ones, into account. It was a struggle to convince Chilean authorities that the Mapuche were making claims for rights that were in fact recognized internationally. If a nation-state does not recognize the rights of indigenous peoples, some Mapuche respondents asked, can it legitimately claim to respect human rights?

For the Mapuche, discontent with the content of democratic citizenship was related to dispossession and conflict dating back hundreds of years, made particularly acute by contemporary conflicts over land, natural resources, and development. There is thus continuity in the Mapuche struggle for cultural rights, territory, and autonomy reaching from before the Pacificación through to the neoliberal democratic context. In recent decades, Latin America has witnessed a shift from assimilationism to multiculturalism as a hegemonic nation-building ideology. Nevertheless, from the perspective of the state, the central goals of citizenship still center on creating a sense of common identity and generating consent among citizens for a given nation-building project. Although states that embrace multiculturalism recognize some indigenous rights, to the extent that they combine recognition of ancestral rights with redistribution of power and resources, indigenous rights continue to be perceived as threats to universalizing citizenship regimes and national development. This was particularly true in Chile over the course of my fieldwork.

This context created fertile ground for Mapuche to envision and put into practice alternatives to neoliberal democratic citizenship. While these have taken a variety of forms, here I examine one in particular: claims for autonomy, or self-determination and self-government. These claims represent an effort on the part of some Mapuche organizations to reclaim their right to subjectivity—the right to determine their own destiny—in the face of ongoing dispossession and systemic racism. As a form of political opposition, they embody "refusal of the common sense understandings which the hegemonic order imposes" (Omi and Winant 1994, 69). Mapuche theorizing of autonomy transcends the traditional citizenship framework, drawing from collective memory and contemporary struggles to project new forms of sociopolitical belonging for Mapuche and those Chileans who wish to join them. Autonomy claims are not necessarily demands to do away with citizenship, but rather to transform it. They often are expressed in terms of strengthening the content of democracy and creating a more inclusive form of belonging; always, they are expressed in terms of historical justice with a vision for what is to come. They articulate the longings of a people with a past, a present, and a future. This analysis points to the fact that the process of subject formation entailed by citizenship is never complete; subjects may participate in their own formation, but they also resist, imagining and actively seeking alternatives to the neoliberal model.

In this chapter I examine the content of demands and proposals for autonomy, showing how they challenge traditional definitions of citizenship by grounding claims in a combination of cultural and political justifications and by asserting a nationhood that transcends the Andes. I contend that for Mapuche autonomy proposals to be successful, the movement will need to grapple with the participation of three groups: Mapuche who work for the state, women, and Chilean allies. I also address interculturality, exploring the role it might play in the construction of an alternative future for the region.

CULTURE, POLITICS, AND DEMANDS FOR AUTONOMY

The Mapuche do not speak in one voice. As Nancy Grey Postero (2007, 11) has written: "Indigenousness—like any identity—is not an uncontested category of domination, but a contingent category negotiated by individual and collective subjects." Although they are subjugated as a group, as in any social group, there are differences among the Mapuche on the basis of gender, class, religion, education, region of residence, political orientation and party, and other factors. Within the movement there are debates over demands, goals, ideology, and strategy. This variance may be partly related to the fact that the Mapuche never had a centralized form of government, even as over centuries of conflict and negotiations with the Spanish and Chileans, alliances and some concentration of power did occur (Haughney 2006). Nevertheless, the absence of centralized governance did not preclude the assertion of common identity or demands for rights, even as some groups privilege civil rights and others collective ones (ibid.). Thus, while distinct sectors prioritize different demands and go about pursuing them in diverse ways (and some may even be pleased with what the state offers), the struggle for the recognition of their rights has been a unifying factor for the Mapuche movement. Although it is not a universal priority, one of the most important of these rights is self-determination, which my respondents discussed in terms of autonomy. Scholars studying similar issues elsewhere in the region (Hale 2006; *NACLA Report on the Americas* 2010; Postero 2007) have shown that recognizing indigenous rights—including some degree of autonomy—is a tactic of neoliberal multicultural states seeking to avoid redistributing power and resources. In Chile, however, recognition remains highly contested, and autonomy an important goal.

Mapuche theorist Victor Naguil (2005), who directed foreign relations for Wallmapuwen, a Mapuche political party established in 2005, has defined "self-determination" as the right allowing peoples or nations to decide the shape of their political future without outside interference.[1] He defines "autonomy" as one route to self-determination, exercised not through the formation of a new state but within the bounds of the existent state in which the people reside. While the state and elites have generally viewed Mapuche proposals for autonomy as a threat to the integrity of the Chilean nation, autonomy as defined by Naguil is not necessarily a proposal to do away with citizenship but rather to transform it, to give citizens—indigenous ones in particular—a voice in what they want their relationship with the state and all that entails (education, development, territorial control, and so on) to look like.

Mapuche organizations are theorizing and working toward autonomy in diverse ways, and in the years I spent working in Chile, discussions of autonomy became more generalized and more sophisticated. I assumed this shift might be related to growing discontent with the state, as was suggested by Maribel Huaiquin, an intercultural health worker, who felt autonomy was important because it would allow the Mapuche to "develop as a people," independent from the paternalistic state that was uninterested in truly addressing the problems faced by Mapuche communities. But far more than the failure of the state, Mapuche respondents hearkened back to a time when their people were autonomous. Wladimir Painemal, a young college-educated member of Wallmapuwen and a writer for *Azkintuwe* (a Mapuche newspaper), argued that problems related to the timber companies, garbage dumps, and development projects took on political significance "because the place where the timber plantation is, is a place [that has] a history. That land has a history, that territory. . . . Many people were taken from those places and the ancient memory remained." Doña Emiliana, an elderly spiritual and cultural leader in a community on the island of Chiloe, epitomized this memory as she recalled how the government appropriated her family's land when she was a child:

And my mother told them, "You, because you are the law, will do what you want with the poor, with the campesino, with the [rightful] owner of the land. . . . You will do what you want to do because you are the big guys; you are the ones who can kill. But one day, you will die all the same. Where will you go? Because you are bad in this world, one day you will be firewood in hell." And it's because of that that I say the ancestors left us with a good memory, and they left us to fight for our own rights. . . . [The government] knows what they've done, the injustices there were before. In the end, they know it all, so . . . they can't become embittered when a lonko tells them the truth, because the time has arrived for things to become clear. Things will be said, and truthfully.

The collective memory of having been autonomous was thus a key factor in aspirations for autonomy. José Antiman of CITEM (Coordinación de Identidades Territoriales Mapuche, the Mapuche Territorial Identities Coordinating Organization) explained: "We were autonomous. . . . We had our own ways of educating children. We had our way of expressing feelings and values. We had our way of practicing medicine. It's a world that was complete, a world that had a structure."

Indeed, the Mapuche were autonomous much longer than most other peoples in Latin America. The agreements reached at parliament with the Spanish confirmed this, and even the Chilean Constitution of 1833 recognized the Mapuche as another nation (Pinto 2003, 113). Only in 1883 was Mapuche territory fully annexed by the Chilean state. Claims for autonomy have recurred since that time. For instance, in the 1930s Manuel Aburto Panguilef, leader of the Federación Araucana, proposed the creation of a Mapuche Republic (COM 2006). And in a 1985 interview (Jiles 1985, 25), Rosamel Millaman, then a leader of Ad-Mapu, the largest and most influential Mapuche organization during the dictatorship, described that organization's project as the pursuit of "autonomy of the Mapuche people, in the sense that we organize ourselves to define our destiny, our path of liberation, without waiting for recipes from this ministry or that organism." This history suggests that demands for autonomy in the early 2000s were not just a product of the conflicts, although the conflicts perhaps reinforced the urgency of the demands. Despite these historical roots, it is important to emphasize that autonomy is a process in construction. Diverse actors and organizations are working (not always in concert with one another) to theorize and, in some cases, begin to put into practice what autonomy might look like for the Mapuche.

Transnational trends have also influenced Mapuche proposals for autonomy. Millaman, who participated in many of these events as part of Ad-Mapu explained that contact with indigenous peoples from Colombia, Panama,

Mexico, the United States, Denmark, and elsewhere in international forums in the early to mid-1980s helped plant the seeds for Mapuche theorizations of autonomy. He cited in particular discussions at the Primer Congreso Indio de Sudamérica in Peru in 1980. Others referred to the autonomous regions of Spain, such as Cataluña and the Basque Country, as models for envisioning Mapuche autonomy, noting, as did Pedro Cayuqueo, a member of Wallma-puwen and editor of *Azkintuwe*: "It is not a requirement to stop being Spanish in order to live in Barcelona or enjoy the citizenship rights of a Catalán." Organizations including Wallmapuwen had contact with groups in those regions as they developed their claims.

Autonomy involves the right to be the author of one's collective destiny. José Antiman explained: "To repair [the] historical and ancestral harms, it is we who have to be the authors. We don't want another author. We are the author. We know the principles. We know our form of life. We'll do the development. We will develop ourselves politically, and we will say, this is the development we want, and we want it with identity. We want it with our way of life, our way of viewing the world." Antiman associated autonomy with the right of the Mapuche to be the subjects and creators of the knowledge that will govern their social world rather than the objects of someone else's development. His words are suggestive of how Mapuche conceptions of autonomy might transcend traditional understandings of citizenship in which cultural differences—and the existence of more than one peoples—are elided to create a homogeneous citizenry in the interest of regularization and control.

A similar sentiment is reflected in the Identidad Mapuche Lafkenche of Arauco's proposal for autonomy (1999): "We hope that in these new times of conflicts, the national voice will emerge that converts us at last into *historical subjects with rights*." The group laments having been treated as the objects of Chilean laws and development and insists that being subjects would entail the right to control their territorial existence "as a way of making our culture, way of life and [way] of understanding the world endure." To the extent that claiming autonomy involves the assertion of the right to be a self-defining collective subject, not just citizen-subjects whose shape is determined by the state, Mapuche theorizing of autonomy goes beyond the traditional framework of citizenship, projecting new forms of sociopolitical belonging. It also does so by claiming a Mapuche nationhood that transcends the modern-day Chile-Argentina border.

In the early 2000s the Mapuche movement was characterized by a tension between cultural and political justifications for rights. This tension was reflected in claims for autonomy as well. Different organizations and theorists tended to emphasize one over the other, and culture and politics were integral to debates over how to represent the collective self. On one side were organizations and leaders who based claims for rights in notions of cultural difference and turned to traditional concepts and practices as a basis for organization and development. This was true of the Coordinadora Arauko Malleko (CAM), the organization considered responsible for most of the attacks on timberlands and other disputed territory. CAM spokesman José Llanquilef declared that the organization pursued territorial recuperation and control because its goal was "the reconstruction of the Mapuche People in all respects, basically in the political and ideological, and also in values, and the cultural and spiritual" (Weftun 2007). He clarified that the CAM's resistance was oriented "toward the structural bases of the oligarchy and capitalism in our territory, above all timber companies and latifundistas," but he also suggested that "everything is interrelated. The struggle for the reconstruction of the Mapuche People is the struggle for RAKIDUAM [autochthonous thought, reflection] and KIMUN [knowledge, wisdom]. Resistance against devastation of the 'environment' is for the recovery of the ITROFIL MOGEN [all the life that exists in the universe; biodiversity], and it is, at the same time, the only way to strengthen Mapuche spirituality. To the extent that our world is recomposed, we will reencounter the Mapuche essence, the Mapuche being."

Hector Llaitul, an imprisoned CAM leader, reinforced this point when he insisted that the CAM's struggle was not the same as a peasant struggle like agrarian reform because "our objective is to exercise territorial control with the object of promoting the autonomous political and economic activities of our communities, promoting our own forms of organization and decision making, for the recuperation of *admapu* [ancestral traditions, laws, and norms], *rakiduam*, and *kimun*" (in Cayuqueo 2008a). Llaitul added that they did not support Western-style exploitation of the land, and their struggle was not about getting land to then become rich capitalists. Instead, it was about "the recuperation of our Nuke Mapu [Mother Earth] and spiritual and ideological decolonization, that is, the real independence of the Mapuche nation. Our central idea is to recover the Mapuche essence."

While actors like Llanquilef and Llaitul are clearly motivated by the ancestral rights of the Mapuche to the land—arguably a political goal—and are opposed to the capitalist system, they justify their claims largely on the basis of cultural distinctiveness; the Mapuche deserve autonomy not only because they were once an autonomous people in this territory but also (and perhaps especially) because they *continue to be* culturally distinct from Chileans. In disputing the notion that all citizens are the same and thus equal as bearers of the same substantive citizenship rights, these views challenge citizenship norms. This perspective resonates with many Mapuche. Indeed, other organizations turned to culture as part of their justificatory strategies and organizational principles. The Consejo de Todas las Tierras, one of the first organizations to promote autonomy after the return to democracy, maintained that its organizational form, in which lawyer Aucan Huilcaman assumed the traditional role of *werken* (spokesperson), was based on Mapuche philosophy and culture. CITEM was organized on the basis of territorial identities, with the rationale that, traditionally, Mapuche who resided in different territories had somewhat distinct cultural and organizational practices. Both of these groups mobilized around a variety of political goals; however, they organized based on the notion of cultural distinctiveness.

Although the CAM considered itself the vanguard of the movement for autonomy and the only organization consequential in its commitment to that goal (Weftun 2007), more than a dozen proposals for autonomy have been written since 1990 (Mariman 2006). Some proposals justify their claims on the basis of cultural difference. For example, the 1999 Identidad Mapuche Lafkenche of Arauco proposal provides an extensive "spiritual and cultural" rationale, citing concepts such as *kimun, lof* (basis of social organization; community), *tuwun* and *kupalme* (Mapuche family norms, linked to the territory), *nor* (how individuals and collectivities should behave, and the rights that entails), *ad* (guidance for the relationship between people and the environment), and Mapuche conceptualizations of development. Although the proposal also gives attention to the juridical basis for autonomy, the cultural rationale is dominant; Mapuche deserve autonomy because they are a living collectivity, culturally distinct from Chileans.

In contrast, advocates of a political rationale for autonomy maintain that while culture is important, it can lend itself to efforts to delegitimate the movement from the outside. The state has engaged in efforts to absorb and water down claims for cultural rights by advocating "diversity" and integrating aspects of Mapuche culture that do not threaten national development or identity into state programs. Elites have been even more reluctant to accept Mapuche claims, basing their rejection in notions of sameness on the one hand (the Mapuche no longer exist as they once did and are essentially the same as Chileans; universal national identity is desirable; and recognition of cultural difference is a violation of equal rights) and difference (Mapuche cultural inferiority) on the other. Such uses of "culture" to deny Mapuche political rights suggests the slippery slope faced by Mapuche who base claims for autonomy on notions of cultural distinctiveness. Opponents of this approach among the Mapuche argue that it is better to base claims for autonomy on political rights—that is, on the fact that the Mapuche historically were and continue to be a people and have the right to determine their own form of sociopolitical belonging. These critics maintain that references to "culture" or "tradition" sometimes border on anachronistic essentialism. For example, Mapuche political scientist José Mariman (1995, 2008) has critiqued cultural affirmations as mythical reconstructions. Humans do not exist outside of culture, he acknowledges, but because of the long history of colonization and urbanization, it is difficult to say what is definitively "Mapuche culture" today. In his view, basing demands in political rights does not entail renouncing culture. Instead, it entails focusing on achieving territorial rights in order to create a new space for exercising culture. Such perspectives recognize the dynamic character of culture; there is no Mapuche "essence" as such, and like any other, Mapuche culture has changed and adopted elements of the "other" over time.

Political claims are given a central place in proposals from the Coordinación de Organizaciones Mapuches (COM) and the Wallmapuwen political party. In 2006, President Bachelet established a nationwide "indigenous debate." Funds were distributed for groups to make proposals to change indigenous policy and improve the relationship between indigenous peoples and the state. The COM, made up of more than thirty organizations, formed in response to this call. Its proposal begins by listing the many instances since the return to democracy in which the Mapuche have in good faith participated in dialogue with the government, observing that despite all the meetings and agreements, the state has continued to foment capitalist expansion and environmental degradation in Mapuche territory and has criminalized Mapuche demands. The proposal declares that Chile's debt with the Mapuche continues to grow, and presents a series of proposals for change revolving around three principal issues: recognition of political rights based on free self-determination, generation of a new form of political participation that guarantees the right to free self-determination and a "just, equitable, and respectful relationship between the Mapuche people and the state," and restitution of land and territorial control (COM 2006, 5). While the COM document concentrated mostly on collective political rights, specific proposals related to economy, education, health, and legislation and justice are presented in terms of *küme mongen*, the Mapuche concept of integral well-being, making it clear that the group seeks a change in the regional culture based, to some extent, on Mapuche norms and values.

Wallmapuwen's 2005 Declaration of Principles draws a distinction between looking at the situation faced by the Mapuche as "an indigenous peasant question" or a "national question." They advocate the latter. The party's ideological principles are fivefold: the Mapuche are a people whose original territory spanned the Andes and who share a culture, history, language, and desire to develop a nation; the Mapuche have the right to self-determination; the Mapuche have the right to restitution of their territory; the Mapuche must engage in a process of national reconstruction including the development of a Mapuche national consciousness; and, as part of this consciousness, Mapudungun must be revitalized as an official language (Wallmapuwen 2005). The party's focus is on political autonomy rooted in territorial identity rather than cultural identity. However, they see common culture as a one of the bases for Mapuche nationhood and endorse several policies related to cultural distinctiveness. For example, they call for the promotion of Mapuche language, recognition of important Mapuche sites, promotion of Mapuche medical knowledge, and development of Mapuche communities, "where it is still possible to find the basis of our own identity reconstruction" (Wallmapuwen 2006, 11).

Nevertheless, the party does not promote particular "Mapuche values" or essential cultural practices. Instead, it focuses on the democratization of Chilean political processes that present obstacles to local decision making. For instance, the party supports decentralization, eliminating the binomial election system, increasing citizen participation in governance, achieving recognition of indigenous peoples, and, significantly, acquiring a statute of regional autonomy for the Araucanía and adjacent comunas with high Mapuche populations, within what the party recognizes as a multinational and multilingual Chile (ibid. 2006; drawing in part from a map accompanying Naguil 2005, the map at the beginning of this book denotes the *comunas* that would be included).[2] The party proposes that autonomy be made operable through a democratically elected regional assembly with proportional representation of all sectors of the regional society (Wallmapuwen 2006).[3]

These steps are important because while the collective rights of the Mapuche as a nation are the motivation for demanding autonomy, and those rights—both political and cultural—permeate the party's proposals and objectives, the party explicitly does not limit the benefits of autonomy to the Mapuche, such that their aims could theoretically appeal to Mapuche and Chileans alike. Although the party's ultimate goal is restitution of the territory and reconstruction of the Mapuche nation as a political entity transcending the Andes, that nation would offer membership to nonindigenous residents as well. This vision is arguably more inclusive than Chilean citizenship in its current form, which denies the collective rights of the Mapuche and tries to fit them into a homogenizing model (despite the recognition of "diversity" in some programs and projects). By asserting a cross-border

Mapuche territory predating Chile and Argentina, it also denaturalizes the nation-state framework (Boccara 2006; Warren 2010). Altogether, the COM and Wallmapuwen proposals do not ignore the importance of common culture as a source of Mapuche peoplehood, but they foreground collective political rights as a basis for autonomy.

With articles titled "Hacia un imaginario de nación" (Toward the imaginary of a nation) and "Mapuches, un pueblo en marcha" (Mapuches, a people in motion), the Mapuche newspaper *Azkintuwe* has been a central voice promoting the idea of a Mapuche nation. Part of this process, writer Wladimir Painemal explained, was to claim the space for Mapuche to write their own history, after centuries of it having been written from the perspective of the dominant. "The people want to read themselves, they want to hear themselves," he said. By writing news from a Mapuche point of view, *Azkintuwe* asserts the Mapuche's collective right to be the tellers of their own history, the interpreters of their own lived experience. As part of interpreting Mapuche history and experience, *Azkintuwe*, similar to Wallmapuwen, has promoted the idea of one Mapuche nation—meaning not just the Mapuche in Gulumapu (Chile) but in Puelmapu (Argentina) as well—Wallmapu as a whole.[4] Pedro Cayuqueo explained the power of recognizing oneself as part of a Mapuche nation that spans the Southern Cone from the Atlantic to the Pacific: "That reality is very forceful when it's always been denied to you. The state denies it to you, history—better said, historiography— denies it to you. . . we ourselves deny it when we [assume] these borders so submissively." This assertion of nationhood involves not only reclaiming Mapuche subjectivity but also envisioning a future for the people, a future that transcends the literal borders of citizenship.

Azkintuwe has been critical of the culturalist approach to autonomy. Cayuqueo explained that he considered religion and culture a dangerous and inadequate base from which to do politics, because they can lead to fundamentalism as well as folklorization. Culture is not fixed; on the contrary, it is always changing, he said. Instead of embracing "caricatures of the Mapuche that come from the nineteenth century or before," he said, "we accept the reality in which we are living and we want to change it." For Cayuqueo the focus on distinct cultural practices and identity as a justification for autonomy is associated with the view that land and territorial origin are essential for maintaining Mapuche identity, as if without the land, the people would no longer be Mapuche. He said older, more traditional leaders often held this view, although there are younger militant leaders such as Llaitul and Llanquilef who root much of their justification for autonomy in this perspective as well.

Cayuqueo and others argue that the movement's focus on land—while it has resulted in the accumulation of more hectares for some communities—has often occurred without a plan for what to do with it. Beyond agricultural production, they asked, what is to be the political use of this territory? In this sense it seems the government's land policy functioned to generate consent among some leaders and to draw attention away from long-range goals. Cayuqueo elaborated an alternative perspective, which he thought was more common in the younger generations, in which being and "thinking as Mapuche" were not necessarily linked to a specific place or piece of land but rather associated with "a consciousness of national belonging that is much more subjective." For him this involved "feeling like a citizen of a country, a Mapuche country. And this makes me feel like a citizen here [in Temuco], in Neuquen, or in Bariloche [cities in Puelmapu]. That is, for me, there's no difference [which side of the border I am on], and I believe in the new generation, this discourse enters much more easily and has to overcome less obstacles." Cayuqueo prefers a political definition of Mapuche identity: they have a right to autonomy and self-determination because they are a nation who historically held those rights (which are recognized internationally). Those rights might have been connected at one point to a particular territory, but the territory does not determine the scope of the rights. Likewise, the people may have shared particular cultural attributes at the time they still held those rights, but those attributes do not have to be the same today for collective political rights to be recognized. The shift away from focusing on land reflects shifting conceptions of citizenship, from one in which the indigenous may make demands on the state as citizens like any other to one in which indigenous rights transcend that relationship, challenging the state and other citizens to envision new forms of sociopolitical belonging.

In turn, culturalists critique people like Mariman and the writers at *Azkintuwe* for losing sight of what makes the Mapuche a distinct people, above and beyond territorial claims. (They might also note that the negation of the importance of land is nerve-wrenchingly similar to the insistence of elites that the Mapuche do not need land to retain their cultural identity). Indeed, despite the critiques of intellectuals like Mariman and Cayuqueo, many Mapuche do turn to cultural identity to give purpose to their activism. César, a leader whose community was fighting for access to sacred sites now located within the borders of a timber plantation, explained that in his view, alongside economic explanations the reason many people have left their communities and lost their identity, even becoming ashamed of who they are, is because sacred places, where Mapuche spirituality was once practiced, have been lost. He drew a link between the cultural-spiritual and the economic.

Not only was his community dealing with land loss, but they had lost access to sites and rituals that in the past had given them a sense of purpose and continuity, helping people make sense of who they were as individuals and part of a collective. César said he could understand people who left and lost their identity, because staying under these circumstances was very difficult.

Taking culture into account can give special potency to political demands and may be especially important as a means to motivate Mapuche to join the movement, just as taking the political into consideration can help get beyond essentialist and folkloric interpretations of indigenous culture, an important step in presenting the Mapuche as a living people with a future to the outside world. Nevertheless, when culture is presented as static and of the past, the movement becomes more vulnerable to critiques from non-Mapuches who argue the Mapuche do not exist anymore and are the same as Chileans. Local elites and the state used culture as an excuse to deny political claims. In this way the culturalist strand of the movement may play into the hands of those who want to deny Mapuche rights. Making a political case for autonomy as the right of a people with a legitimate, historical claim on a given territory to govern itself—rather than basing the claim in cultural difference—is in some ways the more radical approach, but it may also be the more easily argued vis-à-vis those who would use the dynamic character of culture as a reason to deny Mapuche claims.

Altogether, growing insistence on the right to subjectivity, expanding transnational links, and collective memory have made it possible for the Mapuche movement to persevere over time and demands for autonomy to seem increasingly feasible. This is the case even as autonomy remains a project in development, the aspired substance of which is not always totally clear. Mapuche anthropologist Rosamel Millaman has some useful thoughts on ongoing efforts to theorize autonomy. Autonomy, he argued, should be based on autochthonous knowledge, which is neither static nor just of the past. He linked this to the need for Mapuche activists and intellectuals to be mentally autonomous and decolonize the self. Such decolonization, Millaman believed, was the necessary precursor to political and economic autonomy. His thoughts reflect the ongoing tensions between culture and politics in Mapuche theory and practice about autonomy. Surely, most Mapuche working on autonomy would agree with the need to decolonize, mentally and materially. But they might not agree on what that means. What is Mapuche knowledge today? How do Mapuche understand the world? Are Mapuche and Chilean knowledge fully separable? In all likelihood there are many answers to these questions. It is worth noting, though, that the three written proposals reviewed here—from Identidad Mapuche Lafkenche de Arauco, the COM, and Wallmapuwen—each include cultural and political elements, even as they emphasize one over the other in justifying their claims. This suggests that culture and politics are not easily detached from one another. The Mapuche were historically a people with a distinct culture and political autonomy; perhaps because of this, the two types of claims make most sense when made together. Ultimately, it may be a combination of cultural and political justifications for autonomy that stands to constitute the most forceful challenge to the substance of Chilean citizenship, provided that culture is understood as dynamic and accommodating of change.

Not everyone who talked about autonomy spoke in terms of big projects for the future. Some spoke of small, simple ways they and their organizations practiced autonomy. Several associations have experimented with self-management in their territories and communities. Guided by "Mapuche ethical values" and kimun, for example, the Asociación Ñankuchew sought to engage in autonomous community development (Figueroa 2005). Gabriel Ancamil spoke of CITEM's effort to reclaim the *trawun*. He explained: "Trawun means meeting/encounter, and that is what we've generated. We've generated a space of the Mapuche movement's own. To be able to leave the boxing-in of the Chilean state's system of governance a little, and this has permitted us to get together again, look into each other's faces again, and talk about our things internally." Celestino Huentequeo modestly suggested that the school he runs exercised autonomy in administration and decision making, and that experiences like this could one day contribute to autonomy more generally.

While achieving autonomy is a large-scale, long-term project, it is therefore also an everyday practice. It may be in those everyday practices that we get a glimmer of where the cultural and the political meet. I am reminded of Melissa Forbis's (2006) work on women health promoters (*promotoras*) in an autonomous municipality in Chiapas. Forbis shows that although they are part of the overall Zapatista movement for autonomy, through the skills they develop and their everyday actions, the promotoras give meaning to autonomy on multiple levels, challenging inequities and building new forms of relationships in their families, communities, and region. Movement debates about culture and politics can make it seem like the two are discrete elements, and there may be reasons to keep them analytically separate, but in practice they are interconnected. Achieving autonomy will require work on both levels—theorizing it and practicing it in the everyday. Both activities, as Millaman pointed out, require getting autonomy in the head—that is, decolonizing the self, recognizing one's self as a member of a people with an authentic right to autonomy, and becoming able to imagine it as a real possibility.

Despite this, some Mapuche I spoke with were not convinced by what they knew about autonomy—often because they thought it was a separatist claim. Alicia Marín, a mestiza municipal worker from Cautín, emphatically defended Mapuche rights but echoed the rationale of some elites for opposing them when she said she did not think autonomy was feasible because of the extensive "transculturality" in the region (by which she meant cultural and racial *mestizaje*). Andrés Lonkomilla, a state worker in Malleco, identified as "more Mapuche than Chilean." He understood autonomy as "making a Mapuche state independent from the Chilean state," which he felt would lead to "pure problems." He desired instead to "live all together, but respecting one another . . . that they respect you as a person, that [they recognize] there's a difference, and there's a culture behind it." A woman from an *artesanía* association similarly wished "we would struggle all together" as equals, for a better country with more opportunities for all. Comments like these suggest that proponents of autonomy will need to raise consciousness about what it actually means if their movement is to meet with eventual success.

CHALLENGES FOR THE FUTURE

The proposals for autonomy described earlier are relatively incipient, and the Mapuche movement faces many external challenges as its members continue their struggle: the incursion of multinational corporations, the open aggression of many Chileans, and the reticence of the state to recognize the legitimacy of their claims. They also face internal differences regarding goals, strategy, and the roles of culture and politics in the movement. Next I address some additional challenges related to coming to terms with the place of three groups of people in the movement—Mapuche professionals and state workers, women, and Chilean allies. Each of these cases speaks to debates over the right to subjectivity and the role of inclusiveness in movement success. Addressing these challenges would not only increase the likelihood autonomy will one day be achieved but would also contribute to the transformation of the meaning of "belonging" in Chile.

Professionals and Mapuche in the State

Many Mapuche spoke of the "absorption" into the state and co-optation of Mapuche leaders that occurred with the return to democracy and the creation of CONADI (Corporación Nacional de Desarollo Indígena, the National Indigenous Development Agency). Since the Concertación took power, intercultural teacher Pepe Morales explained, it had been trying to "capture" or buy the loyalty of Mapuche involved in the movement; this applied to professionals, who were bought in by being given jobs in the public sector, but also to community members, who were bought in by being privileged with land subsidies. Mapuche respondents lamented that the state had dispersed and pacified sectors of the movement through the creation of programs like Orígenes and scholarships for indigenous students and that some leaders had been sucked into this dynamic, defending the state instead of their communities. While nondegreed leaders were not exempt from this critique, Mapuche activists reserved their strongest criticism for Mapuche professionals who became state employees, suggesting that by submitting to the state's rules and policies, they were betraying the movement.

There is increasing talk, however, of the need for the expertise of technicians and professionals within the movement. Some, like Rosamel Millaman, drew a distinction between Mapuche professionals and intellectuals who are "committed to the struggle" and "those who are functionaries of the interests of the state and the dominant classes." This position begs the question as to whether it is possible to work for the state and also be committed to the Mapuche struggle—a question I contend is of urgent importance as organizations seek to develop the capacity to create viable autonomous institutions. Indeed, while some respondents felt working for the state was completely incongruous with supporting the movement, others suggested that perhaps the movement should not write off those who work for the state. To begin with, young Mapuche often take state jobs related to indigenous policy because employment discrimination makes it difficult to find work elsewhere. Victorino Manque, a leader from the times of Allende, lamented that young, college-educated Mapuche found themselves "selling their knowledge to the *winka*" in order "to not die of hunger." He did not write them off, however. Rather, he saw Mapuche professionals—ranging from engineers and agronomists to lawyers, social workers, and doctors—as essential to achieving the goals of the movement. He explained: "When I was a leader of the Mapuche movement, the majority [was] illiterate, so it was impossible to propose an autonomist proposal, right? Today, no. Today we have the conditions . . . because there are professionals supporting."

The tension surrounding Mapuche professionals was not just that they "sold their knowledge to the winka." Rather, some leaders who had not had access to formal education resented that young professionals had access to state jobs as a result of their academic credentials but lacked important knowledge about and commitment to the Mapuche cause. This resentment was particularly salient in the years immediately following the creation of CONADI, but it seemed to be easing over time. Young scholar Sergio Caniuqueo, who participated in developing the COM proposal, reflected on why this was the case. He spoke enthusiastically of the COM as an example in

which young technicians and professionals had worked together with traditional leaders. I asked why it was possible for this to happen now and not,
say, a decade ago. Caniuqueo responded that sometimes resentment existed
before because the individuals with academic or technical training developed
a technocratic logic, focusing on carrying out projects sponsored by the state
or NGOs. They came to the communities with this logic and a sense that they
had all the answers, and this generated rejection on the part of the communities and traditional leaders. But more recently, attitudinal changes made possible a more productive relationship: "Today technical workers have learned
to be much more humble, to act as systematizers more than possessors of a
truth. . . . And on the other hand, the leaders have admitted there are many
issues they don't understand on a technical level, and as a result it is necessary
to work with a technical worker." It is worth noting that many of the most
forceful autonomy-related initiatives in recent years, including the work of
the Coordinadora Arauko-Malleko, have been orchestrated largely or in part
by college-educated Mapuche who have found through formal education
access to information about autonomy in other countries and contact with
new ideas. As Caniuqueo notes, the knowledge and skills gained by these
individuals can complement the ancestral and organizational knowledge of
lonkos and other leaders.

It is also worth questioning whether working for the state automatically
means you have been co-opted (Park and Richards 2007). Several respondents gave examples of how they resisted from within or used their space in
the state to do more than required. Often this happened in small ways. Both
Gaspar Curamil and Maribel Huaiquin used their positions as intercultural
health facilitators to go far beyond their job descriptions. When Huaiquin got
the job, she was told she was to translate for the doctors, but she also used her
placement to advocate for Mapuche patients in the face of pervasive racism
in the health system. Curamil publicized health problems among Mapuche
and spoke out against the health consequences of police violence. He suffered
recriminations from within the state as a result. Mapuche workers were reflexive about their hybrid positions—being of the people as well as the state.
Curamil claimed he had opposed his bosses in the municipality on several
occasions and was fine with being fired if they obliged him to do anything
he considered unethical. At the same time, he observed that the movement
needed people in different places, both inside and outside the state: "The fight
doesn't just happen in the communities. The fight has to happen also in public
positions, in all environments." He mentioned teachers, mayors, doctors, and
other professionals as being necessary to the struggle. He had been accused
of being a sellout or a traitor for working in the state, showing that debates

over authenticity also play out within the movement. Curamil said he had a clear conscience. He acknowledged, though, that it is hard to balance the two roles, and painful to see how the Mapuche are treated. Sometimes, Curamil said, you just have to do your job, but it was clear this did not make the pain go away.

Some Mapuche who worked for the state had criticisms of the movement. Millaray Catrillanca, a social worker by training, had held various jobs in the public sector since 2002. Once she started working for the state, she said, she realized there was diversity within it. For example, while the maximum authorities might have a particular discourse, middle-range authorities might have greater disposition to work in favor of Mapuche rights. "Sometimes from the outside, you attack [a] person, and sometimes he's not even your enemy," Catrillanca said, "because he could be your ally. Maybe not [in a visible way], but in the process of carrying out a project, a program, in the field, in the operative sense, he could be your ally." When I asked Mauro Panguilef, an Orígenes administrator, what he made of the criticism that his program was created to absorb Mapuche demands and lower the profile of the movement, he said it might have those effects, but it was not created with those objectives. If the movement has problems, he argued, it is because it is not very strong. In his view this is not because of the government, but because the movement needs to engage in its own process of development. These criticisms may be difficult for movement leaders to hear, but taking them seriously would likely strengthen the movement.

A strategy engaging state workers with movement goals would seem sensible. To this end, Catrillanca contended that beyond mobilization, analysis, careful study, and working on public policies from an indigenous perspective were important. There are urgent development needs in Mapuche communities, she said, and if Mapuche professionals do not take charge of this work, it will be left to non-Mapuche. Putting suspicions and resentments aside and taking advantage of the skills and knowledge of Mapuche who have worked in the state but are sympathetic to the movement (as well as other professionals) are likely to be key steps in making autonomy proposals more feasible in the long run, particularly to the extent that such individuals could help create the institutions necessary to put autonomy into play. Indeed, several respondents spoke of the need to create the bases for autonomous Mapuche institutions, a position that acknowledges critiques like Panguilef's. To the extent that many state workers already sympathize with and participate in the movement, or have in the past, this is a dubious division in any case. Still, as Yun-Joo Park and I (2007) have argued, incorporating state workers must be done with openness and care, to avoid squashing non-Western knowledge and limit co-optation.

It is also important to consider the potential contributions of non-Mapuche state workers who are sympathetic to the movement. Several Chilean state workers spoke of the impact working with Mapuche communities had on them as individuals. Emilio Meza, whose job involved supporting micro-enterprises in a municipality in Cautín, observed that even though he had grown up there and had grandparents who lived in the countryside, he had never gotten to know the Mapuche until he started working at the municipality. His attitudes had been transformed as a result of his work: "I recognize that until I started working at the municipality, I didn't have direct contact with Mapuche people. . . . I think I had zero knowledge of the cultural aspect because I never took interest, and also, in the times in which maybe I could have been given an incentive to learn, I wasn't." While laws are necessary to facilitate change, Meza said, it is also necessary to develop awareness among citizens about what it means to recognize indigenous peoples. It was important "that some of us can say the Mapuche really isn't lazy, nor is he an alcoholic, because a lot of people still continue to believe that, but they continue to believe it because [they] haven't had the opportunity to see how they work, to see how sacrificed their life is in the countryside, that it is not easy." Meza felt developing this understanding, as he had, would facilitate greater sympathy with the direction the Mapuche movement had taken and contribute to better relations between Chileans and the Mapuche.

Although he saw interpersonal interactions as essential to transformation, Meza acknowledged the structural barriers faced by Mapuche communities. He observed that his own team, which set up groups of Mapuche and Chilean campesinos in small businesses related to agricultural production, had often proceeded without considering basic needs that had to be met before campesinos could participate productively. The team sometimes criticized Mapuche for not making it into town for meetings, he said, but "it turns out, when we went into the field, we realized, to get to their house, it took us an hour and a half, the roads were horrible." While the municipal workers had a Jeep, Meza added, the Mapuche only had access to a bus that passed once a day. Others had to take two buses to get to town, which required money they don't have. "I think many times one doesn't put oneself in that context, in that reality," he concluded. "I think many times we make the mistake of thinking the difficulty of working with them is for a [cultural] difference, and a lot of times I think it is more . . . a difference of social levels and the needs they have as a person."

Here Meza argues against attributing all types of difference to culture and instead recognizing the intersections of race/ethnicity and economic need. He added that seeing how hard Mapuche campesinos work, especially given the barriers they faced, made him want to work harder for their benefit. Meza's words indicate the possibility of individual change through work in the state apparatus. The Mapuche movement would do well to see people like him as potential allies. Incorporating the participation of Mapuche professionals and state workers—provided that they are willing to prioritize movement goals over state ones—could support the struggle for autonomy by providing a wealth of institutional expertise and skills.

Women

I was visiting Guacolda, an elderly friend in Cautín, who saw several of her children driven into exile during the dictatorship. I sat at her table as she swept the floor and told me stories her grandmother had told her about the occupation. "We women have so much history," she reflected, and I thought about how that history of struggle, work, and courage lived on in women I had met over the previous nine years. Women comprise the second group whose role must be addressed to increase the likelihood that claims for autonomy will one day meet with success. This is not to say women have not played important roles in the movement in the past—they certainly have (see Richards 2003, 2004, 2005). But, as with almost any social struggle, there are issues of gender inequality within the movement that merit resolution. Incorporating indigenous women's rights into the struggle for autonomy would make the challenge to Chilean citizenship stronger and more inclusive.

Gender politics is sensitive terrain. Many Mapuche women feel they have been used by Chileans as a weapon against the Mapuche struggle. This can be seen in the claims of state employees that "at least you can work with the women" and "the women work harder than the men." It is also seen in the use of aspects of Mapuche culture to deny collective rights. For example, university administrator Armando Torres contended: "Among the Mapuche, culturally, the woman was a means of production, an exchangeable good. Well, if we are going to respect Mapuche culture, are we going to let the exploitation of women continue or are we going to say that that is not possible?" This statement demonstrates how elites manipulated the concept of culture to their own ends, as if to say that Mapuche culture were static and women were not/are not exploited in Chilean and other cultures too. Shannon Speed (2006) has described how a similar discourse has shaped the Mexican state's rejection of indigenous rights: the state uses the supposed lack of guarantees for indigenous women's individual rights within indigenous norms as a justification for denying collective rights and autonomy. She notes the irony of this, as the Mexican state has done little that favors indigenous women's rights on any level. She also observes that this strategy denies the simultaneity of indigenous women's experience (the fact that they are always women *and* indigenous) and their desire to both defend their culture and also work within their communities and organizations to promote gender equality.

This context made many Mapuche women reluctant to focus on the specific issues they faced as Mapuche women. In the past, others in the movement sometimes accused women who sought to address such concerns of drawing attention away from more important goals or being brainwashed by winka norms. The women also faced criticisms from Chilean feminists and members of the state women's apparatus, who accused them of defending sexist cultural practices or sought to subsume them within their own political causes (Richards 2005). Still, many Mapuche women insisted that violations of indigenous rights were violations of their rights as women. They asserted their right to be simultaneously women *and* Mapuche—both identifications are central to their subjectivities (Bacigalupo 2003).

Women often saw the Mapuche struggle as their principal one (Richards 2004). This made them critical of state efforts to promote women's rights without simultaneous attention to indigenous rights. For example, Susana Calfucoy, the wife of an imprisoned leader, explained that she did not see Mapuche women's rights included in the government's agenda: "The government talks a lot about women's rights. . . . Where are my rights, then? Don't I, as a woman, have rights to have my husband at home? And they talk about children's rights. Don't my children have rights? . . . I don't believe in women's rights, I don't believe in children's rights, because if we had rights everyone would have them and not just the few. Today we are suffering as women." Calfucoy's words speak to the centrality of the collective struggle to Mapuche women's identities. To the extent that many women I spoke with wanted to deal with gender politics in the movement, it was to better be able to participate to the benefit of the collective.

Nevertheless, some contended that "gender does not exist for the Mapuche," and that the application of the concept represented a form of colonialism (Richards 2005). They argued that, as Oyeronke Oyewumi (1997) has described in the case of the Yoruba, gender is not a salient social division for the Mapuche in the same way it is in Western societies. The fact remains, however, that many women who participate in the movement struggle to do so on equal terms, and their struggle is often made more difficult by men's resistance, which is frequently posited in terms of women's "place" in traditional Mapuche culture. For example, Doña Emiliana observed that her niece, Alba, had inherited bravery and proficiency as a leader from her grand-father, a much-respected lonko. It was Alba who oriented and instructed her cousin, who had recently been named the community's new lonko, in the ways of Mapuche leadership. On the basis of her qualities, Alba should have been lonko, but she could not be because the norms of the community said only a man could hold the position. A couple of years later, Alba's cousin abandoned the community, and they were in search of a new lonko once again. Alba continued to lead in extraofficial ways.

Resistance to women's leadership is based on learned ideas of what a woman is "supposed" to do. These ideas are not necessarily and not only learned in the communities but also in wider organizations and Chilean society. Reflecting on her experience of being criticized by Mapuche men for her leadership role in Mapuche organizations, one leader from the dictatorship era who had since worked for the state in various capacities asked: "Why [is there] so much discrimination when you go outside the community, if within the community, there is leadership on the part of women? Why, when you go outside of the community, do you lose?"

While it is important not to idealize any community as perfectly represen-tative of gender equality (Bacigalupo 2007), I saw such organizational-level issues in action during a trawun hosted by CITEM at a newly constructed community center in the main town of a comuna located in ancestral Pe-wenche territory. When I arrived with some others from Temuco, about thirty-five people, mostly Pewenche from nearby communities, were sitting around the hearth, eating piñones (pine nuts, a Pewenche staple). A member of CITEM who was in his forties told the group this was an opportunity to share thoughts about important issues. He proceeded to talk for a long time; I grew impatient with his run-of-the-mill speech, which went through tirades about the state, foreigners, sociologists, and anthropologists, and did not seem very relevant to the lives of the Pewenche attending the trawun, most of whom were new to CITEM. I had heard similar speeches before but never from members of CITEM, which, as an organization, was very inclusive of diversity among the Mapuche and actively sought and promoted alliances with others. Plus, wasn't the idea to give the Pewenche space to talk about issues important to *them*? Partway through, the man began to fixate on gen-der, calling it a concept imposed by winkas that had nothing to do with the Pewenche, and cautioning them to resist people who came in talking about gender. He went on to discuss other things, but his rant suggested that the antigender discourse is not autochthonous—here was an instance of it being taught to, or at least shared with, a group of rural Pewenche by a member of an organization based in Temuco.

Likewise, when I first met Jorge Millan, the twenty-something son of a leader who was then on trial for terrorism, his eyes popped out when I told him my previous project was about women. Mapuche men and women have their own spaces of responsibility, he said, and it would not be right, for example, for a man to cook because the home is the women's realm (see Bacigalupo 2007). Although Millan did reflect that women were protagonists in the recent conflicts, denouncing the authorities when leaders were imprisoned, such attitudes made it difficult for women to fully contribute their energies, skills, and knowledge to the benefit of the movement.

One day in 2007, I had lunch with Fabiola and Socorro, two women in their thirties who had been active in various Mapuche organizations for years. Socorro had written to me that an organization she was working with wanted guidance on how to start some workshops about gender or complementarity and duality. (In the Mapuche worldview male and female together form a dyad and act in equilibrium with complementary roles [Bacigalupo 2007].) When we spoke in person, Socorro clarified that some of the women thought the concept of gender was appropriate, but others preferred duality or complementarity because their idea was that men would participate as well. Our conversation was interesting, and a little sad. Fabiola wondered aloud if men who say they want to participate in discussions initiated by women do so because they are genuinely interested or because they just want to know what the women are up to. I suggested it was probably some of both. Fabiola looked doubtful and reminded me of a talk I gave at a conference several years earlier, when a Mapuche man objected to the premise of a panel on indigenous women's rights. Fabiola seemed less hopeful about women's place in the movement than she once was, recognizing that power and control affected internal operations. She explained that she and Socorro now say that when they were part of an organization of young Mapuche professionals, they *supported* the Mapuche movement but were not necessarily *part of it*, because when they looked at who made the decisions, it was all men.

I asked what they thought of the idea I had heard other Mapuche women talk about, that sexism is worse in the organizations than in the communities. Fabiola responded that in the organizations she has participated in, the men have learned to listen—or at least they seem like they are listening—but then blow off what the women say, as if it is wrong or insignificant. She laughed ruefully and said, "This seems to be a technique of the modern Mapuche." We talked for a while about how this is a result of men believing that they are the ones who know, understanding themselves as subjects. I asked if what Fabiola was describing was happening in an organization in which she was currently an active participant, and she said yes. I mentioned that days earlier

I had spoken with a male member who said some of the guys thought women did not have the necessary political training to be productive participants. I tried to convince him this belief might be a product of a sexist structure, but he was doubtful. We talked about silencing as a form of symbolic violence, and Fabiola said when she leaves a meeting in which she has not been able to be heard, or has censored herself, she feels undervalued and almost as if she has been physically beaten. Fabiola's and Socorro's comments are similar to what women who were active in earlier generations describe, but different too, especially to the extent that many men in the movement now claim to include women. I eventually agreed to attend a meeting where they would talk through their ideas along with other women representing several organizations.

At the meeting I heard more examples of what Fabiola and Socorro were talking about. Soledad said the most frustrating thing about her organization was that a small group of men ran everything. They did not involve the women when they met with other organizations, for example, and they came to general meetings having decided things ahead of time. When important things happened between meetings, the men did not communicate them to the women. Even though Soledad had a journalism degree, the men only asked the male journalist in the organization to do that type of work. But nor did these women accept uncritically that women's participation should be the same as men's. One suggested that maybe women staying at home and taking care of things there is a support to the movement. A discussion ensued, and someone pointed out that if this was case, the men needed to communicate to their wives what went on at the meetings, and that it should not always have to be the men who attend. Fabiola gave the example of her aunt who had trouble being accepted as the one in her family with more cultural and political knowledge and thus the one who should logically attend organizational meetings. Overall, these young women were pretty united that something needed to be done, and a lot of discussion was given to what to call their concerns: Gender? Duality? Indigenous women's rights? Self-esteem? They seemed to be searching for a way to present it to the men that would not produce conflict and would make clear that they wished to deal with issues of inequality in the movement in order to more fully support it.

Not all men opposed the idea of speaking about gender and changing women's roles. Wladimir Painemal, for example, insisted that recognizing culture as dynamic would be central to the survival of the people, and this meant recognizing that women's roles may change, just as they might use old concepts (like complementarity) for new purposes. And Wallmapuwen includes gender equality in its statement of principles. The question thus becomes how to unite discourse and practice. Perhaps the most repeated line I heard from those who criticized addressing women's issues is that women do so without considering the effects it could have on "the people," that bringing those issues up will only serve to divide "the people." But after more than a decade of going back and forth to Chile and spending a significant time with Mapuche women whose intentions are only to support their people, I have to wonder about the inverse: How can deriding and sidelining women's concerns and participation be thought of as representing the people as a whole? Do not women make up half of the people? What a shame it would be to waste those skills and energies as the goal of autonomy is pursued. As R. Aída Hernández (2009) has noted, women are among those theorizing indigenous futures from a space of nonessentialized indigenous identity; their voices are indispensable to creating an inclusive version of autonomy for the region. To incorporate indigenous women's rights as part of autonomy demands would truly transform the substance of citizenship in Chile, which has not only long denied indigenous rights but also effectively forced indigenous women to choose between their identities as women and as members of a people.

Alliances

The Mapuche have a long and complicated history with alliances, dating back to the decisions of many lonkos to ally themselves with the Spanish, and some with the Chileans, during Chile's war of independence. Yet alliances were a point of contention for many Mapuche activists.[5] This was sometimes related to negative past experiences or to a general frustration with many Chileans' denial of cultural specificity and historical injustices. When I asked schoolmaster Celestino Huentequeo how he reacted to the assertion, common in Cautín, that the area was a "*mescolanza*"—a patchwork or mishmash that made differences irrelevant—he replied:

> It is like trying to forget that at one point we were treated very badly, and to say that this didn't happen, that we never had a problem, which we have had. When they, many times the non-Mapuche, how many times have they said to us, "Look, you are a shitty Indian." . . . So, of course, you hear this in the street, ah? "No, here, it's all fine. We've never had any problems, zero problems, we've lived so well." But no. The history, the reality, when one sees and analyzes things, we've had big problems with racism.

The long history of racism made it difficult for many movement activists to envision working with Chileans. Yet coalitions with Chileans may ultimately be essential to building a movement with the sheer numbers necessary to make demands for autonomy viable.

Mapuche uneasiness about alliances often was related to experiences with Chilean political parties. Mapuche respondents active in the 1960s and 1970s frequently felt used and manipulated by their parties. Even parties on the left, which purported to support many Mapuche claims, were subject to criticism. Rosendo Huenuman, a communist member of Congress during the Allende government, blamed political parties and religion for creating divisions among the Mapuche, arguing that both led the Mapuche to serve the interests of others (Cayuqueo 2008b). He suggested the Mapuche should seek out alliances, but among Mapuche and not with winkas. Even today, Mapuche members of Chilean political parties are often relegated to "ethnic commissions" and their concerns thus marginalized. Some respondents attributed this marginalization to a racist cynicism. Political candidates want Mapuche votes and make promises and space for them within their parties, but once elected, forget the promises. Rosamel Millaman, a member of the Communist Party in his youth, added that in the 1960s and 1970s part of the problem was that racism was simply not considered important within Marxist ideology: "The Left always posited that by solving the social problems of the people, and with their rights and all the rest, racism would disappear. And it seems that this isn't the case. This definitively is not the case."

Nevertheless, particularly by the end of my fieldwork, I had frequent conversations with Mapuche activists about the importance of alliances with non-Mapuches. They often spoke about these in terms of interculturality, which at its most basic level refers to collective and individual-level interactions and mutual influence between Mapuche and Chileans, although some respondents said it entailed mutual respect and recognition as well. The increasing talk about alliances seemed to be due to several factors: the witnessing of broad support for the Chilean student protests of 2006, the support hunger strikers received from diverse sectors in Chile and abroad, and the realization that achieving some sort of cogovernance or autonomy would require convincing others in the region to join them in their quest.

The pitfalls that accompanied alliances during previous eras are often present in people's minds. Even as they recognize the importance of strength in numbers, those who seek to build alliances often have to overcome substantial distrust related to negative past experiences as well as the general difficulty of building alliances, both of which reflect systemic racism. Pedro Cayuqueo, despite being very optimistic about coalition building, gave an example of why doing so was often difficult. In 2006 a Social Forum was held in Chile.[6] Mapuche organizations wanted to call it the Peoples' Social Forum, out of recognition that more than one people were participating, but other organizations resisted, insisting: "This is a Chilean process, we are in Chile."

This suggested to him that although there might be more opportunities for building alliances than in the past, "Chilean society [still] doesn't have the capacity to give space to sociocultural and sociopolitical differences."

When asked how intercultural relations had changed over time, most Mapuche respondents said things were better today. They perceived more respect and interest in learning about Mapuche culture. Sergio Caniuqueo felt relations had improved even since the 1970s and 1980s: "You can't hope racism will disappear overnight, but . . . you hope that with the younger generations, racism diminishes. That is, I, the racism I lived when I was a kid, I don't see so markedly today. That's despite the fact that they categorize us as terrorists, but I don't see that aggressiveness that at one time . . ." I interrupted him, clarifying, "Interpersonally?" Caniuqueo continued: "That's right. In terms of interpersonal relations, I don't see it so strongly anymore." He attributed this change to the work of Mapuche organizations, as a result of which Chileans could no longer simply look at the Mapuche as "little Indians." To some extent, they had to recognize and respect the Mapuche as part of a collective people.

Because discrimination was less openly hostile, Pedro Cayuqueo felt it was easier for the Mapuche to project themselves externally as a political collective rather than turning inward as a "culturalist refuge of one's own." He believed this could facilitate a "much more fluid interethnic relationship," in part because it might lessen the movement's "fixation with land." In his view placing too much emphasis on land was counterproductive:

> I don't think it's saying the land issue is not important. . . . [There are] cultural elements that determine the land is very important for the Mapuche people. But when you do politics what you tend to think . . . is, "Which are the rights claims or struggles that permit us to begin acquiring power?" I don't know any community that has been given land that can tell me, "Now we have power." On the contrary, if the Orígenes Program and the land grants the government has made since 1999 have made anything clear, it's that land doesn't do anything to solve the subsistence economy of the Mapuches in the countryside. That is, it doesn't do it for the Mapuche, just as it doesn't do it for Luchsinger, or for Urban, or for any farmer who is halfway, in quotes, a landowner, who is surviving in the countryside with land. That is, when you [say] . . . Luchsinger is a latifundista, and Urban. . . . They, with their level of income, with their level of agricultural production, if we compare them with the real latifundistas in Argentina, Mexico, or Brazil, they are mere *jornaleros* [day laborers].

What Cayuqueo was getting at was that many medium-scale farmers were also struggling as a result of globalization and the emphasis on large-scale agricultural exports. He observed that the movement's focus on land not only failed to solve "the problem of economic dependency or poverty" but also isolated the Mapuche from potential allies who did not share the demand for land but might share other concerns. Even some victims of *atentados* were potential allies to the extent that they too were being harmed by neoliberal globalization. Rather than construct the *colonos* as the enemy, Cayuqueo felt, it might make sense to reach out to them. (It goes without saying that such alliances would also require a change in colonos' racist attitudes and actions.)

Mapuche communities had in fact built alliances with Chileans in numerous instances since the return to democracy. These included the opposition to the construction of the Ralco dam as well as mobilizations supported by CITEM in the early 2000s to close or clean up garbage dumps located in or near Mapuche communities. These coalitions were not always tension-free, but they existed out of common concern for environmental and health standards. Cayuqueo listed other issues that could generate alliances, including citizen participation, democratization of regional government, and taxing corporations at the regional level. His comments resonate with those of local elites who sought to disassociate Mapuche culture from the land. But whereas elites felt doing so would lead the Mapuche to integrate, Cayuqueo saw deemphasizing land as the key to the creation of a Mapuche nation. For elites, Mapuche culture and its association with land was to blame for high rates of rural poverty. Cayuqueo and others who supported decentering land and cultural essentialism were unambiguous in not blaming the Mapuche for their poverty, however. Instead, they argued that doing so would generate the support necessary to make autonomy a reality.

Despite instances of overlap, Mapuche respondents were careful to draw distinctions between their vision and that of the state or elites. In contrast to the state, which promoted intercultural services in the absence of substantive consideration of indigenous rights, and local elites who saw interculturality as a step backward or as inequality against winkas, Mapuche respondents tended to focus on the need for indigenous rights to be recognized before interculturality was possible. Caniuqueo cautioned: "When you talk about interculturality, basically you are talking about power relations, and if power relations aren't guaranteed in horizontal terms, it is really difficult to talk about it." Nevertheless, he felt invoking interculturality was a good way for the movement to involve Chileans who are disillusioned with aspects of the Chilean system. As an example, he spoke of the appeal the Mapuche approach to healthcare had for some Chileans over the Western approach.

Along similar lines, Millaray Catrillanca sensed substantial demand for intercultural materials among teachers, observing: "There are sectors of

Chilean society that openly accept the indigenous demand." Catrillanca related this sympathy to a broad dissatisfaction with Chilean democracy:

> Today the democratization process is so stalled that if it doesn't advance, I don't think the culture installed by the dictatorship will end. And I don't see democratization advancing. It is a super-structured democratization, with . . . three powers that function, but it doesn't reach the citizens or the culture. . . . Chile, one sees, is conservative, it is a racist, xenophobic country, and in that context obviously, indigenous demands meet up with more walls than doors that open. That is why the allies issue is more important, allies in the nonindigenous world as much as a more diverse perspective [within] the movement.

If the Mapuche movement were able to develop a vision that addressed not only itself but also the country as a whole, Catrillanca felt, it might successfully create the conditions for coalitions that could transform the substance of Chilean democracy.

Others agreed the Mapuche were not the only group looking for alternatives to the present model. As a result of the extreme contradictions generated by neoliberalism, Caniuqueo suggested, more Chileans and Mapuche were developing awareness of their own subordination. He thought the discontent some Chileans felt upon seeing their own demands repressed might make them more open to establishing more positive relationships with the Mapuche: "The fact of being repressed, the fact that your truths do not come out in the news, the fact that if you don't possess capital, your word can't appear in the press. This relation becomes very forceful for the Chilean, and I think in this sense, there are many Chilean people who, although they have not left their racism by the wayside—because racism in the end practically becomes a pathology—they do begin to understand the issue of social demands and that opens a space to generate a new type of relations." Caniuqueo speculated that discontent with neoliberal democracy—along with the substantial efforts of Mapuche organizations to communicate the collective character of their claims—might lead Mapuche and non-Mapuche citizens alike to seriously consider Mapuche proposals for autonomy. In this sense, by generating a system fraught with inequality and environmental destruction and failing to provide a large part of the population with a decent standard of living, the promoters of neoliberalism may be creating the conditions for the types of alliances necessary to make autonomy a real possibility.

I detected some possibilities of support for Caniuqueo's theory in my interviews with local elites. While some saw the growing influence of corporate agriculture and timber companies as inevitable and even desirable, others expressed disappointment with Chile's neoliberal model. Manuel Borja, president of a regional association of agriculturalists, spoke of the hard times falling on medium-scale farmers in the region as a result of global free trade. Colono Rene Ravinet lamented that pine and eucalyptus plantations were beginning to take over in Cautín, destroying autochthonous flora and fauna. He was distressed about the absence of economic alternatives. Malleco education official Gonzalo Lara likewise mourned the loss of the enormous trees and beautiful forests he had regarded with awe as a child, which have been replaced by pine and eucalyptus plantations. Oscar Arias, a councilman from Cautín, complained that timber companies were planting pine and eucalyptus even in fertile areas where crops could be planted or animals pastured, leaving the land "dead" afterward. These observations stand in contrast to the government-promoted development discourse that timber is the only option for the region's degraded land. There was a sense even among these elites that neoliberal development had gone too far in changing the landscape and Mapuche and Chileans' ways of life in the region. Still, for this group to be potential allies for the Mapuche, they would need to be more reflexive about how neoliberalism had affected Mapuche communities in particular as well as how their own privilege depended on the oppression of the Mapuche. They would also need to be educated about the substance of Mapuche claims for autonomy, which many elites regarded with apprehension.

Talk of alliances might seem incongruous with demands for autonomy. Yet nearly all autonomy advocates with whom I spoke went to great pains to explain that autonomy and self-determination were not about driving Chileans out of town. José Antiman explained the position of CITEM: "As the Coordinación, we are not saying the people of other blood leave. No. We want them to become conscious, . . . [to] feel like inhabitants here, and [to] struggle together with us." Pedro Cayuqueo did not see autonomy as jeopardizing the integrity of the Chilean nation. Although he believed the Mapuche had the right to conceive of themselves as a nation, he felt it was important that this nation not be exclusionary. Indeed, in Cayuqueo's vision anyone who resided in the territory would "enjoy the condition being part of that territory provides" such that "those who live here are going to be Mapuche" regardless of their origins. He explained: "From where do we construct nation? Do we construct nation from the cultural or the religious? From the bloodline? Or do we go a little further and construct a nation from a kind of civil conscience of belonging to a collective? I embrace the latter, but not with this idea of bloodline, or racial, or religious purity. . . . A discourse of a Mapuche nation that also invites Chileans to be a part of it, and maybe not only Chileans, is interesting to me."

Cayuqueo was confident many non-Mapuche would want to be a part of this nation. Similarly, Rosamel Millaman did not envision the decolonization and search for autochthonous knowledge of which he spoke above an isolationist or purist undertaking. He argued that the quest for autonomy would never be successful without the support of many people—Mapuche and nonindigenous alike, in Chile and transnationally. Moreover, he argued, autonomy would necessitate taking advantage of the diversity that exists among the Mapuche, and recognizing that diversity, far from disuniting the people, would only enrich the struggle. To the extent that they are about envisioning and putting into practice a new form of belonging for Mapuche as well as Chileans, Argentines, and others who wish to join them, Mapuche claims for autonomy are not an outright rejection of citizenship, but a revisioning of its substance.

Nevertheless, recognizing the potential contributions of Mapuche who have worked for the state, allowing the full participation of women, and building alliances with Chileans are three central challenges that will need to be taken up for Mapuche proposals for autonomy to truly form an alternative to neoliberal democratic citizenship. These challenges must be addressed to convince greater numbers of people to embrace these demands so they are taken seriously and also to prove to potential supporters that this new form of belonging is about inclusion and building a sustainable collective future.

CHILEANS WORKING TOWARD INTERCULTURALITY

Despite general acknowledgment that relations had improved over time, Mapuche respondents suggested that interculturality, in the sense of two peoples coexisting based on mutual knowledge and respect, did not exist in Chile today. As Mapuche, they felt they had long lived interculturally—functioning in two societies that operate on very different logics, learning the cultural codes of the other. They suggested it was Chileans who needed to display greater respect and openness toward the Mapuche and their culture. Even beyond local elites, many Chileans in the Araucanía continued to deny Mapuche existence and identity, often out of what seemed to be willful ignorance (Merino and Pilleux 2003; Merino et al. 2004).

Examples were plentiful over the course of my fieldwork, ranging from the mythical account among colonos that "when my family came here, there was nothing," to the inability of bus ticket agents and clerks to spell Mapuche last names. It is seen in the suggestion of an Austrian who moved to Chile in the 1970s, that one of the hunger strikes was fake (if they were really starving, they would all have long been dead) and in the refusal of an acquaintance in Santiago to believe that police violence takes place in Mapuche communities ("Nah, Patricia, the police and the people get drunk together in those little communities!"). It is seen in the ignorance of an elite councilwoman before a high school Mapuche New Year ceremony in Cautín, when she said to the *machi* who would later lead the ceremony that she should come have her photo taken with a group of politicians for the local paper because "You are also part of this." (The head of the municipal education department quickly interjected, "She's the MOST important part!") It is seen in the leftist woman I met at a party in Temuco, who claimed complete ignorance of police raids in Mapuche communities, asking with eyebrows raised, "This is happening *now?*" Such ignorance of ongoing systemic racism is evidence of the extent to which Mapuche were marginalized in the Chilean South and excluded from imaginings of the collective Chilean self. Hegemonic norms as well as common sense (in the Gramscian sense) constructed Mapuche lived experience and demands as unknowable, illegitimate, or inconsequential to the lives of Chileans. This set a context in which promoting interculturality was very challenging, especially an interculturality based on mutual respect and understanding, rather than the simple insertion of some cultural attributes into state programs.

More than one Mapuche respondent pointed out the irony that even as they discriminated against the Mapuche in their day-to-day lives and resisted recognizing the legitimacy of their ancestral claims, many Chileans in the region—including those who worked for the state as well as owners of hardware stores, livestock sellers, and others—in fact owed their livelihoods to the existence of the Mapuche. This is because indigenous policies and projects generated an important part of the market for their goods. Without the financial resources the region received related to indigenous policies, they said, the region would be depressed and many Chileans out of work. Despite this, few Chileans associated the benefits they derived from the existence of the Mapuche with a need to recognize their status as a people and right to autonomy.

While the Mapuche movement has its own work to do to foment productive coalitions, those coalitions will only be possible if more Chileans recognize the Mapuche and raise their voices in defense of indigenous rights. Some groups of Chileans have displayed willingness to promote interculturality from within civil society. Toward the end of my fieldwork, several organizations emerged in which Mapuche and Chileans worked together in explicitly multiethnic, plurinational coalitions in pursuit of common goals. The members of such organizations reflected not only on how to live together but also on what it means to actively construct an intercultural community. Here I look at the work of some of these organizations, exploring the possibility that interculturality could go beyond state mandates for the inclusion of diversity in policies and programs to actually contribute to a transformation of the meaning of "belonging" in Chile.

Competing visions of interculturality speak to questions of who is allowed to be a knower and what knowledge is accepted as valid in Chilean society today. Interculturality is a field of struggle, intimately related to competing forms of knowledge and the power to define. The institutionalization of interculturality in state policy may be a tactic to generate consent and create neoliberal multicultural subjectivities. However, it may also create spaces for legitimizing Mapuche ways of knowing. I suggest that an interculturality that does the latter would look very different from the version promoted by the Concertación. It would be explicitly antiracist, by which I mean (drawing from Hooker 2009, 92) that it would not only preserve or promote culture but would actively incorporate indigenous rights in an effort to overcome "the real and concrete disadvantages faced by . . . subordinated cultural and racial groups." This version of interculturality would be constructed by Mapuche and Chileans seeking to engage in "epistemological decolonization" (Quijano 2007, 177), build a new kind of society, and transform the content of national belonging—recognizing its multiplicity—from below.

Among the organizations explicitly founded to promote multiculturalism in the region are the Observatorio Ciudadano and a network of citizens called Chile País Multicultural. Chile País Multicultural is sponsored by Avina (a foundation created by Swiss businessman Stephan Schmidheiny, owner of Forestal Millalemu, to support sustainable human development) and promotes recognition of diversity, respectful intercultural relationships, and leadership around these issues.[7] Formerly the Observatorio de los Derechos de los Pueblos Indígenas, the Observatorio Ciudadano changed its name in part to add a focus on intercultural citizenship to its purpose of promoting indigenous rights. Their Campaign for Indigenous Rights and Interculturality in Chile, cosponsored by Chile País Multicultural and funded by Avina, is particularly notable. It involved the creation of visual ads and television and radio spots aimed to intercede in the state-promoted messages in the context of the 2010 bicentennial.[8] The campaign focused on five themes related to recognition: the indigenous were the first inhabitants of the territory and their rights should be recognized; linguistic diversity exists in Chile; cultural diversity exists in Chile; the indigenous have particular rights to political participation; and the indigenous have particular rights to participation in processes of development. Each radio and television spot ended with a message regarding the bicentennial, such as "for a bicentennial with memory" or "for a bicentennial without exclusion." Although the reach of the campaign was limited by funds, it provided an important alternative voice regarding the meaning of interculturality.

I attended an early meeting of another, more informal organization, Pueblo Intercultural (a pseudonym), at a community center in a small city. The gathering occurred around the time of San Juan/We Tripantu. (San Juan is the Catholic Holy Day that replaced the Southern Hemisphere's winter solstice; many rural Latin Americans celebrate it. We Tripantu is the Mapuche New Year celebration that occurs around the same time.) The idea of the organizers was to gather a diverse group of people to talk about what this day meant to them and how they celebrated it with their families, and in the process, to bring together colonos, Mapuche, and Chileans to talk about how they could create a sense of community and common cause. Although all who attended were invited to participate in the discussion, there were three panelists: a German colono and two Mapuche leaders. The event was not anything close to a disaster, but it did make clear what was at stake for the different parties in attempting an intercultural dialogue.

The early part of the evening was dominated by Manolo, a middle-aged man who had recently moved back to the region from Santiago. After the panelists spoke briefly, Manolo aggressively asked the Mapuche men on the panel how they proposed Mapuche and Chileans could live together, adding that the Mapuche also discriminate. He said: 'I also was born here, I also belong to this land and love it. I cry when I hear the national anthem. I feel good when I arrive back from an international trip.'[9] I was fascinated by Manolo's descent into a brand of nationalism with which few Mapuche identify. Sidelong glances and restlessness indicated he was making other people uncomfortable. Later, he suggested the Mapuche needed to change: "They have to organize themselves like we do. It is important for them to be open toward us." As often was the case, for Manolo, interculturality was not about self-reflection but about reflecting on how the Mapuche should be different.

Eventually Esmeralda Marifil, a leader I had known for years and whose fiery temper and unpredictability were widely recognized, became angry. She asked Manolo to forgive her, but his question regarding how we could live together was stupid. There is no respect here, she said, and that is why co-existence is not possible. At the mention of the lack of respect, Manolo interjected: "You just proved it." Marifil went on to explain what it was like to be disrespected in all aspects of your life, every day. She asked: "How am I going to feel integrated if the government doesn't have me in mind?" Manolo said if it consoled her at all, "we are all in the same situation." Even though my own experience with Marifil told me she could be volatile and unpredictable,

I was astounded by Manolo's incapacity to hear what the Mapuche at this event were saying and to recognize their experience was not identical to his.

It is interesting to contrast Manolo's perspective to that of Gabriela Caripan, a leader from a nearby town, who asked the German colono on the panel what *his* proposal would be for how Mapuche, Chileans, and colonos could live together. "How do we make it so space is opened up for the Mapuche? How do we enter into this interculturality game?" she asked. Her question, like Marifil's statement, indicated a perception among some Mapuche that their identity and rights were not given much consideration in the construction of policy or Chilean understandings of interculturality. Rather, what seemed to be promoted was how Mapuche could become more like Chileans. Caripan said that for the Mapuche, interculturality was associated with the state, a political machination more than a movement goal. This event brought home that interculturality as promoted by the Concertación, in terms of getting to know each other and maybe inserting some Mapuche elements into state programs, was a minor priority for many Mapuche. The reflections of Mapuche at this event consistently returned to how the state, corporations, and Chileans were violating Mapuche rights and did not respect them. Their goal was to be recognized as a distinct people with the rights that entails. For the Mapuche at this meeting, it seems, supporting intercultural initiatives first would require recognizing that the different actors coming into this intercultural relationship have unequal power. They seemed to suggest that successful intercultural endeavors would take an explicit position against ongoing dispossession and discrimination, and in favor of indigenous rights. These steps would allow the various actors to come to the table with greater trust and mutual respect.

This vision of interculturality does not always sit easily with Chileans, even those who are Mapuche allies. After the event Andrés, a co-organizer of the event who had a long history of working for Mapuche rights, said it was a positive experience but too dominated by Mapuche issues. In his view this may be true; ultimately one's perspective on interculturality comes down to what makes sense according to one's goals. In a pragmatic sense everyone will have to learn to live interculturally eventually, even if the Mapuche achieve some sort of autonomy or cogovernance. But for the time being, the main goal for many Mapuche was for their rights to be recognized, even if it goes without saying that some Mapuche treated Chileans without respect for their humanity, just as many Chileans, the state, and corporations treated the Mapuche without respect for theirs, and on a much larger scale.

But still, that thirty or so individuals chose to gather on a rainy evening to talk about how they could change intercultural relationships in their comuna might be cause for hope. It certainly gives me hope, particularly in comparison to dismal failures at addressing the conflicts, such as one European NGO's efforts to identify "potenciales de la paz" (potentials for peace), which they defined as people willing to approach the enemy and generate solutions to the conflicts. The Chilean woman who had run the program since it was established in the early 2000s explained that the police and landowners were potentials for peace, but the Mapuche—categorically—were not. In the late 1980s, with a friend, this woman set up an independent project to improve the treatment of *inquilinos*, many of them Mapuche, who worked on fundos in the region. Later she worked for CONADI. She identified with the Concertación politically. It was therefore *chocante* (uncomfortably striking), she said, that the rightist analysis of the conflicts seemed correct to her. When I asked why the Mapuche were not also *potenciales de la paz*, she explained that being one requires putting yourself in the place of the other and the Mapuche were unwilling to do that (whereas, across the board, landowners and the police apparently were).

In her view, there was more discrimination against the landowners than against the Mapuche. Moreover, she said, the police felt vulnerable and scared when they went into the communities. They felt they had to be more delicate and treat the Mapuche differently, and wondered why. To them, stealing was stealing. They wondered if recognizing ancestral rights means that crimes were not the same for all. She added that high levels of poverty among the Mapuche meant that especially among those over age fifty-five, it was difficult to talk about new ideas, and the young just wanted to fight. I was fascinated with how her account was so opposite to Mapuche explanations of the conflicts—but such accounts make sense in the minds of those with epistemic privilege. The absence of analysis of how power shapes social reality in this woman's discourse—and the NGO's work more generally—was striking. The power to define allowed the NGO to categorize all Mapuche as nonpotentials for peace, and they exhibited little desire to analyze the role that dispossession and discrimination (hardly peaceful behaviors) on the part of the state, the police as its henchmen, and landowners played in Mapuche claims. How can peace or intercultural agreement be reached if all participants in a conflict are not considered potential actors in the creation of a solution?

The Pueblo Intercultural event suggested that, however tentatively, people were seeking a different way of belonging in the face of neoliberalism. As Andrés said at the event, "[our city] is a group of ghettos that doesn't manage to form a community." A number of the Chilean women in attendance sought common ground in their interest in spirituality, natural medicine, and environmentalism. While the association of the indigenous with spirituality and nature is of course problematic in its essentialism, at the very least it shows some willingness on the part of these Chileans to see value in the Mapuche. One of the women summed it up by saying, "we all want a better life," which is perhaps the most basic form of commonality from which to build a mutual project challenging neoliberal hegemony.

Toward the end of the evening with Pueblo Intercultural, Marcela Navarro, who works for the Observatorio, suggested that recognizing the other implies recognizing yourself, and this has to do with citizenship and our relationship with a state that does not take account of us. I wondered why this discussion, like so many others in Chile, came back to the state. Why should reflecting on who we are as a people and how we treat the "others" among us require reflecting on our relationship with the state? But of course the two are related. The state has promoted a particular version of Chilean identity that is more atomizing than community-building. It excludes the Mapuche, but many Chileans also feel excluded, or at the very least, not reflected. The oft-repeated apprehension about not being taken into account signals something important about the character of the neoliberal state. This apprehension, as well as events like the one sponsored by Pueblo Intercultural, are about insisting on an identity that challenges the one promoted by the state— it is about how we imagine community, and as my friend Pancho once said, demanding a say in "what we want this thing to look like." Finally, though, it is important to note how difficult it is going to be to build an intercultural future, particularly among the region's most elite. What do we do, for example, with the local historian in Malleco, a career military man who tells us there were never many Mapuche in the area, not a drop of blood was spilt, and in fact those who were there happily helped the Chileans "pacify the territory"? What possibilities for interculturality exist when there are people who believe that version of history?

I am compelled to reflect on some of the quandaries that initially motivated this study. In 2003, having focused my research on Chile for nearly five years, I wanted to understand the politics of racial identity for Chileans. I wanted to understand this because nothing in Chile made sense according to the dominant racial ideologies of the rest of Latin America. The myth of mestizaje was not hegemonic, but nor was the myth of a white nation along the lines of a white Argentina. Rather, it seemed Chileans simply refused to look very deeply at all into their individual and collective heritage. They were *chilenos nomás,* "just Chileans." Part of me naively felt that if Chileans would recognize their Mapuche roots, rather than denying them, discrimination against the Mapuche would be somehow alleviated. But over the course of conducting this research, I was confronted with new questions: Why does it matter for Chileans to recognize the aspects of indigenous identity and culture that have been absorbed as part of "lo chileno"? Would acknowledging their Mapuche heritage bring them any closer to respecting indigenous rights? I now suspect that convincing Chileans to recognize their Mapuche elements, without a clear concomitant emphasis on antiracism and the legitimacy of indigenous rights, would simply lend to continued denial of Mapuche difference (as in the "we're all mestizo" argument) or a watering down of Mapuche claims.

On its own, intercultural discourse does little to challenge the substance of citizenship. It facilitates the generation of consent among the Mapuche for neoliberal development. Yet, to project a form of belonging that goes beyond the exclusionary norms of citizenship, the Mapuche need Chilean allies— they need Chileans to also express dissatisfaction with Chilean democracy as it currently stands. This alone is not enough, however, and it is here that the concept of interculturality may help the Mapuche movement build alliances. This version of interculturality would look very different from that promoted by the state, which is aimed at the Mapuche and not the rest of the nation. When recognition of Mapuche rights and acknowledgment of dispossession and discrimination do not form the starting point for intercultural coalitions, inequality is perpetuated. To facilitate alliances and contribute to the transformation of social life in southern Chile, Chileans would have to acknowledge historical and contemporary power differentials, recognize the legitimacy of indigenous rights, and be explicitly committed to antiracism.

As the Bolivian anthropologist Xavier Albó pointed out at the 2006 Latin American Network of Legal Anthropology conference, recognition of the "plural" aspect of the nation—the fact that more than one people legitimately exist within the borders of the state—necessarily must exist before interculturality is possible. I once heard Aucan Huilcaman, the leader of the Consejo de Todas las Tierras, make essentially the same point: under conditions in which there is denial that indigenous peoples exist—as reflected in interpersonal life and encoded in the absence of constitutional recognition and legal recognition of indigenous rights—true interculturality cannot exist. I am suggesting that Chilean citizens raising their voices to express not only dissatisfaction with Chilean democracy but also outrage about systemic racism against the Mapuche could contribute to the eventual substantive recognition of indigenous rights. This could include the right to autonomy, which would benefit the Mapuche as well as Chilean citizens of the region.

AUTONOMY AND THE FUTURE

Mapuche proponents of autonomy recognized this struggle as a long-term project. The project has been helped along by access to education (and the educated not abandoning these claims) and transnational networks. It is also facilitated by the ways memory lives on in the everyday experience of the Mapuche. Of course, memory lives on in part because dispossession continues in new forms and the historical debt has not been paid. At the same time, claims for autonomy are part of a forward-looking collective project. The debates over culture and politics they entail are ultimately debates over how to represent the collective self as a subject deserving of rights, rather than citizen-subjects whose rights are determined from the outside. In this sense Mapuche theorizing of autonomy projects forms of belonging that challenge the traditional framework of citizenship. That the assertion of these rights is perceived as a threat to economic interests as well as the epistemological position that upholds them means this will be a long-term struggle. The proposals for autonomy presented here may seem overly optimistic to some, but I would argue that time will tell. If the movement comes to better accommodate the participation of women as well as Mapuche who work in the state—the skills, energy, and knowledge of whom can only strengthen the movement—and build coalitions with Chileans (who can provide the numbers necessary to force the state to acknowledge the legitimacy of these claims), the goal of autonomy may one day be achieved in ancestral Mapuche territory. The most important point is that these claims represent a people asserting itself as a people, resisting a history of colonial dispossession in all its forms, including neoliberal multicultural citizenship.

CHAPTER 7

SYSTEMIC RACISM, SUBJECTIVITIES, AND SHARED FUTURES

In March 2011, as popular struggles erupted across the Middle East, U.S. president Barack Obama visited Chile. "At a time when people around the world are reaching for their freedoms," he observed, "Chile shows that, yes, it is possible to transition from dictatorship to democracy, and to do so peacefully" ("Obama in Chile" 2011). The strength of this transition—the so-called Chilean Miracle—frequently has been attributed to the neoliberal model instituted by the dictatorship and left in place by the Concertación governments. In this book I have sought to trouble the association between neoliberalism and the strength of democracy by addressing the consequences of the Chilean Miracle for the Mapuche people. The Mapuche case shows that the Chilean transition has not involved an improvement in the substantive experience of democracy for many indigenous people. Instead, despite the establishment of some multicultural policies and the promotion of diversity, for many Mapuche, Chile's neoliberal democracy has represented the perpetuation of colonial dispossession and structural racism.

Racial and cultural hierarchies have been pivotal in shaping social rela-

tions in the Araucanía over time. They pose urgent dilemmas for the substance and future of Chilean democracy. This chapter represents an epilogue
of sorts, reflecting on the situation post-2010, when Sebastián Piñera took
over leadership of the country. I summarize the book's findings and analytical contributions, then I speak briefly to two routes to change: the pursuit of
indigenous rights claims in international forums and the formation of antiracist intercultural coalitions for change. Finally, I address what the Chilean
case can add to broader debates about rights, racism, and democracy.

THE PIÑERA GOVERNMENT

In March 2010, Sebastián Piñera assumed the presidency of Chile. A
member of the Renovación Nacional (National Renovation Party), he was
the first rightist to win this position since the return to democracy. What
would become of indigenous policy under Piñera? A year into his administration, it seemed the neoliberal multicultural agenda would persevere,
with some alterations, mainly involving the individualization of indigenous
claims and intensification of efforts to integrate indigenous subjects into the
free-market economy.

Piñera's campaign materials displayed a willingness to engage the Concertación's commitment to multiculturalism while simultaneously echoing
some of the attitudes held by local elites in my study. The section on indigenous peoples in his "Program of Government" is subtitled "The Value of
Multiculturalism" (Piñera 2009). The first line reads: "One of the great assets
of the country is its multicultural richness to which our original peoples contribute." The document criticizes the Concertación for its lack of effectiveness in "taking advantage of this potential," specifying that its policies failed
to create a context in which the indigenous could "participate in the opportunities provided by economic development and at the same time maintain
their identity and culture." The Concertación's policies were excessively
"ruralizing," the document alleges, tying indigenous identities and cultures
to the land. Piñera intended to eliminate these tendencies, meaning that his
government would shift away from restituting land, abolish aspects of the
land policy they felt incentivized violence, privilege subsidies for individuals
rather than communities, and create opportunities to access the market.

In one sense Piñera's program suggests that a discursive commitment to
multiculturalism had become more or less a given. The document also ex-
hibits the long-standing tendency to patronize the indigenous, referring to
"our" original peoples, for example. The commitment to multiculturalism is
very thin; it is discussed in terms of "development with identity," reflecting
some aspects of Mapuche demands at the return to democracy rather than the

more substantive claims for collective cultural and political rights that had become widespread in the movement by the early 2000s. Indeed, the word "rights" does not appear in the document's discussion of indigenous peoples at all. Nor is adherence to the recommendations and requirements of various UN bodies, observers, and documents to which Chile is obliged—such as the recommendations of the Special Rapporteur on the Rights of Indigenous Peoples, the Convention Against Racial Discrimination, ILO 169, or the Declaration on the Rights of Indigenous Peoples—mentioned at all (Pantel 2010). This suggests that Piñera's government planned to continue to ignore international norms with regard to indigenous rights.

In addition, the program suggests an indigenous policy that would be individualizing and oriented toward production (ibid.). The assertion that Concertación policies "tied" the indigenous to the land echoes the narratives of the local elites in this study, and the decision to subsidize individuals making land claims but not communities signals an intention to take collective rights off the table. Early indications suggested that Piñera stayed true to the promise to deemphasize land. In 2010 the administration did not spend all the money that had been allocated in the land fund, leaving 115 communities that had been prioritized by the Bachelet administration for the restitution of lands with unresolved claims (Acción et al. 2010). One of Piñera's first steps vis-à-vis the Araucanía was to name Andrés Molina *intendente* of the Araucanía. Molina's professional background was in management at two timber companies. He was an important representative of business in the region, having previously served as the regional president of CORMA (Chilean Wood Association) as well as director and president of Corparaucanía (Association for the Productive Development of the Araucanía). His appointment was interpreted as an indication that the Piñera administration would privilege private sector interests over indigenous rights in the region.

In his first State of the Nation Address on May 21, 2010, Piñera again used patronizing rhetoric, observing: "Our original peoples are an integral part of Chile." He announced two lines of programming that his government would engage regarding the Mapuche. The first was a "historic reencounter with the Mapuche people." Within this category would be included passage of Constitutional Recognition, modification of CONADI to create "a real Indigenous Development Agency" (what that might entail was unclear), and reformation of the land policy to include training, technical help, and "associability." In a nod to local elites, Piñera said his government would retain a clear position against violence "promoted by minorities within the communities and indigenous territories," thereby upholding the good-bad Indian dichotomy that is a prominent feature of neoliberal multiculturalism.

The second line of programming consisted of the Plan Araucanía. A general plan to address the region's failure to develop along the lines of the rest of the country, the Plan Araucanía was initially proposed in 2009, before Piñera was president, apparently by a group of business leaders, university presidents, and representatives of a few Mapuche associations. Piñera adopted it as his own and details were announced in 2010. The plan notes that the Araucanía has the lowest GDP per capita in country, lower levels of income and higher poverty and illiteracy rates than the rest of the nation (particularly among the Mapuche), and virtually no foreign investment. The plan aims to make the region the country's seventh most competitive by 2022, while also "harmonizing" economic development with "the cultural reality of the region" (Gobierno de Chile 2010, 3). It makes special note that these objectives will be accomplished in part through decentralization, such that regions and municipalities will be in charge of anything they "can do better" than the central government (ibid., 25). It is geared around five axes: the "indigenous situation," education, health, economy/production, and infrastructure.

Specific objectives relating to the indigenous, some of which were mentioned in the May 21 speech, include a "reencounter with the Mapuche people, to recover trust and put value in their culture," creating channels of participation and consultation and facilitating the implementation of ILO 169; regularizing land titles; making land transferred to the Mapuche more habitable by providing water, housing, electricity, fences, and so on; assuring food security; creating "commercial alliances" between small-scale farmers and businesses that might demand their products; setting up programs for microentrepreneurs; strengthening education with Mapuche content and language; incorporating intercultural education in at least 45 percent of schools in the region; and improving intercultural health centers. All together, the plan sounds like the epitome of neoliberal multiculturalism.

The Plan Araucanía, as well as the May 21 speech, immediately attracted critics. The plan's authors assert that over seventy thousand hectares transferred to Mapuche communities and individuals by CONADI were "commercially unproductive" and that more than 85 percent lacked access to water for irrigation or human use. Essentially, through this plan, the Piñera government was accusing CONADI of handing over land that had no productive value. Domingo Namuncura, a director of CONADI under Frei, observed that this accusation is a "veiled questioning of the Indigenous Law," and the focus on "commercial alliances" a backhanded strategy to make those lands available to commercial actors in the region, through rental agreements or other types of "association." Others, such as Senator Eugenio Tuma, observed that putting these assertions on the table is preparation for doing away with the land policy altogether. José Aylwin, co-director of the Observatorio Ciudadano, suggested the tenor of the plan is that something must be done with the land the Mapuche have abandoned, rather than improving policies—an echo of elite discourses about Mapuche lack of deservedness throughout this book (all in Abrigo 2010). The Piñera administration's concerns about productivity in this regard are not far off from the old "suicide belt" narrative so prevalent in the region. Nevertheless, reflecting on the May 21 speech, Aylwin (2010) also observed that the Piñera government is maintaining (and in some cases deepening) many of the Concertación's social policies, including indigenous ones, as well as its economic policies. In the speech Piñera said he would prioritize ending "excessive inequalities" alongside developing "an economy that is free, competitive, and open to the world," based on exportation of raw materials.

Although Piñera made no explicit reference to Mapuche rights in the May 21 address or his campaign materials, his administration has been forced to confront them in several ways. The lack of justice entailed by the antiterrorist law led to another hunger strike in 2010, this one conducted by thirty-four Mapuche prisoners and lasting for almost three months. The Piñera administration turned a blind eye to the strike, even as it was occurring at the same time that the same number of copper miners was being rescued by the government in the north with much fanfare. Toward the end, with the pressure from the Catholic Church and others, the government engaged in negotiations with the hunger strikers, promising among other things to recharacterize violations of the antiterrorism law as violations of the criminal code. They followed through on this promise in several cases, but the Mapuche continued to be charged under the antiterrorism law in new cases. At the end of 2010 forty individuals remained without liberty under the antiterrorism law (whether in prison preventatively, serving a sentence, or under house arrest).[1]

A major case that would show how the Piñera government planned to deal with terrorism charges was brought to sentencing in Cañete (in the Bío-Bío Region) in 2011. This sentence was much anticipated because it would signal whether the new government would keep its word after the hunger strike. In February the court absolved fourteen Mapuche accused of "terrorist arson." It found four of them, including Héctor Llaitul, a leader of the Coordinadora Arauko-Malleko (CAM), and three other members, guilty of an attack on prosecutor Mario Elgueta in 2008 but removed the "terrorist" characterization from that crime ("Tribunal de Cañete" 2011). The sentencing took place a month later, and Llaitul was sentenced to twenty-five years in prison. The other three were sentenced to twenty years each. These were the longest sentences ever applied in the context of the conflicts. While the government had asked that the charges be recharacterized, it only did so at the end of the trial, after the special privileges accorded to prosecutors under the antiterrorism law (secret witnesses, wiretapping, and so on) had been used throughout the process ("Justicia Chilena" 2011). That is, recharacterization of the charges had only symbolic effects at best, as the entire case had already been built, and guilt established, based on the procedures associated with the antiterrorism law. Moreover, it was made clear that harsh penalties—the harshest ever—could be handed down whether the charges involved terrorism or not. The Supreme Court later modified the charges and reduced the sentences to fifteen years for Llaitul and eight for the others, but the sentences remained comparably long ("Suprema rebaja" 2011).

Beyond the use of antiterrorism legislation to criminalize Mapuche claims, the state continues to struggle to meet its obligations under ILO 169. For example, even though Piñera said his administration would prioritize passage of constitutional recognition, the version sent by the executive to the legislature was very similar to the one initiated by rightist senators in 2009, asserting a singular, indivisible, and multicultural Chilean nation. The insistence on singularity and indivisibility demonstrates continued apprehension that recognizing indigenous peoples as peoples threatens the integrity of the nation. The writing of this version, like many others, did not involve any prior consultation with indigenous peoples. Indeed, consultation and participation represent a second area in which the state has struggled to meet the requirements set forth in ILO 169 and the UN Declaration. Toward the end of the Bachelet administration, "Supreme Decree 124" was passed to establish consultation and participation for indigenous peoples on government decisions that affect them. However, according to the Instituto Nacional de Derechos Humanos de Chile (INDH), an autonomous state agency created in 2009, this decree is not adequate to meet those requirements (in Toledo Llancaqueo 2011). It was not a product of consultation; it restricts the issues that can be consulted about, gives the administration decision-making power about what consultation will entail, establishes very limited time frames in which it is supposed to happen, and explicitly excludes investment projects (such as megaprojects for electric dams, the timber industry, or agriculture). In March 2011, when the Piñera government announced a "historic process" of consultation, presumably as part of its "reencounter" with the Mapuche, it specified that this process would be based on Decree 124 (ibid. 2011).

In the judicial sphere there have been some appellate court decisions in the Chilean South to the benefit of the Mapuche in which indigenous rights have been recognized, often with specific reference to ILO 169. The Supreme

Court has revoked many of those decisions (Acción et al. 2010), but in one case, in January 2011, the Court confirmed an appellate court decision that when the Comisión Regional de Medio Ambiente (COREMA) approved the installation of a garbage dump near Mapuche communities in the Región de Los Ríos (to the south of the Araucanía), it did so illegally and arbitrarily. COREMA had failed to consult with the communities and ascertain their informed consent, in violation of Chilean environmental laws as well as ILO 169 (Vargas 2011). In general, the Piñera government seems to have chosen to follow the route of the Concertación while deemphasizing land claims and the concept of rights as much as possible, putting strong emphasis on the export-based economy, and giving substantial import to the role of regional business.[2]

CONTRIBUTIONS

I have shown that the multicultural policies and discourses that emerged in response to conflicts over resources and indigenous rights in the Chilean South involve a re-visioning of the racial project (the ways racial and cultural inequalities are built into the state) and an effort to create particular types of citizen-subjects. In various ways, different groups of people accommodate, reject, or resist the state's efforts to create citizens who consent to its objectives. These local attitudes and actions are essential to understanding the consequences of that racial project. Based on these general findings, I make five interrelated analytical contributions. First, the shape and content of neoliberal multiculturalism depend on national and local context. Second, racial oppression and the economic system are mutually constituting, and indigenous demands respond to that reality. Third, the structural *and* the subjective are crucial to analyzing struggles over rights and resources. Fourth, memory, symbolic violence, and epistemic privilege play central roles in the maintenance of systemic racism and coloniality. Fifth, top-down efforts to construct particular types of subject-citizens are likely to be accompanied by groups of people struggling from below to assert their right to be self-constructing subjects. Together, these contributions point to the critical need to find more authentically inclusive alternatives to neoliberal democratic citizenship.

The Chilean Miracle entailed constructing an economy based largely on the export of raw materials and agricultural products. In the Araucanía this model is embodied by the timber industry and development projects that create the infrastructure to support the export economy, such as roads, hydroelectric dams, and airports. These initiatives have had devastating effects on Mapuche communities. They entail the continued appropriation of Mapuche land and resources for the enrichment of others, and contributed to the conflicts that intensified over the course of the Concertación governments. The Concertación's response to the conflicts reflected the transnational discourse of neoliberal multiculturalism, but it also was conditioned by its own goals in the global economy, Mapuche demands, and the particularities of Chilean history. On the one hand, the Concertación created programs and policies that responded positively to Mapuche demands related to development or diversity. On the other, it harshly penalized Mapuche actions that favored principles of autonomy, self-governance, and territorial control.

The changing policies and discourses that make up the Chilean version of neoliberal multiculturalism represent a shift in the racial project, previously exemplified by colonialism and warfare and later the general erasure of the indigenous and the continued appropriation of their land. Michael Omi and Howard Winant (1994, 56) have defined a "racial project" as the "effort to reorganize and redistribute resources along particular racial lines," accompanied by a given "interpretation, representation, or explanation of racial dynamics." In terms of the organization and distribution of resources, neoliberal multiculturalism in Chile uses ancestral Mapuche territory for the enrichment of elites and corporations in the global economy. In terms of how racial dynamics are explained, neoliberal multiculturalism involves the creation of two subject positions for the Mapuche, which reflect the categories delineated by Charles Hale (2002, 2006): the authorized Indian and the terrorist. This shift in how racial understandings were built into the state clearly did not signal the eradication of systemic racism, and in many respects it reinforced it. Massive outmigration, dispossession, lands depleted of water and nutrients, lack of control over natural resources, inability to contribute to decisions that affect them, criminalization of demands: these are the consequences of the Chilean Miracle for the Mapuche.

Examining the perspectives of local elites and some state workers demonstrates that the move toward neoliberal multiculturalism as a racial project is multifaceted and sometimes contested. While local elites readily embraced the notion of Mapuche as terrorists, they rarely granted legitimacy to even the watered-down version of multiculturalism promoted by the Concertación. Instead, they argued that the Mapuche were culturally inferior, poverty the cause of their woes, and integration the solution. The intransigence of these attitudes as part of the regional social imaginary reflected entrenched racism as well as elites' efforts to preserve what they perceived to be their interests. Their tenacity in resisting multiculturalism and Mapuche claims for collective rights had important implications for the possibility of transforming racial and ethnic relations. Like the national and transnational discourses that shape political decision making, local elites' narratives were deeply rooted in a history of economic and political depredation that is an integral part of systemic racism. In this sense these narratives played dual, contradictory roles: local elites' rejection of even superficial forms of recognition threatened to undermine the state's neoliberal multicultural project, but their calls for the Mapuche struggle to be criminalized and refusal to recognize indigenous rights in a more meaningful, material way actually provided sustenance to state neoliberal goals. Examining beliefs and attitudes in the Araucanía shows that racism is produced and reinforced not just in a top-down manner but also through everyday beliefs and interactions.

Analytically, my findings demonstrate that, despite being a transnational project, the specific contours of neoliberal multiculturalism depend on contextual factors at the national and local levels. Indeed, the Chilean case stands in contrast to depictions of neoliberal multiculturalism elsewhere in the region (see Andolina, Radcliffe, and Laurie 2005; Assies, Ramirez, and Ventura Patiño 2006; Hale 2006; Hooker 2009; Horton 2006; Postero 2007; various contributions in Leyva, Burguete, and Speed 2008). In much of Latin America, multicultural policies—including constitutional recognition, passage of ILO 169, intercultural education and healthcare, participation and consultation, and in some cases limited autonomy and collective land rights— accompanied neoliberal reforms in the 1980s and 1990s. Chile, however, was slow to engage in even symbolic recognition. In part, this was due to the fact that in Chile, neoliberalism was imposed much earlier, during the Pinochet dictatorship, and its imposition depended less on the active consent of the people. But the reluctance to recognize was also related to other historical factors, including the long-term existence of a border between Chilean and Mapuche territory, the understanding of racial-ethnic identity in dichotomous terms, and the erasure of indigenous presence in favor of social class as a marker of social distinctions. This confluence of factors led Concertación governments to favor an assimilationist model that presented indigenous issues as produced by poverty alone until quite recently. These factors shaped attitudes toward the Mapuche in civil society as well. To the extent that the Concertación embraced recognition, it did so reluctantly—diversity might be recognized but opportunities for participation, consultation, and autonomy were drastically limited compared to cases like Bolivia and Nicaragua, however imperfect they may be (Hooker 2009; Postero 2007). The relative absence of decentralization—a common feature of neoliberal reforms elsewhere—also contributed to these limitations.

The conflicts have contributed to a readiness to embrace the punitive aspects of neoliberal multiculturalism and a particularly drastic construction of the *indio insurrecto* as terrorist (a subject position made readily available by the legacy of the dictatorship). Indigenous movements in other parts of the region may be turning inward or looking beyond recognition to focus on material claims (Burguete 2008; *NACLA Report on the Americas* 2010), and recognition as it stands does little to challenge underlying social relations anywhere in the region (Hale 2006; Postero 2007). But the Mapuche in Chile still very much intertwine the two types of demands, faced as they are with an extraordinarily narrow scope of "permissible" behavior and ever-intensifying repression of rights claims.

It is perhaps not surprising that "context matters." Surely there are differences among the other cases in the region as well, and despite the particularities of the case, neoliberal multiculturalism is the racial project that has come to accompany, and facilitate the workings of, the Chilean Miracle. Nevertheless, being attentive to context highlights that, despite transnational components and consistencies, neoliberal multiculturalism depends on local particularities for its effectiveness. Paying attention to those specificities allows us to avoid reifying neoliberal multiculturalism. It also shows that transnational aspects of the discourse do not overdetermine state-citizen relations at the local level, and it suggests the continued importance of the national and local (as opposed to transnational capital and discourses alone) in understanding systemic racism in the contemporary world.

My findings highlight the ways economic objectives and racial inequality are intertwined. This is true at the state level, where neoliberal policies in the Araucanía were built on dispossession that began with the original colonial assault, and where the state response to Mapuche objections to this reality was to categorize them as terrorists. It is equally true at the level of local subjectivities, where elites resisted multiculturalism in order to avoid reckoning with the structural inequalities that have benefited them at the expense of the Mapuche. I want to emphasize, though, that it is not enough to argue that racial ideologies are used to justify the current socioeconomic system. Rather, racial oppression and the economic system are mutually constituting. That is, racist ideologies are used to legitimize the way the economic system operates at the expense of particular groups, perpetuating the colonial relationship. At the same time, the economic system itself creates and perpetuates categories of racial difference. These links are manifest in transnational, national, and local discourses and practices, and they helped sustain the acute situation in the Araucanía. Just as racism and the economic system are intertwined, Mapuche demands have long combined recognition of ancestral rights with redistribution of power and resources.

Those demands are reflective of struggles over resources and rights in the Araucanía, and the differences in worldview that make them so intense. It is only in looking at state discourses and practices as well as local subjectivities that these struggles can be understood. Constructing the Mapuche as terrorists let the state, local elites, and timber company owners alike ignore past and present racism and elide the fact that they might be in unjust possession of Mapuche land. Constructing the Mapuche as terrorists permitted them to avoid addressing what many believe are legitimate claims to the preservation or recuperation of Mapuche territory, biodiversity, worldview, and collective political rights. An issue that merits national discussion and a political solution was instead criminalized. Simultaneously, by carefully delimiting through policy the rights they were willing to recognize, the Concertación created "acceptable" ways of being Indian and generated consent for multicultural goals. These multicultural policies, together with the use of antiterrorism legislation to sanction Mapuche who step out of line, demonstrate how race is built into the neoliberal project.

Examining local narratives shows elites also resisted recognizing these rights, but for somewhat different reasons. Whereas the government designed policies that would not threaten national development or identity, local elites were more concerned about their own relative privilege. By attributing conditions in Mapuche communities to flaws in their culture and asserting they needed to integrate, local elites, in a way, recognized the Mapuche as a collectivity. They worked hard to delegitimize Mapuche collective and cultural claims, simultaneously calling into question the Concertación's multicultural agenda. Elite narratives in the face of the multicultural project demonstrate how entrenched racism informs practices and beliefs at the local level. Thus even though multiculturalism, in Chile anyway, is a new, transnationally influenced racial project involving the recognition of some rights but not others, if this project fails, it is not only because those policies fail to engage socioeconomic redistribution or more substantive claims for collective rights but also because of resistance in the region to incorporate even symbolic principles of interculturality into everyday practice. The intentions of the central state are certainly limited, but entrenched racism at the local level is a major factor in the failure to recognize indigenous rights—one that, as in the case of the terrorism charges, sometimes provides the state with a ready excuse to limit the scope of recognition.

Memory, symbolic violence, and epistemic privilege are crucial elements in the maintenance of systemic racism as a part of state policy as well as in everyday life. The construction of "acceptable" ways of being Indian, and the refusal to engage the legitimacy of other claims, itself functions as symbolic violence, legitimizing dispossession and coloniality in the name of national development and the rule of law. Local elites' memories and versions of history are likewise used to justify their privilege in the Araucanía, thus sustaining systemic racism more broadly. Similarly, epistemic privilege functions at the level of the state to justify "Chilean" ways of knowing and facilitate the imposition of neoliberal development in ancestral Mapuche territory. Locally, epistemic privilege makes elites' claims more "believable" than Mapuche ones in the context of particular conflicts. It is only in looking at subject formation as well as local subjectivities that we can see the complex ways in which symbolic violence, memory as a form of it, and epistemic privilege contribute to the perpetuation of systemic racism. Examining symbolic violence and epistemic privilege shows how racism and coloniality are maintained, even as they change in form.

Finally, state efforts to create particular types of citizen-subjects do not go unanswered. In the Araucanía, local elites' and Mapuche views came into conflict with one another, but both groups actively asserted their right to be self-constructing subjects in this changing political context, relying on memory and knowledge claims to sustain particular positions relative to each other and the state. Both groups relied on the dialectics of sameness and difference in asserting their claims. The Mapuche claimed the right to difference when they demanded collective and cultural rights, but they also claimed the right to the civil protections held by all Chilean citizens (to not be held to a different legal standard, for example). Local elites, in contrast, justified the inequalities that benefited them on the basis of purported Mapuche cultural inferiority but asserted sameness in order to call the legitimacy of Mapuche collective claims into question.

Multicultural reforms were not aimed at transforming the subjectivities of local elites. Nevertheless, elite resistance to these reforms represents an effort to assert themselves as subjects. We might argue that the most sensible option for Mapuche and many colono farmers would be to form alliances as a manner of protecting themselves from the impacts of neoliberal agricultural policies. However, the entrenched racism in the region seemingly made it impossible for most colonos to identify their interests with those of Mapuche communities. They instead chose to identify with a national conservative elite. Of course, many Mapuche are also suspicious of such alliances, given the history of dispossession and other abuses in the region. Neoliberal multiculturalism *was* about creating self-governing indigenous subjects who would not challenge state goals in the global economy. Mapuche who asserted the right to resist were confronted with state violence. Authorized ways of being Indian meanwhile were defined so narrowly that there was little room for interlocution between the state and Mapuche as valid political actors. By utilizing this strategy, the Concertación avoided entertaining the legitimacy of Mapuche demands as political claims, instead reducing them to social claims that could be resolved through handouts and development-oriented solutions.

While some Mapuche accommodated the subject position laid out for them by the Concertación governments, many others refused to consent. Sometimes the same individuals and communities consented in some ways and resisted in others. Refusal is another important element in understanding whether or not the multicultural project succeeds. Time and again, through their praxis, rights claims, and plans for their future, Mapuche individuals and communities demanded to be taken into account as subjects of the social world, and as a people with all the rights that entails. Although the Chilean Miracle has had particular racial consequences, Mapuche activists insisted there is continuity in their struggle for cultural rights, territory, and autonomy reaching from before the Pacificación to the present day. Still, the neoliberal democratic setting, in which the state and local elites refused to recognize the legitimacy of their claims, created an urgent context for Mapuche to theorize and put into practice ideas about territorial control, autonomy, and self-determination that could serve as alternatives to neoliberal democratic citizenship.

The articulation of a coherent political project on the part of Mapuche movement actors has been made difficult by the absorption of leaders into state agencies and projects, the creation of divisions within the movement on the part of the state, differences in philosophy and tactics, and conflicts within the movement itself. The centrality the state seems to play in efforts to articulate such a project is also problematic. Recognition from the state is important but only if substantive rights to self-determination and the redistribution of power and resources accompany it. As Andrea Smith (2010) and many contributors to Leyva, Burguete, and Speed (2008) insist (in keeping with the notion of epistemological decolonization), perhaps more important than recognition on the part of states is recognition from other indigenous peoples and subjugated groups. To the extent that Mapuche movement actors are articulating such a project, however fraught with difficulties and contradictions the process may be, they insist on the interconnections between recognition and material equality, and reclaim the right to be subjects in their own right, rather than subjectified by state objectives. Their demands and actions demonstrate that despite the dehumanization entailed by systemic racism and ongoing dispossession, some people do resist, actively seeking new, less oppressive collective futures.

Systemic racism persists in Chile, even as it has changed in form. Multicultural policies in Chile are low on substance, and everyday racism is reinforced by the new paradigm. Only Mapuche and their allies have been accused of terrorism, and over the course of my fieldwork, only Mapuche individuals died in the context of the conflicts. This changed in the early morning hours of January 4, 2013, when Werner Luchsinger, a cousin of Jorge, and his wife, Vivian McKay, were killed in an arson attack on their property.[3] The event occurred in the context of protests commemorating the anniversary of the death of Matías Catrileo, which had occurred nearby in 2008. The fire was started after Luchsinger shot one of the protesters, a young machi from the area. President Piñera visited the scene, announcing that, in addition to applying the antiterrorism law, a new antiterrorism police unit, specially formed to address these conflicts, would be created ("Arson Deaths" 2013). Mapuche individuals and organizations and their allies quickly repudiated the deaths. Public outcry against the Mapuche was immediate, however, and tended to universalize the Mapuche as savages and terrorists. This drew some Mapuche and their allies to question why police violence and the Mapuche deaths it has incurred (including that of Catrileo) have not resulted in similar outcry or consequences. This event, so tragic, also in some sense had to have been anticipated in the region—the lack of adequate state response to Mapuche claims, the unsustainable tension surrounding the conflicts, finally came to this. It is a tragedy that was preventable through state action and respect for indigenous rights, and it is this, along with the loss of life, that leaves many with a heavy heart.

These facts have to make us question the laudatory treatment afforded the Chilean transition. The struggle for a more just democracy continues. That the economic system and racism are intertwined and operate at multiple levels is central to my findings, and it will necessarily inform future struggles—in Chile and in other places where inequality has intensified after neoliberal transitions to democracy. I now turn to two strategies already being engaged in the Mapuche case, which are essential to continued resistance to neoliberal racism in Chile and elsewhere.

TOWARD A BETTER FUTURE: BIFOCAL ACTIVISM

Racism and coloniality endure in Chile, at the level of state policy as well as everyday discourse and actions. Since this situation entails human suffering, change is desirable. What a transformed Chile would look like is another matter and would likely involve a lot of trial and error. Still, initiatives that have taken place elsewhere in the Americas indicate some potential first steps. The new constitutions of Bolivia and Ecuador explicitly refound their countries as unitary and plurinational states, and the first article of Bolivia's recognizes the existence of autonomies. The territory of Nunavut in Canada now

has more than ten years of experience putting a version of indigenous autonomy into practice, and of course there are a number of Mapuche theorists
and activists with a range of ideas about what they would want a changed
system to look like. In addition to continuing that praxis-oriented work, I
suggest that achieving change—making it possible that autonomy or some
other substantive transformation in the relationship between Mapuche and
the Chilean state and society could actually occur—will require continued
activism on the transnational and local levels.

In light of the state's failure to uphold indigenous peoples' human rights,
some organizations and communities are using transnational institutions
to try to force the debate onto the national scene (while recognizing that
the state may not necessarily follow the recommendations and mandates of
transnational actors and courts).[4] One way they have done so is to invite international NGOs, such as FIDH or Human Rights Watch, to conduct inves-
tigative reports on the human rights situation in the Chilean South. Likewise,
both the previous and current UN Special Rapporteurs on the Rights of Indigenous Peoples, Rodolfo Stavenhagen and James Anaya, have visited Chile
to investigate the status of indigenous peoples and the extent to which Chile
meets its international obligations regarding their rights. As outside observations, these visits draw attention to the conflicts and let the state know the
international community is aware of ongoing abuses.

Organizations have also made complaints to various entities in the UN
and Inter-American systems. These include, among many others, a report to
the Committee Against Torture documenting cases of police violence against
indigenous people and other forms of discrimination (CINTRAS et al. 2011);
a request for a hearing with the Inter-American Commission on Human
Rights (IACHR) regarding abuses committed against Mapuche and Chilean
advocates of Mapuche rights (Aylwin and Yañez 2008); a request from the
lonkos of Temucuicui and Rofue to the IACHR to obligate the Chilean state
to stop police abuses (particularly of children) in their communities (Catrillanca and Jineo 2009, 2010); and a request, made during the Lagos administration and finally sent by the IACHR to the Inter-American Court of Human
Rights in 2011, to hear a case against the Chilean state for discriminatory
application of the antiterrorist law (Observatorio Ciudadano 2011).

One major instance in which Mapuche communities and Chilean NGOs
successfully used the UN system involved the UN Committee for the Elimination of Racial Discrimination (CERD).[5] Countries that sign on to the
Convention for the Elimination of All Forms of Racial Discrimination are
required to make periodic reports to the committee documenting their efforts to meet the expectations specified therein. In the early 2000s Chile was

long overdue in filing its progress report. A group of Mapuche communities involved in socioenvironmental conflicts together with several NGOs, including the Observatorio Ciudadano and RADA (Red de Acción por los Derechos Ambientales, Action Network for Environmental Rights), sent a complaint to CERD regarding the disproportionate location of garbage dumps and water treatment plants in or near Mapuche communities, contending this was tantamount to environmental racism. CERD took up the complaint in 2007 and in 2008 informed the Chilean government that it was required to respond to the complaint and submit its periodic report. If Chile did not submit its report, CERD would evaluate the situation based on the organizations' complaints alone. The session was scheduled for August 2009, and the government finally submitted its report in June, at which point CERD postponed its examination until August of 2010. According to Blaise Pantel, coordinator of the Observatorio's Indigenous Rights Program at the time, that the CERD examined Chile at all was a product of the actions of Mapuche and Chilean civil society organizations. This brought Chile's violations of the convention to light in the international community and led to a series of strong recommendations from CERD, including that the state revise the antiterrorism law to prevent its use against people engaged in social protest and demand-making, put into practice the recommendations of the rapporteurs, recognize indigenous rights in the constitution, establish racial discrimination as a crime, prevent, investigate, and punish police abuses against the Mapuche, and so on (Observatorio Ciudadano 2010).

A 2011 case may be suggestive of how the Piñera administration will deal with complaints made to the international system. A group of Chilean NGOs was given a hearing before the IACHR regarding incidents of violence against Mapuche children. They delineated a number of serious complaints, including the use of the antiterrorist law against minors, injuries suffered by children hit with rubber bullets or tear gas by police, and illegal interrogations in schools when parents were not present, as well as harassment, torture, and kidnapping. Miguel Ángel González, director of Human Rights for Chile's Foreign Ministry, spoke on behalf of the Piñera government, arguing that these accusations were "generic, extreme, grave, and subjective." He rejected the "catastrophic" picture painted by the organizations and claimed to know of only three cases in which Mapuche youngsters had been involved in the conflicts. (All were cases in which the youngsters had broken the law in some way.) He invited the IACHR to come see for itself the reality of Mapuche children in Chile. The IACHR reportedly planned to do so in the near future ("Denuncian ante la CIDH" 2011). Clearly, the Piñera government was not willing to assume responsibility for these human rights violations.

The use of international organizations and resources as a strategy to hold the government accountable for Mapuche rights is not new, though it seems to have been stepped up in recent years. It is not a perfect strategy, because UN and OAS (Organization of American States) agencies have little power to hold nation-states accountable (although theoretically, Inter-American Court of Human Rights decisions are binding). This was made very clear with the construction of the Ralco dam. In 2003, Chile made a number of commitments before the IACHR to the Pewenche women resisting the dam's construction. But in 2004 the dam was opened before most of those promises had been met. These included creating a new comuna in the Alto Bío-Bío, establishing mechanisms to solve Pewenche communities' land problems, strengthening an indigenous development area in the region, facilitating Pewenche participation in an area forestry reserve, adopting environmental protections, compensating the women, and starting a consultation process regarding constitutional recognition and ratification of ILO 169. Aside from the first, none of these measures were fully completed before the dam was opened, and some have not been satisfied to this day (Observatorio de Derechos de los Pueblos Indígenas 2005). To some extent, more than a guarantee that states will respect indigenous rights, in publicizing rights violations internationally, these efforts serve to challenge Chile's democratic reputation. They also help put the issue on the public agenda within Chile, in part because the media seems more willing to pick up a story about the Mapuche if outside observers are talking about it, and in part because the Chilean justice system has proved unwilling to take up communities' and organizations' complaints.[6]

The second strategy I want to emphasize is efforts to build antiracist intercultural coalitions from below. Some Mapuche and Chileans have already begun to do this. Indeed, it seems more Chileans are willing to stand up in defense of Mapuche rights. For example, ten thousand people marched in Santiago in 2010 in support of the hunger strikers ("Más de 10 mil personas" 2010). It might be that more Chileans on the left are willing to speak out in defense of the Mapuche now that the Right is in power. Certainly this was true of Concertación politicians during the 2010 hunger strike. Those efforts sometimes smelled of political opportunism. Nevertheless, dissatisfaction with the content of Chilean democracy seems to have made more Chilean citizens willing to entertain the legitimacy of Mapuche claims. Still, much work is yet to be done, particularly in the Araucanía. The formation of coalitions of Mapuche and Chileans working together to create intercultural dialogue and action, expressing a desire for a more substantive democracy as well as an end to systemic racism, could generate the pressure necessary to convince the government to recognize indigenous rights, which stands to benefit Mapuche and Chilean citizens alike. But intercultural coalitions will only be effective if they put Mapuche demands at their center and are explicitly antiracist—that is, not only recognizing diversity but also advocating the redistribution of power and resources necessary to undo the systematic disadvantages faced by the Mapuche and other racially and culturally subordinated groups. This change will require a commitment to epistemological decolonization (Quijano 2007) and a willingness to challenge the selective memories of the dominant, transforming their collective understandings of the past (Hooker 2009). Otherwise, such coalitions are in danger of simply reproducing assimilationist, colonializing rhetoric whereby Mapuche are expected to fit into Chilean norms and worldviews.

As an extreme and yet in some ways paradigmatic case, Chile provides important lessons regarding the persistence of racism in democracies around the world and its relationship to the transnational ideology of neoliberalism. The multicultural policies that have become a prominent feature of many contemporary democracies actually reinforce racism by building on historical patterns and introducing new discourses and practices that work to the detriment of indigenous peoples and other subjugated groups. The reticence of people to put principles of interculturality and equality into practice at the local level likewise contributes to the obstinacy of racism. That reticence— or refusal—can give governments an excuse to limit the scope of reform. Nation-states are central actors in the perpetuation of systemic racism, as are people who benefit from it on the ground. My findings thus speak to the importance of integrating macro-level and micro-level analysis, of focusing on the structural as well as the subjective, in analyzing struggles over rights and resources in today's world. While acknowledging the influence of transnational trends and discourses, my analysis shows the continued relevance of the nation-state—and local communities—as we seek to understand how new racial discourses interact with enduring social hierarchies.

Yet struggle will continue, in Chile and elsewhere, as human beings try to live out their lives in dignity and sustainability and seek to have a say in what they want their world to look like. Not everyone will resist in all contexts, but where domination exists, so do the seeds of struggle. Of course, to resist is not necessarily to succeed, as actors with power seek to retain it. What resistance does indicate, as María Lugones tells us, is a subject at work, exercising the self creatively.[7] To struggle is to assert the self, an act of rebellion in the face of oppression and subject formation. Mapuche who struggle (and their Chilean and transnational allies alongside them), like so many throughout the world, insist through their actions that another world is possible, if we only imagine it and have the courage to accompany our collective imaginings with action.

NOTES

Chapter 1. Race and the Chilean Miracle

1. Geographically, the Araucanía is better described as located in South-Central Chile. However, the region is colloquially understood and described as in the Chilean South, and so I refer to it as such throughout this book.

2. "Mapuche" is both singular and plural in the Mapuche language (Mapudungun). Therefore I do not generally refer to "Mapuches" in this text, although my respondents and other authors sometimes pluralized Mapuche in that way.

3. "Intercultural" and "multicultural" are used interchangeably in Chile. I provide further discussion of these terms in chapter 4.

4. The Mapuche communities that Orígenes works with are those recognized formally by CONADI (Corporación Nacional de Desarollo Indígena, National Indigenous Development Agency). Many of these communities are reducciones originally established through the *títulos de merced* I describe in chapter 2, but the 1993 Indigenous Law also established procedures for the legal recognition of communities founded more recently, thus accommodating communities that have subdivided and/or purchased land in new locations, and even groups of indigenous individuals who have joined together and identified as communities to derive state benefits as such.

5. Unless otherwise noted, translations from Spanish to English (from interviews, field notes, and other primary and secondary sources) are my own. Single quotation marks (as well as the indented list in this paragraph) denote lines reconstituted from my field notes. Double quotation marks denote audio-recorded transcriptions or verbatim notes.

6. Like other respondents throughout this book, Gonzalo is protected through the use of a pseudonym and removal of identifying characteristics. More details on methodological issues appear later in this chapter.

7. In Chile most regions are made up of two provinces, each of which contains several comunas.

8. The myth of mestizaje refers to the notion that people of European, indigenous, and African roots all came together to form one new, harmonious, and homogeneous race, superior to its component parts.

9. Figures from the Instituto Nacional de Estadísticas and Programa Orígenes

(INE and Orígenes 2005) and the Ministerio de Planificación (MIDEPLAN 2006a). The indigenous represent 6.6 percent of the total population in Chile; 87.2 percent of the indigenous are Mapuche. The remaining 12.8 percent is comprised by the Aymara (7.8 percent of the total) and seven other peoples. There is a small Afro-descendent population in Chile; however, they are not counted in official statistics.

10. Some portions of this section originally appeared in somewhat different form in Park and Richards 2007, and are reproduced with Park's permission here.

11. "Consultation" is considered important as a means of assuring that the indigenous are involved in administrative and legislative decisions that affect them, their territories, and their resources, and that states either come to joint agreement with them or garner their informed consent before acting (INDH [Instituto Nacional de Derechos Humanos; National Institute of Human Rights] in Toledo Llancaqueo 2011). "Participation" is sometimes used in a similar sense and also refers to being involved in establishing priorities, design, delivery, and evaluation of policies and programs of various sorts. "Autonomy" is a type of self-determination that is discussed throughout the book, particularly in chapter 6.

12. Bolivia might be unique in having entered a "postmulticultural" period, although other scholars, focusing on the high Andes in particular, have noted a similar shift in movement claims and objectives. In addition, some have begun to refer to a "postneoliberal" (if not postmulticultural) moment. They argue that the global economic crisis that began in 2008 shows neoliberalism is untenable, and the election of leftist governments throughout Latin America even before then demonstrates neoliberalism's waning hegemony. I take issue with both of these arguments. In the first case, many of the policies put in place to stabilize the 2008 crisis did more to retrench neoliberalism than reform it. In the second, we need look no further than the Concertación, particularly the socialist governments of Ricardo Lagos and Michelle Bachelet, to see that being "leftist" does not necessarily signal a lack of affinity for free-market capitalism. Even the Concertación's relatively successful efforts to reduce poverty were inflected by the neoliberal objective of helping citizens access the market, rather than exercise social rights (Schild 2000). While some countries in the region may have entered a "postneoliberal" period, Chile is not among them.

13. One notion that seems to echo through some of the recent literature on the limits of recognition is that the indigenous were somehow duped into believing that what they needed was formal recognition. It seems to me, in contrast, that indigenous movements have long seen demands for recognition and socioeconomic redistribution as inextricably linked. Formal recognition is one important step, and indigenous movements have consistently insisted that it be accompanied by substantive change. Likewise, it must be remembered that multiculturalism itself has been an important demand of many indigenous movements, albeit one made more complex in the context of neoliberalism (Horton 2006; Speed 2008).

14. Writing in the U.S. context, Feagin uses the term "white racial frame." I remove the racial marker "white" here to facilitate the usefulness of the concept in the Latin American context.

15. Even among elites, there are different racial projects that are difficult to understand as reflective of the same frame or ideology (even recognizing that there are always competing elements within a given ideology). The interests of political elites at the national level may not always match those of local elites.

16. Andrea Smith's (2010) work drawing Native Studies into conversation with queer theory's notion of the "subjectless critique" may also be instructive here. Smith agrees that displacing the subject ("the native" in this case) can usefully focus our analyses on the broader social relations (settler colonialism) that have produced that subject. However, she also cautions that this critique can serve to disguise the power (epistemic and otherwise) of the white supremacist, settler subject, and she argues that what may be more helpful is an "identity plus" politics, marking "all identities and their relationship to the fields of power in which they are imbricated" (ibid., 63).

17. *Atentados* refers to the "attacks" on colonos' or Chileans' property, often involving land occupations or arson, purportedly committed by Mapuche.

18. The letter "k" often replaces the Spanish "c" in Mapuche spellings like "Arauko" and "Malleko." Likewise, Mapuche often removed accent marks from Mapuche proper nouns that would carry them in Spanish. I follow that convention in this book.

19. I struggled with the ethical and epistemological implications of using pseudonyms for those who asked to be indentified. This was especially true of Sergio Caniuqueo, Pedro Cayuqueo, Rosamel Millaman, and Wladimir Painemal's reflections (made as theorists of autonomy and not as participants in particular conflicts) in chapter 6. As another exception, the four appear by name in that chapter.

20. Sometimes spelled *wingka* or *wigka*, in Mapudungun, *winka* refers to outsiders. Its etymology is thought to be *we* (new) + *inka* (Inca) and carries the negative connotation of "usurper" or "thief." Today it is often used to refer to all nonindigenous Chileans.

Chapter 2. Contested Memories, Symbolic Violence, and the History of the Araucanía

1. According to José Bengoa (2004), there were ethnic differences among those who lived in central Chile at the time of the Spanish arrival, and the Spanish called them by diverse names. The Aconcagua Valley represents the northern limit for those with a similar ("Mapuche") cultural and linguistic background. "Many of the original peoples that inhabited the Central Valley did not manage to survive" as a result of war and epidemics. "Others did so through mestizaje and the assimilation of their customs with those of the invader, working for Spanish *encomenderos*" (ibid., 77). (*Encomenderos* were individuals endowed by colonial authorities with a number of *pueblos de indios*—semiautonomous indigenous villages—from which they collected cash and labor tributes, ostensibly in exchange for protection and religious instruction.) Still, in 1779, when the Archdiocese of Santiago conducted its first census, 15.4 percent of the population of the Santiago *corregimiento* (administrative subdivision) was mestizo, and 13.4 percent was indigenous (most residing in *pueblos de indios*). Sol Serrano (2002, 47) maintains that the pueblos de indios in Chile's Central Valley were early on "dissolved into the hacienda." In her studies of nineteenth-century social institutions, she has found no references to the indigenous among the peasants of the Central Valley, nor evidence of languages other than Spanish. Nevertheless, Alvaro Jara (1956) noted that an 1813 census conducted by the Archdiocese of Santiago listed 26,153 Indians, and the Archdiocese of Concepción, 22,299 more. Still, the fact remains that the indigenous population of central Chile had decreased drastically by the 1800s. As a result, "Central Chile saw itself as the image of the whole country.

The generalized mestizaje . . . , the transformation process of the indigenous into the 'Chilean people,' was not the same as what occurred at the frontiers, on the borders, where the indigenous remained as such in spite of everything" (Bengoa 2004, 92).

2. Here Arauco refers to Mapuche territory in general.

3. Pinto maintains that this was the case despite the Guerra a Muerte, and that the change in strategy around 1830 was due more to Mapuche resistance to integration than anything else. He suggests that "Guerra a Muerte" is somewhat of a misnomer: "In our opinion, more than a 'war to the death,' this movement, which occurred between 1814 and 1830, reflects the defense of local interests on the part of a well-established regional society that was not disposed to submit to the centralizing projects of the ruling class that was beginning to decide the destiny of Chile from Santiago. The Mapuche people did not remain at the margin of this resistance, despite the express willingness of some leaders and intellectuals of the epoch to include them in the nation-building project [proyecto de país] they were formulating" (Pinto 2003, 23).

4. It seems to me that Pinto's evidence is a little more mixed than he acknowledges and sometimes indicates that few saw the Mapuche as their equals. For example, while peaceful means of interaction (parlamentos, missions) were advocated, the Mapuche were still frequently described as brutes, barbarians, or hordes (e.g., Pinto 2003, 82). Nevertheless, his analysis contributes to a better understanding of the process by which Chilean attitudes toward the Mapuche changed over time.

5. See Vicuña MacKenna's 1884 Elisa Bravo, an account of a young woman thought to have possibly survived an 1849 shipwreck near Puaucho on the Isla Huapi (in the present-day comuna of Saavedra, on the Pacific Coast of Cautín), for potent examples of such rhetoric.

6. The war itself also eventually became transnational, as Mapuche fought against the ongoing Pacificación in Chile and the 1879 Conquest of the Desert in Argentina.

7. Arribanos was the denomination given to Mapuche who resided in the central plains of the region.

8. Pinto (2007) has suggested that the Mapuche initially were able to take advantage of the new markets that resulted from the growing Chilean population in the region but then suffered disproportionate consequences of the worldwide depression in the 1930s, which coincided with the rapid deterioration of their soil.

9. León (2005) has written at length about this phenomenon.

10. Palacios argued that the Chilean race was a mixture of indigenous and Visigoth roots, which he considered superior to the Spanish.

11. Barr-Melej (2001) does not directly address the integration of the Mapuche in his book. However, in a personal communication (February 2009) he said he found no evidence that the nationalist ideology he analyzes was used to integrate indigenous subjects. Likewise, Sergio Caniuqueo suggests that the dominant discourse of this period was one of Mapuche disappearance, rather than mestizaje or integration (personal communication February 6, 2012; see also Caniuqueo 2006).

12. Almagro is credited with the "discovery" of Chile. Urrutia was a Chilean general at the time of the Pacificación.

13. Mapuche organizations that fought against usurpation included the Federación Araucana, founded by Manuel Aburto Panguilef in 1919. At a 1935 congress the organization demanded return of usurped territory, in addition to creation of indigenous institutions and election of Mapuche representatives (Ray 2007). In the

mid-1930s the Corporación Araucana was created. Led by Venancio Coñoepan, it focused on gaining access to the state. (Coñoepan was minister of land and colonization under President Carlos Ibáñez for five months in 1952, and two other members of the Corporación Araucana were deputies in Congress.) The organization was a formidable opponent to division of community lands. Other important early organizations include the Sociedad Caupolican Defensora de la Araucanía, founded in 1910, which focused on integration. (Corporación Araucana was its successor.) The Unión Araucana, founded in 1926, was linked to the Capuchins and focused on integration and the elimination of social ills. The Frente Único Araucano, founded in 1938, was linked to the Popular Front (a left-wing coalition). The Asociación Nacional Indígena, founded in 1953, was another voice on the left within the Mapuche movement (Caniuqueo 2006; Foerster and Montecino 1988; Ray 2007).

14. Bernardo O'Higgins was a revolutionary and the first leader of independent Chile.

15. Certainly the concept of "terra nullius" has shaped many settler societies, including Australia as well as several in the Americas. "Terra nullius" has a legal meaning in international law, but it is the fantasy of terra nullius and how it informs the memories of the descendants of settlers that I am interested in here.

16. Fabien Le Bonniec (2009a) has shown that, contradictorily, in nineteenth-century writings on Araucanian territory a "virgin forest" discourse coexisted with ones that emphasized Chilean security and development. He follows Sara McFall (2002) in suggesting that this may be because Mapuche land use was less intensive than European-style farming, often involving cattle ranching over broad expanses of land, and thus had less impact on the landscape.

17. Stephen Lewis (1994) has shown how as early as 1883, Chilean authorities like President Domingo Santa María rescripted the Pacificación as a peaceful process involving not warfare but the Mapuche simply being convinced by the good treatment of the Chileans that further resistance to becoming part of the Chilean nation was futile.

18. The Steins' conflicts with the community claiming the fundo became more intense when, after agreeing to sell it, they sought police protection to harvest trees on the property. One night while they were still living in the house, two Molotov cocktails were thrown through the window, starting a fire that the Steins were able to extinguish.

19. Mestizo nationalism refers to movement, and in some cases state, discourses that elevated the notion of the mestizo nation as a source of collective pride and resistance to neocolonial domination.

20. In general, inquilinaje was much less common in the Chilean South than in central Chile. The agricultural labor force in the region was more mobile and seasonal (Klubock 2006).

21. Despite the affinity of many Mapuche with the Left during this period, it is important to note, as does Caniuqueo (2006, 104, 107), that there were even in the 1960s and 1970s currents pointing to the limits of the relationship between the Mapuche and the Left as well as explicitly anticommunist discourses in Mapuche communities. The latter were based on fear of disruptions to Mapuche social order as well as a sense of loyalty to the patron.

22. Mallon (2005) suggests that by not simply returning fundos to their pre–

agrarian reform owners, emphasizing economic "efficiency" and actually allowing some beneficiaries of agrarian reform to keep their plots, the dictatorship's agrarian officials were able to retain an image of objectivity, even as they laid the groundwork for the intensification of export-based industrial farming and forestry.

23. Personal communication with Wladimir Painemal, 2009.

24. Research on the dictatorship's indigenous policy is scant, as Cristian Martínez and Sergio Caniuqueo (2011) attest. Nevertheless, new research reveals that concurrent with the efforts to dismantle the communities, the dictatorship fostered some policies to promote integration, which garnered approval from some Mapuche sectors. One example is the Proyecto de la Frontera (Border Project), whereby the regime established a health center, a school, and a police outpost in each sector of the cordillera, in an effort to integrate the most remote parts of the indigenous south into the nation. The project simultaneously addressed the isolation of these communities and generated confidence in public institutions, particularly at the municipal level (Caniuqueo 2011). The dictator also occasionally mobilized the notion of mestizaje, once referring to the Mapuche as "one of the essential components in the formation of our nationality" (Foerster 2001).

25. See also Rosamel Millaman's poignant account of these issues in Hale and Millaman 2006.

26. The military actively pursued him but ultimately mistakenly assassinated another man, and Don Rosendo went into exile in East Germany.

27. In the 2000s a fire was set on Rohrer's property, thought to be the action of Mapuche activists.

28. Hanssen's family has farmed in Malleco since the early 1930s. In the late 1990s they bought a fundo on which they planted fruit trees. Soon after, a neighboring Mapuche community expressed interest in buying the fundo through CONADI. Hanssen and his family explained that it was not for sale. Some time passed, and the community approached him again, asking for permission to occupy the fundo. Hanssen denied permission, saying he would remove them with the help of the police, which is what happened. The mobilizations continued; in 2000 an ambush resulted in injuries to a member of Hanssen's extended family. Shortly thereafter, the family was harvesting with police protection when suddenly the field started burning in several places. Responsibility was never determined. In the end the family sold the fundo to CONADI and, according to Hanssen, it sits abandoned today.

29. Although they were the exception, a few local elites disagreed with the portrayal of peaceful coexistence. Oscar Arias, a councilman in Cautín, agreed that the Mapuche took the Pacificación "almost submissively," but he observed that later, they were not given opportunities. They were welcome to spend their money in the cities, but if any collective decisions had to be made or problems resolved, they were not included in the process. Carlos Castro, the center-left mayor of a comuna in Malleco, said things were worse in the past but seemed to blame Mapuche ignorance: "The Mapuche really felt discriminated against. . . . He didn't recognize what his rights were." Nor did the state have the resources to deal with the issue, he claimed. Arias disagreed with the notion that the Mapuche were lazy, arguing: "The Mapuche is hard-working too, not all of them, but . . . when they have the opportunity, they work." He added that Mapuche women in particular are hardworking, and suggested that this was even truer in the past: "Before, the head of the house just drank *mate*. . . .

The woman was the one who did the garden . . . the one who did everything, but the man was always lazier." These views suggest variation in local elites' interpretations of the past. Nevertheless, they are filled with internal contradictions: things were worse in the past, but it was due to Mapuche ignorance; the Mapuche were not given opportunities, but the men were, in fact, quite lazy. Such views suggest openings in the reception of the Mapuche at the local level, but they also reinforce the obstinacy of historical frameworks that justify racial inequality.

30. "Mapuchitas" is the diminutive for "Mapuche women." It is a derogatory term.

Chapter 3. Neoliberalism and the Conflicts under the Concertación

1. Personal communication with Diane Haughney, February 17, 2012.

2. In the Araucanía at least nineteen landfills, 70 percent of the total, are located within or alongside Mapuche communities (Ray 2007).

3. This is not to say that there is not variance among Mapuche organizations and communities in terms of development strategies and priorities. Some communities have welcomed state programs like Orígenes, INDAP (Instituto Nacional de Desarrollo Agropecuario, National Agricultural Development Agency) soil improvement programs, and municipal microenterprise initiatives relatively uncritically. Others focused on looking for sustainable, autochthonous alternatives to planting pine and eucalyptus. And although the dominant discourse in the movement is anti–neoliberal development, there are differences among organizations regarding what an alternative approach might look like. For example, the Coordinadora Arauko-Malleko focuses on acquiring ancestral lands in order to pursue autonomous development from a Mapuche perspective. In contrast, members of the Wallmapuwen political party were focused less on land recuperation and more on political autonomy. I spoke with some of them who felt a limited form of exogenous timber plantation was acceptable, so long as environmental concerns are taken into account and profits benefit the Mapuche nation.

4. In the end the initiative was not implemented in Currarehue.

5. Historically, and today, these interactions have occurred mostly in Spanish. However, Sergio Caniuqueo and Fabien Le Bonniec have recorded some field data on *winka* landowners who did learn and function in the Mapuche language (personal communication with Caniuqueo).

6. Particular individuals and communities were more or less cognizant of the distinction between land and territory. Fabien Le Bonniec (2009b) has noted that the concept of territory, along with others like "nation" and "people," has entered Mapuche discourse relatively recently. (He says "territory" emerged in the mid-1990s, although Haughney [2006] observed use of the term in Mapuche proposals for the Indigenous Law several years earlier.) I think Le Bonniec would agree that even if how these concepts are expressed changes over time, the claims themselves have a historical continuity reaching back to before Chilean colonization of Mapuche lands.

7. While the transnational aspects of the Mapuche movement remain understudied, it is worth noting that Mapuche have participated in international indigenous congresses dating back to the time of Venancio Coñoepan (Foerster and Montecino 1988). The first UN Decade of the World's Indigenous People (1995–2004) brought substantial global attention to indigenous rights, and some Mapuche participated in

related activities and forums, including drafting the Declaration on the Rights of Indigenous Peoples. Indigenous rights organizations have welcomed Rodolfo Stavenhagen and James Anaya, UN Special Rapporteurs on Indigenous Rights, to Chile to investigate the status of indigenous rights claims. Some organizations have links to NGOs in other countries. The Mapuche diaspora produced by the dictatorship has provided publicity for the Mapuche cause in Europe and elsewhere as well.

8. Although many fundo owners also planted timber and some agrobusinessmen invested in the industry, the scale of their wealth generally did not compare to that of timber company owners. Still, that these actors came together in calling for the government to apply antiterrorist legislation against the Mapuche indicates their perceived common interests.

9. As these conflicts and the actors involved are well documented in the public sphere, I do not use pseudonyms in these descriptions.

10. Castro et al. (1999) put these figures at 120 families on 860 hectares; either way, the situation was dismal.

11. Personal communication with Eduardo Mella, February 28, 2012.

12. Numerous scholars have written about the cultural politics of indigenous authenticity; for a good review, see Jackson and Warren 2005. In the Mapuche context Ana Mariella Bacigalupo (2007) has written about debates over authenticity as they impact the discourse and practices of *machi* (Mapuche shamans). Chapter 5 in this book contains a more complete discussion of local elites' use of tropes about authenticity to invalidate Mapuche claims.

13. See also Spivak 1994 on the epistemic violence of (and complicity of intellectuals in) constructing the colonial subject as "other."

14. Martín Correa (2009) has provided a succinct history of the ongoing claims of Pillan, dating back to the late 1800s. In 2009, Juan Mendoza Collio was killed by a Special Forces police officer in the context of conflicts in that area.

Chapter 4. Constructing Neoliberal Multiculturalism in Chile

1. No one I know of has collected this data for the entire Concertación period. The total number depends on who we are counting—those accused under the antiterrorist law or those accused under civil and criminal codes as well, those directly involved with *atentados* or those arrested during protests, those who have been condemned or those who are in jail or under house arrest but still awaiting trial or sentencing. In any case, the Instituto de Estudios Indígenas (2003) counted 209 charged as of October 2003 (not necessarily under the antiterrorist law). Between November 2001 and October 2003, thirty-one were accused of violating that law. Fourteen were imprisoned as of October 2003, all but one "preventatively." As of January 2010, the end of the Concertación period, the Observatorio Ciudadano recorded fifty-two Mapuche (a couple were non-Mapuche sympathizers) in jail (either already sentenced or preventatively incarcerated while investigations proceeded) as well as another twenty-two under house arrest or subject to other restrictions on their freedom of movement (again, this number includes individuals who have been sentenced as well as those whose rights were restricted preventatively). The vast majority of these seventy-four were accused and/or processed under the antiterrorist law.

2. Information on the trials is drawn mostly from Toledo 2007, HRW and ODPI 2004, and ODPI 2005.

3. The Chilean legal system was "modernized" in 2000, and the new system allows for mistrial petitions. However, the plaintiffs' use of this option has been widely criticized, as it was intended as a resource for the accused.

4. In 2009, I was told a version of events that supported the innocence of the lonkos. According to my source, Pichun and Norin were negotiating with CONADI for a land grant at the time. Just as they were arriving at an agreement, some of the leaders of the CAM decided to set these fires. Pichun and Norin were not guilty, according to my source, but they were loyal to the leaders of the CAM and took the fall for them.

5. Several of the accused in this case went into hiding rather than being tried under the antiterrorism law.

6. In fact, the antiterrorism law was revised during the Aylwin government, and it was those revisions that included crimes against property as part of the definition of terrorism.

7. The government was largely successful in debilitating the CAM, but this has not meant the end of the conflicts as other actors, organizations, and communities, including many of those listed in chapter 3 and an alliance of lonkos founded in 2009 and led by Lonko Catrillanka of Temucuicui, continued occupying lands and drawing attention to violations of Mapuche rights in other ways. The CAM has been fraught with internal conflicts for much of its existence as well, with important members either quitting the organization or being forced out over ideological differences. By the time of this writing, the CAM had become a shell of what it once was.

8. The military justice system closed the investigation of the officer who killed Lemun without charging him. In June 2009 a military tribunal found Walter Ramírez, the officer who killed Catrileo, guilty of using unnecessary force resulting in death; in August 2010 he was condemned to three years and a day. However, Ramírez would not be incarcerated during that period but instead was required to sign in with the authorities once a month. In 2010, Miguel Jara Muñoz, the officer who killed Mendoza Collio, was found to have used undue force resulting in death. The military prosecutor requested a sentence of fifteen years in jail. Prosecuting attorneys also accused the police of trying to cover up the case ("Fiscal Militar" 2010). Jara Muñoz was condemned to five years and a day in 2011, but that decision was revoked by a martial court in 2012, which found that he had acted in legitimate self-defense.

9. My companion and I drove past the home of a protected witness. The place was surrounded by an electrified security fence, taller than your average fence in the campo, with a big gate as well. As we were driving out, a 4x4 filled with police passed us, going the other direction, to do their hourly check on the witness.

10. In 2002, Lagos responded to the complaints of the Right by declaring that Mapuche who occupied fundos would not be allowed to access money from CONADI's Land Fund.

11. "Alerta en Arauco" (2000); "La intifada mapuche" (2001); "Mapuches amenazan" (2001); "Comunidades indígenas en pie de guerra" (2001). The Chiapas quotation is from "La intifada mapuche."

12. The Chilean funds were not "fresh funds" but rather money that would have already been spent on indigenous communities by various state agencies.

13. Many of the funds in the last category were dedicated to programs for state workers.

14. The lack of indigenous participation in the design of Orígenes to some extent stands in contrast to IDB efforts to promote consultation. Although funded in part by the IDB, a subcontractor working for the Chilean government designed the program and the design process adhered to the modus operandi of the Chilean government rather than IDB ideals.

15. Not every community had projects in every area, however; nor did the program, initially anyway, reach all communities.

16. I remind the reader that single quotation marks here indicate lines reconstituted from my field notes. Double quotation marks denote audio-recorded transcriptions or verbatim notes.

17. According to Verónica Valdivia and Rolando Álvarez (2011), the role of municipal governments in service delivery first became prominent during the dictatorship. At that time, municipal reform was undertaken to depoliticize demands for social rights and to encourage citizens to see the municipalities as the main providers of socioeconomic assistance and participation (rather than the central state and political parties, respectively).

18. Participants limit the amount of land they dedicate to forestry in part because of the twenty or so years between planting and harvest; they need to use the rest of their land for crops that will contribute annual income.

19. Seguel (2003b) has documented many other cases of what he calls "terrorism against Mapuche."

20. Repsol is the Spanish oil company in conflict with a Mapuche community in Argentina over contamination. Endesa is the Spanish company that built Ralco and other dams in the Alto Bío-Bío. Benetton has had an ongoing land conflict with a Mapuche community in Argentina. José Bunster was a banker, latifundista, and major wheat producer in the Araucanía.

Chapter 5. Local Elites Confront Multiculturalism

1. State workers represent a mixed group to the extent that some reinforced dominant discourses and others aligned themselves with Mapuche claims.

2. María Eugenia Merino and Mauricio Pilleux (2003) have done work getting at class differences. They show that while Chileans in the Araucanía express stereotypes and prejudices across all social strata, semantic strategies differ by social class. For instance, members of middle and upper strata are more likely to see themselves as victims of Mapuche actions, and members of lower strata are more likely to displace responsibility for dispossession onto others. Middle and lower strata often see value in Mapuche of the past while evaluating contemporary Mapuche as somehow degenerate. Members of lower strata also tend to express prejudice directly, while middle and upper strata do so more implicitly.

3. Local elites from one comuna in Cautín tended to argue that the existence of special policies meant that the Mapuche were no longer discriminated against. They also suggested that everyone was mixed together and thus essentially the same. They did not however, express the heated opposition to indigenous policies that their contemporaries from Malleco (and those involved in conflicts in Cautín) did. This may be related to the relative absence of intense conflict in their comuna. It might also

suggest subtle differences in how the relationship between Mapuche and Chileans has developed over time in different parts of the region, or it might simply mean that they were savvier in responding to my questions.

4. In reality, the price for which land in conflict was sold to CONADI was almost always much higher than market value. Still, Isler may have been correct when he asserted no one would buy the land if CONADI did not.

5. Ordóñez, along with Jorge Luchsinger, compared their situation to that of white farmers in Africa. Ordóñez drew a parallel between southern Chile and Zimbabwe, while Luchsinger, in an interview in *Qué Pasa* magazine, said: "The Mapuche is crafty, he's twisted, disloyal, and abusive. . . . Do you know what happens in Africa with the natives? . . . In Africa, the sequence is to burn the barns, then they set the patron's house on fire, and if the European still doesn't abandon the house, they kill him. That is what is left for me. . . . They already burned the houses down. Now the only thing left is for blood to flow" (Corvalán 2005).

6. Still, unlike many landowners, Marcial said he had "a very positive attitude with respect to the Mapuche. For me it is a people that I feel close to, and I lament very much being [involved in] a fight against them. It is not a fight against them, it is a fight against terrorist expression, that a few of them practice." Although it is true that a limited number of Mapuche have participated in the more aggressive tactics, Marcial misses that the criminalization of Mapuche claims and their characterization as "terrorist" affects and offends most Mapuche.

7. It is worth noting that this critique also was common among Mapuche who had applied for land subsidies via approved procedures and waited many years to see any results. One man told me: "They've helped the most rebellious, and they haven't ever worked, and they don't help the good people."

8. Paradoxically, elites also criticized traditional Mapuche culture as "uncivilized," which they used as another reason to deny Mapuche claims.

9. Centros de Madres, or local Mothers Centers, existed in Chile long before the dictatorship. Social organizations as well as spaces for learning new skills and information, the centers also often served as a base for governments to generate support among poor and working-class women (Richards 2004). Wives of political and military leaders visited the centers during the dictatorship, "teaching" poor women how to economize and manage their homes. The irony of rich women teaching poor women how to "get by" was surely not lost on the purported beneficiaries.

10. The reader is reminded that while double quotation marks indicate audio-recorded transcriptions or verbatim notes, single quotation marks denote lines reconstituted from field notes.

11. According to the 2006 CASEN, the poverty rate in the Araucanía was substantially higher than that of the rest of the country for the indigenous and nonindigenous alike. Still, there was a gap: 24.7 percent of the indigenous were poor versus 18.2 of the nonindigenous. (I could not find these figures disaggregated by rural and urban populations.)

12. The income upon which these statistics are built includes earnings as well as state subsidies.

13. I do not think this was true; it is my understanding that the amount of Orígenes funds a community received was determined by the total number of families in the community.

14. In Chile it is mostly the Mapuche who drink *hierba mate* tea. *Sopaipillas* are sweet fried bread. The *nguillatun* is a Mapuche ceremony of thanks and petition.

15. Further, Álamos used the word "Mapucha," a derogatory term that is used to mock or demean. "Mapucha" does not correspond to the vocabulary the Mapuche use to identify themselves. Nor does it follow Spanish language rules, whereby a proper noun that ends in "e" only takes on gender in the pronoun that precedes it.

16. The concept of "cultural agreements" is from Calhoun 2002.

Chapter 6. Autonomy, Interculturality, and a More Inclusive Future

1. As of March 2012, the party had yet to gather the five thousand signatures necessary to become a legally recognized party in the Chilean system.

2. Encoded in the Constitution, the binomial system is a legacy of the Pinochet dictatorship. Each legislative district has two representatives. The winning coalition must win at least two-thirds of the vote to win both seats, even if their candidates come in first and second. This system was set up to effectively give the Right veto power in the legislature, because the Left was unlikely to ever win more than two-thirds of the vote in a given district. The system works against parties, such as the Communists, who have refused to join one of the two big political coalitions (Haughney 2006). It would obviously work against small parties like Wallmapuwen.

3. Wallmapuwen's proposal for regional autonomy draws from a proposal written by the Liwen Mapuche Studies and Documentation Center at the beginning of the 1990s.

4. *Azkintuwe* first appeared in print in October 2003, and although funds for the print edition have been inconsistent, it has maintained an active Web presence since that time. Several of its editors and writers are members of Wallmapuwen, and although *Azkintuwe* is not an official news organ for the party, their views on autonomy and nationhood are closely aligned.

5. Transnational alliances did not inspire as much uneasiness as did those with Chileans. This is probably related to the long history of transnational solidarity. The movement has relied on support and publicity from organizations like Human Rights Watch, Amnesty International, the United Nations, and Federación Internacional de Derechos Humanos (FIDH). Chilean and Mapuche NGOs like the Centro de Políticas Públicas y Derechos Indígenas, the Observatorio de Derechos Indígenas, and the Catholic Church's legal team worked to bring these transnational actors to formally observe human rights abuses in the region.

6. National Social Forums are an offshoot of the World Social Forum, an annual meeting of movements and organizations from around the globe that emerged in response to the World Economic Forum in an effort to share experiences and collectively reflect on resisting neoliberalism, under the slogan: "Another World Is Possible."

7. According to Forbes.com's list of world billionaires, in 2003, Schmidheiny donated all shares from GrupoNueva, worth one billion dollars, to Viva Trust (the yields of which fund Avina). Nevertheless, the fact that Avina was born of timber industry profits has given some individuals and groups pause before accepting its funding.

8. See derechosindigenaseinterculturalidad.cl for the materials produced by the Campaign for Indigenous Rights and Interculturality.

9. I remind the reader that single quotation marks denote lines reconstituted from my field notes. Double quotation marks indicate audio-recorded transcriptions or verbatim notes.

Chapter 7. Systemic Racism, Subjectivities, and Shared Futures

1. Another interesting development related to terrorism charges involved the WikiLeaks documents revealed in 2010. The documents showed Chile had sought and received FBI support in investigating Mapuche organizations for ties with the FARC, ETA, and other terrorist or separatist organizations. That Chile sought FBI support was not a surprise; this was already known from State Department documents. However, the documents also showed U.S. ambassador Paul Simons was categorical in his rejection of the idea that the Mapuche were terrorists and their construction as such on the part of the government, elites, and the media (Gallego-Díaz 2010).

2. Social protest also broadened under Piñera's government, most notably in the form of the student movement (which started under Bachelet) and the movement against the construction of hydroelectric dams in the far south. These protests demonstrate not only generalized discontent with the content of Chilean democracy but also a renewed willingness on the part of the state to use violence against its citizens. Pancho, a longtime Mapuche supporter, observed, "The positive thing is that [Chilean] people no longer think [Mapuche complaints about state violence] are exaggerations. Rather, they've been able to see the police making use of [rubber bullets, birdshot, and tear gas] in the plain light of day and on TV."

3. In April 2012 an officer died of a gunshot wound received during a police raid in a community in Malleco. Although the death was originally blamed on Mapuche, it appears the officer was shot by another officer.

4. This strategy reflects what Margaret Keck and Kathryn Sikkink (1998) have termed the "boomerang effect," whereby movements reach out to transnational groups to pressure states into national-level changes.

5. Most information in this paragraph is from a personal communication with Blaise Pantel, April 1, 2011.

6. Personal communication with José Aylwin, April 12, 2011.

7. Discussion led by Lugones, University of Georgia Institute for Women's Studies, November 10, 2006.

GLOSSARY

Words in Mapudungun and Spanish

ad: guidance for the relationship between people and the environment

admapu: ancestral traditions, laws, and norms of the Mapuche

Araucanía: ancestral Mapuche territory; now the name of the ninth administrative region of Chile

Araucanos: the Mapuche, as called by the Spanish conquistadors

asistencialismo: a social system dominated by reliance on state subsidies and programs

atentado: attack on colonos' or Chileans' property, purportedly committed by Mapuche

auto-atentados: self-attacks, or the suggestion that some atentados were staged by colonos or timber plantation guards

boleadoras: Mapuche slingshots

botada: left to waste; often used to suggest that Mapuche lands were left messy and abandoned

campesino: peasant

colonos: descendants of European settlers who immigrated to the Araucanía after the Pacificación

comuna: municipality, in the cases addressed in this book, usually made up of a small town and surrounding rural areas

comuneros: community members

consejero/a: municipal councilman or councilwoman

convivencia: coexistence

corridas de cercos: running fences; shifting the location of a fence so as to appropriate part of a neighbor's property as one's own

Frontera: the border between Mapuche and Chilean territory; also used to refer to the Araucanía more generally

fundos: medium- to large-scale farms

Gulumapu: Mapuche territory west of the Andes (the Chilean side)

Indio: Indian, often used pejoratively

inquilinaje: tenant farming

inquilinos: tenant farmers

insurrecto: insurrectionary

intendente: the top regional authority, appointed by the president

itrofil mogen: all of the life that exists in the universe; biodiversity

juzgados de indios: the court system set up in 1930 to deal with Mapuche land and property

latifundistas: large-scale landowners

lonko: leader; literally "head" in Mapudungun

machi: Mapuche shamans/healers/spiritual leaders

Mapudungun: the Mapuche language

mediería: half-sharing of various sorts

mestizaje: an assimilationist ideology of cultural and racial mixing between those of indigenous, European, and African descent

mestizo: an identity based on the ideology of *mestizaje*

Mirista: member of the Movimiento de Izquierda Revolucionaria

mucho mosto, mucha música y poca pólvora: "a lot of alcohol and music and a little gunpowder," an expression attributed to Cornelio Saavedra, commanding general of the Pacificación

Nuke Mapu: Mother Earth

Pacificación: Pacification; the war waged by Chile against the Mapuche in the mid- to late 1800s

parlamentos: Encounters at which Mapuche and Spanish (and later Chilean) authorities established agreements regarding borders and other conditions of peace; also refers to the agreements themselves, which can be considered treaties between sovereign nations

permitido: authorized

Pewenche: Mapuche who reside in the cordillera

Puelmapu: Mapuche territory east of the Andes (the Argentine side)

rakiduam: autochthonous thought; reflection

reducciones: land reductions

rewe: wooden altar belonging to a machi

ruka: traditional Mapuche home, usually with walls of adobe or *coliwe* (native bamboo) branches, a thatch roof, and an open hearth

tierras antiguas: ancestral lands

títulos de merced: deeds that established the lands that would belong to the Mapuche after the Pacificación

trabajar a medias: to half-share

trawun: meeting; encounter

Wallmapu: Mapuche nation and territory; includes people and territory on both sides of the Andes

We Tripantu: Mapuche New Year, celebrated near the Southern Hemisphere's winter solstice in late June

winka: sometimes *wingka* or *wigka*, refers to outsiders, all nonindigenous Chileans; etymology thought to be *we* (new) + *inka* (Inca); often carries negative connotation of usurper or thief

BIBLIOGRAPHY

Abrigo, David. 2010. "Namuncura: (Gobierno) busca que la tierra indígena pueda ser comprada, arrendada o vuelta a enajenar." *Azkintuwe*. December 23. Online at http://www.azkintuwe.org/dic_2302.htm. Accessed on January 4, 2013.

Acción et al. 2010. "El estado de los derechos humanos en Chile: Visión y desafíos desde la sociedad civil y los pueblos indígenas." Report.

Acevedo, Paulina. 2009. "Entregan carta a Bachelet pidiendo se investigue violencia policial contra niños Mapuches." *Azkintuwe*. October 22. Online at http://www.azkintuwe.org/oct221.htm. Accessed on January 4, 2013.

Al-Ali, Nadje Sadig. 2007. *Iraqi Women: Untold Stories from 1948 to the Present*. London: Zed Books.

"Alerta en Arauco por temor a ola de violencia mapuche." 2000. *El Sur*. October 1.

Almendras, Graciela. 2008. "Villalobos: 'Los pueblos originarios en Chile desaparecieron.'" *Azkintuwe*. September 1. Online at http://www.azkintuwe.org/sept1-2.htm (reprinted from *El Mercurio*). Accessed on January 4, 2013.

Andolina, Robert, Sarah Radcliffe, and Nina Laurie. 2005. "Development and Culture: Transnational Identity Making in Bolivia." *Political Geography* 24 (6): 678–702.

Aretxaga, Begoña. 2000. "Playing Terrorist: Ghastly Plots and the Ghostly State." *Journal of Spanish Cultural Studies* 1: 43–58.

"Arson Deaths in Chile Spark Anti-Terror Measures." 2013. *The Guardian*. January 4. Online at http://www.guardian.co.uk/world/2013/jan/04/arson-chile-land-dispute. Accessed on January 22, 2013.

Assies, Willem, Luis Ramírez, and María del Carmen Ventura Patiño. 2006. "Autonomy Rights and the Politics of Constitutional Reform in Mexico." *Latin American and Caribbean Ethnic Studies* 1: 37–62.

Auyero, Javier. 2003. *Contentious Lives: Two Argentine Women, Two Protests, and the Quest for Recognition*. Durham: Duke University Press.

Aylwin, José. 1998. "Indigenous People's Rights in Chile." Canadian Association for Latin American and Caribbean Studies, 28th Congress. Vancouver. March 19–21.

———. 2001. "El acceso de los indígenas a la tierra en los ordenamientos jurídicos de América Latina: Un estudio de casos." Document prepared for Agricultural

Development Unit, Economic Commission for Latin American and the Caribbean (ECLAC).

———. 2002. "Política públicas y pueblos indígenas: El caso de la política de tierras
del estado chileno y el pueblo mapuche." Working paper. University of Texas–
Austin. Center for Latin American Social Policy (CLASPO).

———. 2007. "La política del 'nuevo trato': Antecedentes, alcances y limitaciones."
In *El gobierno de Lagos, los pueblos indígenas y el "nuevo trato": Las paradojas de la de-
mocracia chilena*. Edited by José Aylwin and Nancy Yáñez, pp. 29–58. Santiago:
LOM.

———. 2010. "El mensaje de Piñera y los derechos humanos." Online at http://www
.monitoreandoderechos.cl/node/48. Accessed on April 8, 2011.

Aylwin, José, and Nancy Yáñez. 2008. "Request for Public Audience at CIDH."
Online at http://www.monitoreandoderechos.cl/ficha/130. Accessed on April 9,
2011.

Bacigalupo, Ana Mariella. 2003. "Rethinking Identity and Feminism: Contributions
of Mapuche Women and Machi from Southern Chile." *Hypatia* 18 (2): 32–57.

———. 2007. *Shamans of the Foye Tree: Gender, Power, and Healing among Chilean Mapuche*. Austin: University of Texas Press.

Barr-Melej, Patrick. 2001. *Reforming Chile: Cultural Politics, Nationalism, and the Rise of
the Middle Class*. Chapel Hill: University of North Carolina Press.

Becker, Marc. 2011. "Correa, Indigenous Movements, and the Writing of a New
Constitution in Ecuador." *Latin American Perspectives* 38 (1): 47–62.

Bell, Percival. 2001. "Es un error de diagnóstico creer en subversión mapuche." *El
Sur*. February 11.

Bello, Álvaro. 2007. "El Programa Orígenes y la política pública del gobierno de
Lagos hacia los pueblos indígenas." In *El gobierno de Lagos, los pueblos indígenas y el
"nuevo trato": Las paradojas de la democracia chilena*. Edited by Nancy Yáñez and José
Aylwin, pp. 193–220. Santiago: LOM.

Bengoa, José. 1985. *Historia del pueblo mapuche: Siglo XIX y XX*. Santiago: Ediciones
Sur.

———, ed. 2004. *La memoria olvidada: Historia de los pueblos indígenas de Chile*. Santiago:
Cuadernos Bicentenario (Presidencia de Chile).

Best, Steven, and Douglas Kellner. 1991. *Postmodern Theory: Critical Interrogations*.
New York: Guilford.

Boccara, Guillaume. 2006. "The Brighter Side of the Indigenous Renaissance." *New
World, New Worlds*. Online at http://www.nuevomundo.revues.org/2405. Accessed on April 24, 2012.

———. 2007. "Etnogubernamentalidad: La formación del campo de la salud intercultural en Chile." *Chungara, revista de antropología chilena* 39 (2): 185–207.

Bonilla-Silva, Eduardo. 2001. *White Supremacy and Racism in the Post–Civil Rights Era*.
Boulder: Lynne Reinner.

Bosques para Chile. 2010. "Nuestros principios." Online at http://www.bosquespara
chile.cl/bosques.asp?id=293&ids=296. Accessed on March 7, 2010.

Bourdieu, Pierre, and Loic Wacquant. 1992. *An Invitation to Reflexive Sociology*. Chicago: University of Chicago Press.

Brysk, Alison. 2000. *From Tribal Village to Global Village: Indian Rights and International
Relations in Latin America*. Stanford: Stanford University Press.

Burguete, Araceli. 2008. "Gobernar en la diversidad en tiempos de multicultural-ismo en América Latina." In *Gobernar (en) la diversidad: Experiencias indígenas desde América Latina. Hacia la investigación de co-labor.* Edited by Xochitl Leyva, Araceli Burguete, and Shannon Speed, pp. 15–64. Mexico City: CIESAS/FLACSO-Ecuador y Guatemala.

Calhoun, Craig. 2002. "Imagining Solidarity: Cosmopolitanism, Constitutional Patriotism, and the Public Sphere." *Public Culture* 14 (1): 147–71.

Campaña por los Derechos Indígenas y la Interculturalidad en Chile. Online at http://www.derechosindigenaseinterculturalidad.cl. Accessed on March 7, 2010.

Caniuqueo, Sergio. 2005. "Antagonismo en las percepciones territoriales: Un marco de interpretación." Unpublished manuscript.

———. 2006. "Siglo XX en Gulumapu: De la fragmentación del Wallmapu a la uni-dad nacional Mapuche. 1880 a 1978." In *¡ . . . Escucha, winka . . . ! Cuatro ensayos de historia nacional Mapuche y un epílogo sobre el futuro.* Edited by Pablo Marimán, Sergio Caniuqueo, José Millalén, and Rodrigo Levil, pp. 129–217. Santiago: LOM.

———. 2008. "Particularidades en la instauración de colonialismo chileno en Gulu Mapu, 1884–1950: Subordinación, alianzas y complicidades." Unpublished manuscript.

———. 2011. "La dictadura y las respuestas organizativas Mapuches, 1973–1989." Presentation at 19th Jornadas de Historia de Chile. Universidad Diego Portales, Santiago, Chile.

Caron, Bruce. 2003. *Community, Democracy, and Performance: The Urban Practice of Kyoto's Higashi-Kujo Madang.* Santa Barbara: The New Media Studio. Online at http://junana.com/CDP/corpus/TOC.html. Accessed on February 16, 2012.

Carruyo, Light. 2007. *Producing Knowledge, Protecting Forests: Rural Encounters with Gender, Ecotourism, and International Aid in the Dominican Republic.* University Park: Pennsylvania State University Press.

Carvajal, Andrés, José Peralta, and Carlos Ribera, eds. 2006. *A desalambrar: Historias de mapuches y chilenos en la lucha por la tierra.* Santiago: Editorial Ayun.

Casanueva, Fernando. 1998. "Indios malos en tierras buenas: Visión y concepción del mapuche según las elites chilenas del siglo XIX." In *Modernización, inmigración y mundo indígena: Chile y la Araucanía en el siglo XIX.* Edited by Jorge Pinto, pp. 55–131. Temuco, Chile: Universidad de la Frontera.

Cash, John. 2004. "The Political/Cultural Unconscious and the Process of Reconcil-iation." *Postcolonial Studies* 7 (2): 165–75.

Castro, Milka, Debbie Guerra, Roberto Morales, Eduardo Parry, and Rodrigo Sepúlveda. 1999. "Informe colegiado de difusión pública: Comunidad 'Temulemu.'" Report for the Colegio de Antropólogos de Chile. Online at http://www.mapuche.info/mapuint/temulemu.html. Accessed on February 24, 2012.

Catrillanca, Juan, and Domingo Jineo. 2009. Letter to CIDH (Solicitud de me-dida cautelar), November 5. Online at http://www.monitoreandoderechos.cl/ficha/134. Accessed on April 9, 2011.

———. 2010. Letter to CIDH, June 15. Online at http://www.monitoreandoderechos.cl/ficha/135. Accessed on April 9, 2011.

Cayuqueo, Pedro. 2005. "Mapuches, un pueblo en marcha." *Azkintuwe* 2 (13): 12–15.

————. 2008a. "El único camino posible es la experiencia antisistémica y rebelde" (interview with Héctor Llaitul Carillanca, CAM Leader). *Azkintuwe.* April 21. Online at http://www.azkintuwe.org/abril18_01.htm. Accessed January 4, 2013.

————. 2008b. "Rosendo Huenuman: El último parlamentario Mapuche." *Azkintuwe.* July 28. Online at www.azkintuwe.org/jul28_01.htm. Accessed on January 4, 2013.

————. 2009. "Gobierno impulsa registro de ADN de presos políticos Mapuches." *Azkintuwe.* January 28. Online at http://www.azkintuwe.org/ene28_006.htm. Accessed on January 4, 2013.

Chamosa, Oscar. 2008. "Indigenous or Criollo: The Myth of White Argentina in Tucumán's Calchaquí Valley." *Hispanic American Historical Review* 88 (1): 71–106.

CINTRAS et al. 2011. "Informe intermedio de organizaciones no gubernamentales sobre el seguimiento de las observaciones finales del comité contra la tortura al estado de Chile." Santiago.

Comisión Asesora en Temas de Desarrollo Indígena. 1999. *Informe.* Santiago: Ministerio de Planificación (MIDEPLAN).

"Comunidades indígenas en pie de guerra." 2001. *El Austral.* November 9. Online at http://www.mapuche.info/news02/austral011109.html. Accessed on January 4, 2013.

"Conflicto Mapuche: 69% cree que el gobierno debe endurecer medidas contra activistas." 2002. *La Tercera.* March 6.

Coñuepan Arcos, Venancio. 2009. "6 carabineros dados de baja por robo y asalto a forestales Arauco, acciones eran cometidas para que culparan a indígenas Mapuche de la zona." Public statement.

Coordinación de Organizaciones Mapuche (COM). 2006. "Propuestas de organizaciones territoriales Mapuche al estado de Chile. Temuco, Gulumapu." Unpublished proposal.

Cope, R. Douglas. 1994. *The Limits of Racial Domination: Plebian Society in Colonial Mexico City, 1660–1720.* Madison: University of Wisconsin Press.

Correa, Martín. 2009. "Asesinato de Jaime Mendoza Collío: Ni accidente ni hecho aislado."*Azkintuwe.* September 21.

————. n.d. "El fundo Santa Margarita, su origen, historia y su relación con las comunidades mapuches vecinas y colindantes." Working paper.

Correa, Martín, and Eduardo Mella. 2010. *Las razones del illkun/enojo: Memoria, despojo y criminalización en el territorio mapuche de Malleco.* Santiago: LOM/Observatorio.

Correa, Martín, Raúl Molina, and Nancy Yáñez. 2005. *La reforma agraria y las tierras Mapuches: Chile 1962–1975.* Santiago: LOM.

Corvalán, Patricio. 2005. "Los días de furia de Jorge Luchsinger." *Qué Pasa.* June 18.

Cuadra, Ximena. 2010. "Anteproyecto de investigación para estudios de maestría." Unpublished paper.

"Denuncian ante la CIDH casos de violencia contra niños Mapuches." 2011. *El Mostrador.* March 25.

Díaz, Cecilia. 1984. "Mapuches e italianos en Malleco: Relaciones interetnicas en 80 años de historia." In *Documentos de trabajo 16.* Santiago: Grupo de Investigaciones Agrarias, Academia de Humanismo Cristiano.

DuBois, W. E. B. [1903] 1969. *The Souls of Black Folk.* New York: Signet.

Dufey, Alberto. 2000. *La emigración suiza en la Araucanía (Chile), un caso de integración acelerada. Aspectos socio-económicos.* Victoria: Ediciones Impresos Regional.

Escobar, Arturo. 2007. "Worlds and Knowledges Otherwise: The Latin American Modernity/Coloniality Research Program." *Cultural Studies* 21 (2–3): 179–210.

Feagin, Joe R. 2006. *Systemic Racism: A Theory of Oppression.* New York: Routledge.

Federación Internacional de Derechos Humanos (FIDH). 2006. "La otra transición chilena: Derechos del pueblo Mapuche, política penal y protesta social en un estado democrático." Report from International Mission. April.

Figueroa, Noelia, ed. 2005. *Aprendizajes para la autogestión territorial Mapuche: Experiencias de cinco organizaciones territoriales indígenas.* Hualpán, Chile: FOS.

"Fiscal militar pidió 15 años de cárcel para carabinero que mató a Jaime Mendoza Collío." 2010. September 11. Online at http://www.azkintuwe.org/nov_091 .htm. Accessed on January 4, 2013.

Foerster, Rolf. 2001. "Sociedad mapuche y sociedad chilena: La deuda histórica." *POLIS* 1 (2).

Foerster, Rolf, and Sonia Montecino. 1988. *Organizaciones, líderes, y contiendas mapuches (1900–1970).* Santiago: Ediciones CEM.

Forbis, Melissa. 2006. "Autonomy and a Handful of Herbs: Contesting Gender and Ethnic Identities through Healing." In *Dissident Women: Gender and Cultural Politics in Chiapas.* Edited by Shannon Speed, R. Aída Hernández, and Lynn Stephen, pp. 176–202. Austin: University of Texas Press.

Forestal Mininco. 2010. "Plan de buena vecindad." Online at http://www.mininco .cl/Comunidad/planBV.htm. Accessed on March 7, 2010.

Foucault, Michel. 1983 [1982]. "The Subject and Power." In *Michel Foucault: Beyond Structuralism and Hermeneutics.* Edited by Hubert L. Dreyfus and Paul Rabinow, pp. 208–26. Chicago: University of Chicago Press.

Frankenberg, Ruth. 1993. *White Women, Race Matters: The Social Construction of Whiteness.* Minneapolis: University of Minnesota Press.

Gallego-Díaz, Soledad. 2010. "Chile pidió ayuda al espionaje de EE UU frente a los mapuches." *El País* (Spain). December 13.

Gedicks, Al J. 1993. *The New Resource Wars: Native and Environmental Struggles against Multinational Corporations.* Boston: South End Press.

Gil, Antonio. 2009. "Piñera reclama una segunda 'Pacificación de la Araucanía'." *Azkintuwe.* August 9.

Gills, Barry, Joel Rocamora, and Richard Wilson. 1993. *Low Intensity Democracy.* London: TNI/Pluto Press.

Gobierno de Chile. 2008. "Re-Conocer: Pacto Social por la Multiculturalidad." Government document.

———. 2010. "Plan Araucanía." Online at http://www.planaraucania.cl. Accessed on April 8, 2011.

González, Héctor. 1986. "Propiedad comunitaria o individual: Las leyes indígenas y el pueblo mapuche." *Nutram* 3: 10–11.

Gordon, Colin. 1991. "Governmental Rationality: An Introduction." In *The Foucault Effect: Studies In Governmentality.* Edited by Graham Burchell, Colin Gordon, and Peter Miller, pp. 1–51. Chicago: University of Chicago Press.

Gould, Jeffrey L. 1998. *To Die in This Way: Nicaraguan Indians and the Myth of Mestizaje, 1880–1965.* Durham: Duke University Press.

Gramsci, Antonio. 1971. *Selections from the Prison Notebooks*. New York: International Publishers.

Grass, Antonio. 2001. "Las empresas forestales y los problemas del pueblo mapuche." In *Territorio mapuche y expansión forestal*. Edited by Sara McFall, pp. 63–66. Temuco/Concepción, Chile: Instituto de Estudios Indígenas (Universidad de la Frontera)/Ediciones Escaparate.

Gustafson, Bret. 2002. "Paradoxes of Liberal Indigenism: Indigenous Movements, State Processes, and Intercultural Reform in Bolivia." In *The Politics of Ethnicity: Indigenous Peoples in Latin American States*. Edited by David Maybury-Lewis, pp. 267–308. Cambridge: Rockefeller Center for Latin American Studies.

Hale, Charles R. 2002. "Does Multiculturalism Menace? Governance, Cultural Rights, and the Politics of Identity in Guatemala." *Journal of Latin American Studies* 34: 485–524.

———. 2004. "Rethinking Indigenous Politics in the Era of the 'Indio Permitido.'" *NACLA Report on the Americas* 38 (2): 16–21.

———. 2006. *Más que un indio: Racial Ambivalence and Neoliberal Multiculturalism in Guatemala*. Santa Fe: School of American Research Press.

Hale, Charles R., and Rosamel Millaman. 2006. "Cultural Agency and Political Struggle in the Era of the Indio Permitido." In *Cultural Agency in the Americas*. Edited by Doris Sommer, pp. 281–304. Durham: Duke University Press.

Hartsock, Nancy. 1990. "Foucault on Power: A Theory For Women?" In *Feminism/Postmodernism*. Edited by Linda J. Nicholson, pp. 157–75. New York: Routledge.

Haughney, Diane. 2006. *Neoliberal Economics, Democratic Transition, and Mapuche Demands for Rights in Chile*. Gainesville: University Press of Florida.

———. 2007. "Neoliberal Policies, Logging Companies, and Mapuche Struggle for Autonomy in Chile." *Latin American and Caribbean Ethnic Studies* 2 (2): 141–60.

———. 2008. "Contending Visions of Rights, Development, and Nation: The Concertación and the Mapuche Movement in Chile." Paper presented at Native American and Indigenous Studies Conference. Athens, Georgia, April 10–12.

Hernández, R. Aída. 2009. "Indigeneity as a Field of Power: Possibilities and Limits of Indigenous Identities in Political Struggle." Address at Contested Modernities: Indigenous and Afro-descendent Experiences in Latin America, Lozano Long Conference. University of Texas at Austin. February 26–28.

Hill Collins, Patricia. 1998. *Fighting Words: Black Women and the Search for Justice*. Minneapolis: University of Minnesota Press.

Hooker, Juliet. 2009. *Race and the Politics of Solidarity*. New York: Oxford University Press.

Horton, Lynn. 2006. "Contesting State Multiculturalisms: Indigenous Land Struggles in Eastern Panama." *Journal of Latin American Studies* 38 (4): 829–58.

Human Rights Watch and Observatorio de los Derechos de los Pueblos Indígenas (HRW and ODPI). 2004. "Undue Process: Terrorism Trials, Military Courts, and the Mapuche in Southern Chile." Report.

Identidad Mapuche Lafkenche de la Provincia de Arauco. 1999. "De la deuda histórica nacional al reconocimiento de nuestros derechos territoriales." Online at http://rehue.home.xs4all.nl/act/act188.html. Accessed on January 31, 2012.

Illanes, Maria Angelica. 2003. "Los mitos de la 'diferencia y la narrativa historiográfica chilena.'" In *Revisitando Chile: Identidades, mitos e historias*. Edited by

Sonia Montecino, pp. 588–92. Santiago: Cuadernos Bicentenario (Presidencia de La República).

Instituto de Estudios Indígenas. 2003. *Los derechos de los pueblos indígenas en Chile: Informe del Programa de Derechos Indígenas.* Santiago: LOM.

Instituto de Estudios Políticos (IDEP). 2003. "Encuesta IDEP." Online at http://www.unab.cl/idep. Accessed in June 2003.

Instituto Nacional de Derechos Humanos (INDH). 2011. *Informe Anual 2010: Situación de los derechos humanos en Chile.* Santiago: INDH.

Instituto Nacional de Estadísticas (INE). 2007a. "Cambios estructurales en la agricultura Chilena: Análisis Intercensal 1976–1997–2007." Santiago: INE.

———. 2007b. "Censo Agropecuario y Forestal Resultados Por Comuna." Online at http://www.ine.cl/canales/chile_estadistico/censos/censos_agropecuarios/censo_agro pecuario_07.php. Accessed on April 8, 2012.

INE and Programa Orígenes. 2005. "Estadísticas sociales de los pueblos indígenas en Chile: Censo 2002." Santiago.

Jackson, Jean, and Kay Warren. 2005. "Indigenous Movements in Latin America, 1992–2004: Controversies, Ironies, New Directions." *Annual Review of Anthropology* 34: 549–73.

Jara, Alvaro. 1956. *Legislación indigenista de Chile.* Mexico City: Instituto Indigenista Interamericano.

Jiles, Pamela. 1985. "Mapuches: El reflejo mejor de la tierra." *Análisis* (August 6) 13: 24–25.

Jordan, Glenn, and Chris Weedon. 1995. *Cultural Politics: Class, Gender, Race, and the Postmodern World.* Oxford: Blackwell.

"Justicia Chilena condena a 25 y 20 años de cárcel a dirigentes Mapuche." 2011. *Azkintuwe.* March 22. Online at http://www.azkintuwe.org/20110322_003.htm. Accessed on January 4, 2013.

Keck, Margaret, and Kathryn Sikkink. 1998. *Activists beyond Borders: Advocacy Networks in International Politics.* Ithaca: Cornell University Press.

Klubock, Thomas Miller. 2004. "Labor, Land, and Environmental Change in the Forestry Sector in Chile, 1973–1998." In *Victims of the Chilean Miracle: Workers and Neoliberalism in the Pinochet Era, 1973–2002.* Edited by Peter Winn, pp. 337–87. Durham: Duke University Press.

———. 2006. "The Politics of Forests and Forestry on Chile's Southern Frontier, 1880s–1940s." *Hispanic American Historical Review* 86 (3): 535–70.

"La intifada mapuche. Se agrava el levantamiento indígena." 2001. *El Mercurio.* February 4.

La Tercera. 2002. "Conflicto mapuche: 69% cree que el gobierno debe endurecer medidas contra activistas." March 6.

Laurie, Nina, Robert Andolina, and Sarah Radcliffe. 2003. "Indigenous Professionalization: Transnational Social Reproduction in the Andes." *Antipode* 35 (3): 463–91.

Lavanchy, Javier. 1999. "Perspectivas para la comprensión del conflicto mapuche." Online at http:// http://www.archivochile.cl/Pueblos_originarios/hist_doc_gen/POdocgen0006.pdf. Accessed on January 4, 2013.

Le Bonniec, Fabien. 2009a. "Del 'Territorio Independiente Araucano' al Wallmapu: Transformaciones sociales y ambientales del paisaje de la Frontera entre los siglos XIX y XXI." In *Paisaje, espacio y territorio: Reelaboraciones simbólicas y re-construcciones identitarias en América Latina*. Edited by Nicolas Elison and Mónica Martínez Mauri, pp. 47–67. Quito: Abya Yala.

————. 2009b. "Etnografiar el territorio: Discursos, contextos, procesos y actores en la conformación de las territorialidades Mapuche." Unpublished manuscript.

Leiva, Claudio. 2008. "El origen de las tierras en conflicto." *La Nación Domingo*. August 31.

León, Leonardo. 2005. *Araucanía: La violencia mestiza y el mito de la pacificación, 1880–1900*. Santiago: Universidad Arcis.

————. 2007. "Tradición y modernidad: Vida cotidiana en la Araucanía (1900–1935)." *Historia* (Santiago) 40 (2): 333–78.

Lewis, Stephen E. 1994. "Myth and the History of Chile's Araucanians." *Radical History Review* 58: 112–41.

Leyva, Xochitl, Araceli Burguete, and Shannon Speed, eds. 2008. *Gobernar (en) la diversidad: Experiencias indígenas desde América Latina. Hacia la investigación de co-labor*. Mexico City: CIESAS/FLACSO-Ecuador y Guatemala.

Liberona, Flavia. 2000. "Bosques de verdad para Chile." *Movimiento Mundial por los Bosques Tropicales Boletín* 39. Online at http://www.wrm.org.uy/boletin/39/Chile.html. Accessed on February 13, 2012.

Libertad y Desarrollo. 2001. "Frente al terrorismo del siglo XXI." *Temas Públicos* 546. September 14.

Lucero, José Antonio. 2009. "Decades Lost and Won: Indigenous Movements and Multicultural Neoliberalism in the Andes." In *Beyond Neoliberalism in Latin America?* Edited by John Burdick, Philip Oxhorn, and Kenneth M. Roberts, pp. 63–81. New York: Palgrave Macmillan.

Mallon, Florencia. 1996. "Constructing Mestizaje in Latin America: Authenticity, Marginality, and Gender in the Claiming of Ethnic Identities." *Journal of Latin American Anthropology* 2 (1): 170–81.

————. 2005. *Courage Tastes of Blood: The Mapuche Community of Nicolás Ailío and the Chilean State, 1906–2001*. Durham: Duke University Press.

"Mapuches amenazan." 2001. *El Austral*. February 6.

Mariman, José. 1995. "La organización Mapuche Aukiñ Wallmapu Ngulam." Online at http://www.xs4all.nl/~rehue/artjmar2.html. Accessed on September 29, 2008.

————. 2006. "¿Etnonacionalismo Mapuche?" Paper presented at 26th International Congress of the Latin American Studies Association. San Juan, Puerto Rico.

————. 2008. "Reacción chilena a la demanda mapuche de autodeterminación-(interna) o autonomía." Presentation at Native American and Indigenous Studies Association Conference. Athens, Georgia, April 10–12.

Marín, Francisco. 2009. "José Alywin, Observatorio Ciudadano: 'Reconocimiento constitucional de pueblos indígenas es engañoso.'" *Azkintuwe*. March 10. Online at http://www.azkintuwe.org/marz11_01.htm (reprinted from http://www.elciudadano.cl). Accessed on January 4, 2013.

Marshall, T. H. [1950] 1992. *Citizenship and Social Class*. Concord, Massachusetts: Pluto Press.

Martínez Neira, Christian, and Sergio Caniuqueo. 2011. "Las políticas hacia las comunidades mapuche del gobierno militar y la fundación del Consejo Regional Mapuche, 1973–1983." *Veriversitas* 1 (1): 146–86.

"Más de 10 mil personas marcharon en Santiago por los derechos del Pueblo Mapuche." 2010. *Azkintuwe*. October 12. Online at http://www.azkintuwe.org/oct_0121.htm. Accessed on January 4, 2013.

McFall, Sara. 2001. "Expansión forestal: Una amenaza para la territorialidad." In *Territorio mapuche y expansión forestal*. Edited by Sara McFall, pp. 43–56. Temuco/Concepción, Chile: Instituto de Estudios Indígenas (Universidad de la Frontera)/Ediciones Escaparate.

———. 2002. "Paisajes visuales, ópticas distintas: cambios en el medio ambiente y la territorialidad Mapuche." In *Territorialidad mapuche en el siglo XX*. Edited by Roberto Morales, pp. 301–23. Temuco, Chile: Instituto de Estudios Indígenas (Universidad de la Frontera).

Merino, María Eugenia, and Mauricio Pilleux. 2003. "El uso de estrategias semánticas globales y locales en el discurso de los chilenos no mapuches de la ciudad de Temuco." *Estudios Filológicos* 38: 111–19.

Merino, María Eugenia, Rosamel Millaman, Daniel Quilaqueo, and Mauricio Pilleux. 2004. "Perspectiva interpretativa del conflicto entre mapuches y no mapuches sobre la base del prejuicio y discriminación étnica." *Persona y Sociedad* 18 (1): 111–27.

Milkman, Ruth. 1997. *Farewell to the Factory*. Berkeley: University of California Press.

Ministerio de Planamiento (MIDEPLAN). 2006a. Encuesta de Caracterización Socioeconómica Nacional (CASEN). Santiago.

———. 2006b. *Memoria nuevo trato, 2000–2006*. Santiago: Gobierno del Presidente Ricardo Lagos Escobar.

Moraga Vásquez, Eduardo. 2003. "Figueroa a contraluz." *Revista el Campo* (*El Mercurio* suppl.). June 9.

NACLA Report on the Americas. 2010. "Introduction. After Recognition: Indigenous Peoples Confront Capitalism." *NACLA Report on the Americas* (September–October): 11–12.

Nagengast, Carole. 1994. "Violence, Terror, and the Crisis of the State." *American Review of Anthropology* 23: 109–36.

Naguil, Victor. 2005. "Walmapu tañi kizüngunewün." *Azkintuwe* 2 (14): 12–14.

Namuncura, Domingo. 2008. "El retorno del espíritu colonialista." *El Mostrador*. September 7.

Narváez, Luis, and María Alonso. 2006. "Juan Agustín Figueroa: El patrón intocable del sur." *La Nación Domingo*. May 28.

National Security Archive (NSA). n.d. "On [the] 30th Anniversary of Argentine Coup: New Declassified Details on Repression." Online at http://www.gwu.edu/~nsarchiv/NSAEBB/index.html#Latin%20America. Accessed on February 13, 2012.

———. n.d. "The Case against Pinochet: Ex-dictator Indicted for Condor Crimes." Online at http://www.gwu.edu/~nsarchiv/NSAEBB/index.html#Latin%20America. Accessed on February 13, 2012.

"Obama in Chile Hails Latin American Progress." 2011. *BBC News online*. March 21. Online at http://www.bbc.co.uk/news/world-latin-america-12813996. Accessed on January 4, 2013.

Observatorio Ciudadano. 2010. "Observaciones finales del Comité para la Eliminación de la Discriminación Racial de la ONU al estado de Chile." Cartilla 3 Derechos Humanos en Chile.

————. 2011. "Casos de aplicación de ley antiterrorista contra dirigentes mapuche son trasladados a jurisdicción de la Corte Interamericana de Derechos Humanos." Online at http://www.mapuexpress.net/?act=news&id=7370. Accessed on March 27, 2012.

Observatorio de Derechos de los Pueblos Indígenas (ODPI). 2005. "Los derechos de los pueblos indígenas en Chile: Balance del 2004." Working paper. Temuco, Chile.

Omi, Michael, and Howard Winant. 1994. *Racial Formation in the United States: From the 1960s to the 1990s*. New York: Routledge.

Ong, Aihwa. 1996. "Cultural Citizenship as Subject-making." *Current Anthropology* 37 (5): 737–62.

Ortiz, Patricio. 2007. "Intercultural Bilingual Education, Indigenous Knowledge, and the Construction of Ethnic Identity: An Ethnography of a Mapuche School in Chile." PhD diss., University of Texas at Austin.

Oyewumi, Oyeronke. 1997. *The Invention of Women: Making an African Sense of Western Gender Discourses*. Minneapolis: University of Minnesota Press.

Palacios, Nicolás. 1904. *Raza chilena*. Valparaiso, Chile: Impr. i Litografía Alemana de Gustavo Schäfer.

Paley, Julia. 2001. *Marketing Democracy: Power and Social Movements in Post-dictatorship Chile*. Berkeley: University of California Press.

Pantel, Blaise. 2010. "El programa de gobierno 2010: Un retroceso en material de derechos de pueblos indígenas." Online at http://www.observatorio.cl/node/149. Accessed on April 8, 2011.

Park, Yun-Joo. 2006. "The State, Mapuche Communities, and Multicultural Social Policy: A Comparative Study of Three Intercultural Hospitals in Chile." PhD diss., University of Texas at Austin.

Park, Yun-Joo, and Patricia Richards. 2007. "Negotiating Neoliberal Multiculturalism: Mapuche Workers in the Chilean State." *Social Forces* 85: 1319–39.

Pinto, Jorge. 2003. *La formación del estado y la nación, y el pueblo mapuche: De la inclusión a la exclusión*. Santiago: Dibam.

————. 2007. "Expansión económica y conflicto mapuche: La Araucanía, 1900–1940." *Revista de Historia Social y de las Mentalidades* 1 (11): 9–34.

Piñera, Sebastián. 2009. "Programa de gobierno: Pueblos originarios." Online at http://www.gob.cl/programa-de-gobierno/seguridades/pueblos-originarios/. Accessed on April 8, 2011.

————. 2010. "Del Chile del bicentenario al país de la oportunidades." Online at http://www.gob.cl/especiales/mensaje-presidencial-21-de-mayo/. Accessed on April 8, 2011.

Polletta, Francesca. 2006. *It Was Like a Fever: Storytelling in Protest and Politics*. Chicago: University of Chicago Press.

Portelli, Alessandro. 1991. *The Death of Luigi Trastulli and Other Stories: Form and Meaning in Oral History*. Albany: State University of New York Press.

Portes, Alejandro. 1997. "Neoliberalism and the Sociology of Development: Emerging Trends and Unanticipated Facts." *Population and Development Review* 23 (2): 229–60.

Postero, Nancy Grey. 2004. "Articulations and Fragmentations: Indigenous Politics in Bolivia." In *The Struggle for Indigenous Rights in Latin America*. Edited by Nancy Grey Postero and Leon Zamosc, pp. 189–216. Sussex: Academic Press.

———. 2007. *Now We Are Citizens: Indigenous Politics in Postmulticultural Bolivia*. Stanford: Stanford University Press.

Quijano, Anibal. 2000. "Coloniality of Power, Eurocentrism, and Latin America." *Nepantla: Views from South* 1 (3): 533–80.

———. 2007. "Coloniality and Modernity/Rationality." *Cultural Studies* 21 (2–3): 168–78.

Radcliffe, Sarah A., and Nina Laurie. 2006. "Culture and Development: Taking Culture Seriously in Development for Andean Indigenous People." *Environment and Planning D: Society and Space* 24: 231–48.

Ray, Leslie. 2007. *Language of the Land: The Mapuche in Argentina and Chile*. Copenhagen: International Work Group for Indigenous Affairs (IWGIA).

Reiman, Alfonso. 2001. "Expansión forestal: La visión desde el movimiento mapuche." In *Territorio mapuche y expansión forestal*. Edited by Sara McFall, pp. 33–40. Temuco/Concepción, Chile: Instituto de Estudios Indígenas (Universidad de la Frontera)/Ediciones Escaparate.

Reuque Paillalef, Rosa Isolde. 2002. *When a Flower Is Reborn: The Life and Times of a Mapuche Feminist*. Durham: Duke University Press.

Richards, Patricia. 2003. "Expanding Women's Citizenship? Mapuche Women and Chile's National Women's Service." *Latin American Perspectives* 30: 41–65.

———. 2004. *Pobladoras, Indígenas, and the State: Conflict over Women's Rights in Chile*. New Brunswick: Rutgers University Press.

———. 2005. "The Politics of Gender, Human Rights, and Being Indigenous in Chile." *Gender and Society* 19: 199–220.

———. 2006. "The Politics of Difference and Women's Rights: Lessons from Pobladoras and Mapuche Women in Chile." *Social Politics* 13 (1): 1–29.

———. 2007. "Bravas, Permitidas, Obsoletas: Mapuche Women in the Chilean Print Media." *Gender and Society* 21: 553–78.

———. 2010. "Of Indians and Terrorists: How the State and Local Elites Construct the Mapuche in Neoliberal Multicultural Chile," *Journal of Latin American Studies* 42: 59–90.

Roberts, Bryan R., and Alejandro Portes. 2006. "Coping with the Free Market City: Collective Action in Six Latin American Cities at the End of the Twentieth Century." *Latin American Research Review* 41 (2): 57–83.

Robinson, William I. 2001. "Social Theory and Globalization: The Rise of a Transnational State." *Theory and Society* 30: 157–200.

Ross, Amy. 1999. "The Body of the Truth: Truth Commissions in Guatemala and South Africa." PhD diss., University of California at Berkeley.

Salinas, Maximiliano. 2003. "Historia e identidades desde el mestizaje." In *Revisitando Chile: Identidades, mitos e historias*. Edited by Sonia Montecino, pp. 554–61. Santiago: Cuadernos Bicentenario (Presidencia de La República).

Schild, Verónica. 1998. "New Subjects of Rights? Women's Movements and the Construction of Citizenship in the 'New Democracies.'" In *Cultures of Politics/*

Politics of Cultures. Edited by Sonia E. Alvarez, Arturo Escobar, and Evelina Dagnino, pp. 93–117. Boulder: Westview Press.

————. 2000. "Neo-liberalism's New Gendered Market Citizens: The 'Civilizing' Dimension of Social Programs in Chile." *Citizenship Studies* 4 (3): 275–305.

Schwartz, Barry. 2007. "Collective Memory." In *Encyclopedia of Sociology.* Edited by George Ritzer, pp. 588–90. New York: Blackwell-Wiley.

Seguel, Alfredo. 2002. "Invasión forestal y etnocidio Mapuche." Online at http://www.mapuexpress.net/?act=publications&id=2634. Accessed on February 13, 2012.

————. 2003a. "El poder fáctico de las empresas forestales en Chile. ¿A quién se enfrenta el pueblo Mapuche?" Online at http://www.mapuche.info/fakta/repor taje030129.html. Accessed on February 13, 2012.

————. 2003b. "Radiografía al conflicto forestal en el Gulumapu." Online at http://www.mapuexpress.net/?act=publications&id=2634. Accessed on February 13, 2012.

————. 2005. "Modelo forestal chileno y pueblo Mapuche: Las posiciones irreconciliables de un conflicto territorial." Online at http://www.mapuexpress .net/?act=publications&id=224. Accessed on February 13, 2012.

Sepúlveda Navarro, Rosa, and Adelmo Millaqueo Millapán. 2004. "Informe diagnóstico y de intervención, comunidad Cacique José Guiñón, Ercilla." Servicio Salud Araucania Norte, Angol, Chile. Unpublished report.

Serrano, Sol. 2002. "Foro: Identidad y mestizaje." *Revista Cultura,* no. 29.

"6 Carabineros dado de bajo por hurta de madera." 2009. *El Sur.* July 23.

Smith, Andrea. 2010. "Queer Theory and Native Studies: The Heteronormativity of Settler Colonialism." *GLQ: A Journal of Lesbian and Gay Studies* 16 (1–2): 41–68.

Smith, Dorothy. E. 1979. "A Sociology for Women." In *The Prism of Sex: Essays in the Sociology of Knowledge.* Edited by Julia A. Sherman, pp. 135–87. Madison: University of Wisconsin Press.

Speed, Shannon. 2006. "Rights at the Intersection: Gender and Ethnicity in Neoliberal Mexico." In *Dissident Women: Gender and Cultural Politics in Chiapas.* Edited by Shannon Speed, R. Aída Hernández Castillo, and Lynn M. Stephen, pp. 203–21. Austin: University of Texas Press.

————. 2008. *Rights in Rebellion: Indigenous Struggle and Human Rights in Chiapas.* Stanford: Stanford University Press.

Spivak, Gayatri. 1994. "Can the Subaltern Speak?" In *Colonial Discourse and Post-Colonial Theory: A Reader.* Edited by Patrick Williams and Laura Chrisman, pp. 66–111. New York: Columbia University Press.

Stahler-Sholk, Richard. 2007. "Resisting Neoliberal Homogenization: The Zapatista Autonomy Movement." *Latin American Perspectives* 34 (2): 48–63.

Stern, Steve J. 2004. *Remembering Pinochet's Chile: On the Eve of London 1998.* Durham: Duke University Press.

"Suprema rebaja condenas a comuneros mapuches y éstos mantienen huelga de hambre." 2011. *La Tercera.* June 4. Online at http://diario.latercera.com/2011/06/04/01/ contenido/pais/31-71518-9-suprema-rebaja-condenas-a-comuneros-mapuches -y-estos-mantienen-huelga-de-hambre.shtml. Accessed on March 26, 2011.

Tauran, Erasmo. 2012. "Temucuicui Autónoma deja reclamo de fundos de René Urban en manos de comunidad vecina." Online at http://www.biobiochile

.cl/2012/02/01/temucuicui-autonoma-deja-reclamo-de-fundos-de-rene-urban -en-manos-de-comunidad-vecina.shtml. Accessed on February 24, 2012.

Taylor, Diana. 1997. "Making a Spectacle: The Mothers of the Plaza De Mayo." In *The Politics of Motherhood: Activist Voices from Left to Right*. Edited by Alexis Jetter, Annelise Orleck, and Diana Taylor, pp. 182–96. Hanover: University Press of New England.

Terwindt, Carolijn. 2004a. "El desafío del monopolio de violencia." Translation of master of laws thesis, Utrecht University, the Netherlands.

———. 2004b. "Legitimación de violencia en el sistema." Translation of chapter 8, in "Puzzle of Violence: A Discourse Analysis after the Legitimization of Violence in the Mapuche Conflict in Chile." MS thesis, Utrecht University, the Netherlands.

Toledo Llancaqueo, Victor. 2007. "Prima ratio. Movilización mapuche y política penal. Los marcos de la política indígena en Chile 1990–2007." *Observatorio Social de América Latina (OSAL)* 8 (22): 253–93.

———. 2011. "Instituto de DDHH Chile: 'Decreto 124 sobre consultas indígenas no satisface obligaciones internacionales.'" Public statement, Centro de Políticas Públicas y Derechos Indígenas, March 28. Reproduced at http://www.mapu express.net/content/news/print.php?id=6710 Accessed on January 4, 2013.

"Tribunal de Cañete absuelve a mapuches de principales cargos imputados por la Fiscalía." 2011. *Azkintuwe.* Online http://www.azkintuwe.org/feb_2203.htm. February 22. Accessed on January 4, 2013.

Tuhiwai Smith, Linda. 1999. *Decolonizing Methodologies: Research and Indigenous Peoples.* London: Zed Books.

U.S. Department of State. 2007. "Country Reports on Terrorism." Online at http:// www.state.gov/s/ct/rls/crt/2007/103710.htm. Accessed on November 10, 2008.

Valdés, Marcos. 2000. "Análisis de coyuntura." Online at http://www.mapunet.org/ mapunet/coyuntura/coyuntura2.htm. Accessed on April 17, 2001.

Valdivia, Verónica, and Rolando Álvarez. 2011. "El municipio entre democracia y dictadura: Ciudadanía y despolitización en la historia reciente de Chile." Presentation at 19th Jornadas de Historia de Chile. Universidad Diego Portales, Santiago, Chile.

Van Cott, Donna Lee. 1994. "Indigenous Peoples and Democracy: Issues for Policy-makers." In *Indigenous Peoples and Democracy in Latin America.* Edited by Donna Lee Van Cott, pp. 1–28. New York: St. Martin's Press.

———. 2000. *The Friendly Liquidation of the Past: The Politics of Diversity in Latin America.* Pittsburgh: University of Pittsburgh Press.

Vargas, José Luís. 2011. "Fallo a favor de comunidades Mapuches invalida autorización para instalar basurero en Lanco." *Azkintuwe.* Online at http://www .azkintuwe.org/ene_0601.htm. Accessed on January 4, 2013.

Vicuña MacKenna, Benjamin. 1884. *Elisa Bravo, o sea el misterio de su vida, de su cautividad y de su muerte con las consecuencias políticas i públicas que la última tuvo para Chile.* Santiago: Imprenta Victoria.

Vilas, Carlos M. 1996. "Neoliberal Social Policy: Managing Poverty (Somehow)." *NACLA* 24 (6): 16–25.

Villalobos, Sergio. 2000a. "Caminos ancestrales." *El Mercurio.* September 3.

———. 2000b. "Errores ancestrales." *El Mercurio.* May 14.

Wade, Peter. 1997. *Race and Ethnicity in Latin America*. Chicago: Pluto Press.

Wallmapuwen. 2005. "Declaración de principios: El partido al que aspiramos." Online at http://www.wallmapuwen.net/lecturas-complementarias/. Accessed on March 20, 2012.

———. 2006. "El Nacionalismo Mapuche como programa político." Online at http://www.wallmapuwen.net/lecturas-complementarias/. Accessed on March 20, 2012.

Warren, Sarah D. 2009. "How Will We Recognize Each Other As Mapuche? Gender and Ethnic Identity Performances in Argentina." *Gender and Society* 23 (6): 768–89.

———. 2010. "Urban Indigenous Identities and Claims for Collective Rights in Chile and Argentina." PhD diss., University of Wisconsin.

Weftun. 2007. "Aclarando verdades y mentiras sobre la CAM: Entrevista al vocero de la CAM, Jose Llanquief." Online at http://www.nodo50.org/weftun/documentos/entrevistas/verdades_y_mentirasago07.html. Accessed on February 14, 2012.

Williams, Christine. 2006. *Inside Toyland: Working, Shopping, and Social Inequality.* Berkeley: University of California.

Williams, Raymond. 1981. *Culture*. London: Fontana.

Winn, Peter, ed. 2004. *Victims of the Chilean Miracle: Workers and Neoliberalism in the Pinochet Era, 1973–2002*. Durham: Duke University Press.

Wolfreys, Jim. 2000. "In Perspective: Pierre Bourdieu." *International Socialism Journal* 87 (Summer). Online at http://pubs.socialistreviewindex.org.uk/isj87/wolfreys.htm.

Wolin, Sheldon S. 1989. *The Presence of the Past: Essays on the State and the Constitution.* Baltimore: Johns Hopkins University Press.

Yashar, Deborah J. 1999. "Democracy, Indigenous Movements, and the Postliberal Challenge in Latin America." *World Politics* 52 (1): 76–104.

Zeitlin, Maurice, and Richard Earl Ratcliff. 1988. *Landlords and Capitalists: The Dominant Class of Chile*. Princeton: Princeton University Press.

Zúñiga, A. 2001. "Los otros mapuches." *El Mercurio*. April 4.

INDEX